Eldercare Issues in China and India

The contributors to this book present case studies of elder care in China and India, and draw comparisons between the two – illuminating some of the key issues facing the two largest Asian countries as they develop rapidly.

Caring for the elderly is a major challenge for all countries, and one which is of acute concern for rapidly developing economies. Development tends to run counter to long-established cultural norms of family-based caring and filial piety, even as it also tends to lead to longer life expectancy. Taking a range of methodological and conceptual approaches to understanding these challenges, the contributors present a multifaceted understanding of elder care issues in both India and China. They focus in particular on caregiving within families and at care homes – and the impacts these have on quality of life and the experience of caregiving for both caregivers and the aged themselves.

An invaluable collection for scholars and students of gerontology and aging in Asia, that will also be of great interest to scholars with a broader interest in global trends in caregiving.

Longtao He is an associate professor in the Research Institute of Social Development at Southwestern University of Finance and Economics, Chengdu, China. His research interests focus on qualitative health research, medical social work, and social work ethics. He has published a sole-authored book titled "Care Work, Migrant Peasant Families and Discourse of Filial Piety in China" with Springer Nature. His articles appear in Qualitative Health Research, Journal of Religion & Health, Applied Research in Quality of Life, British Journal of Social Work, European Journal of Ageing, BMJ Open, Journal of Ageing and Social Policy, and so on.

Jagriti Gangopadhyay is currently an Assistant Professor at the Manipal Centre for Humanities, Manipal Academy of Higher Education (MAHE). She is also the faculty coordinator for the Center for Women's Studies. She did her PhD from the Indian Institute of Technology Gandhinagar. For her research, she has received funding from the Indian Council of Social Science Research, India, National Commission for Women, India, Center for Southeast Asian Studies, Kyoto University, Japan, and the University of Saskatchewan, Canada. Recently she was also awarded the Shastri Publication Grant by Shastri Indo Canadian Institute for her published monograph, "Culture, Context and Aging of Older Indians: Narratives from India and Beyond, published by Springer. She has published in journals of international and national repute such as Journal of Cross-Cultural Gerontology, Springer, Adoption Quarterly, Taylor and Francis, Ageing International, Springer, Indian Journal of Medical Ethics and Contributions to Indian Sociology, Sage.

Routledge Studies on Asia in the World

Routledge Studies on Asia in the World will be an authoritative source of knowledge on Asia studying a variety of cultural, economic, environmental, legal, political, religious, security and social questions, addressed from an Asian perspective. We aim to foster a deeper understanding of the domestic and regional complexities which accompany the dynamic shifts in the global economic, political and security landscape towards Asia and their repercussions for the world at large. We're looking for scholars and practitioners – Asian and Western alike – from various social science disciplines and fields to engage in testing existing models which explain such dramatic transformation and to formulate new theories that can accommodate the specific political, cultural and developmental context of Asia's diverse societies. We welcome both monographs and collective volumes which explore the new roles, rights and responsibilities of Asian nations in shaping today's interconnected and globalized world in their own right.

The Series is advised and edited by Matthias Vanhullebusch and Ji Weidong of Shanghai Jiao Tong University.

Indian Migrants in Tokyo
A Study of Socio-Cultural, Religious and Working Worlds
Megha Wadhwa

Green Finance, Sustainable Development and the Belt and Road Initiative
Edited by Fanny M. Cheung and Ying-yi Hong

Asia and Europe in the 21st Century
New Anxieties, New Opportunities
Edited by Rahul Mishra, Azirah Hashim and Anthony Milner

China's Western Frontier and Eurasia
The Politics of State and Region-Building
Zenel Garcia

Eldercare Issues in China and India
Edited by Longtao He and Jagriti Gangopadhyay

Find the full list of books in the series here: https://www.routledge.com/Routledge-Studies-on-Asia-in-the-World/book-series/RSOAW

Eldercare Issues in China and India

Edited by Longtao He and
Jagriti Gangopadhyay

LONDON AND NEW YORK

First published 2022
by Routledge
4 Park Square, Milton Park, Abingdon, Oxon OX14 4RN

and by Routledge
605 Third Avenue, New York, NY 10158

Routledge is an imprint of the Taylor & Francis Group, an Informa business

© 2022 selection and editorial matter, Longtao He and Jagriti Gangopadhyay; individual chapters, the contributors

The right of Longtao He and Jagriti Gangopadhyay to be identified as the authors of the editorial material, and of the authors for their individual chapters, has been asserted in accordance with sections 77 and 78 of the Copyright, Designs and Patents Act 1988.

All rights reserved. No part of this book may be reprinted or reproduced or utilised in any form or by any electronic, mechanical, or other means, now known or hereafter invented, including photocopying and recording, or in any information storage or retrieval system, without permission in writing from the publishers.

Trademark notice: Product or corporate names may be trademarks or registered trademarks and are used only for identification and explanation without intent to infringe.

British Library Cataloguing-in-Publication Data
A catalogue record for this book is available from the British Library

Library of Congress Cataloguing-in-Publication Data
A catalog record has been requested for this book

ISBN: 978-1-032-18379-4 (hbk)
ISBN: 978-1-032-18381-7 (pbk)
ISBN: 978-1-003-25425-6 (ebk)

DOI: 10.4324/9781003254256

Typeset in Galliard
by Knowledge Works Global Ltd.

Contents

List of figures	vii
List of tables	viii
List of contributors	ix
Acknowledgment	xii

1 Introduction: Eldercare Issues in Contemporary Chinese and Indian Societies 1
LONGTAO HE

SECTION I
Eldercare and Filial Piety in China and India 11

2 The Extension of Xiao 13
MARIUS MEINHOF AND YIMING ZHANG

3 Eldercare, Filial Piety within the Joint Family System of Urban India 31
JAGRITI GANGOPADHYAY

SECTION II
Family Care for Elders in Chinese and Indian Societies 53

4 A Comparative Study of Caregiving Experiences between Family Caregivers of Elderly Cancer Patients in China and India: A Qualitative Meta-synthesis 55
LONGTAO HE AND HAN WU

5 Filial-Piety-Based Family Care in Chinese Societies 89
ZHUOPENG YU AND BOYE FANG

SECTION III
Institutionalized and Formal Eldercare in China and India 105

6 Stigmatization of the Elderly and the Influence of NIMBY
  in Community-Based Eldercare Institutions 107
  FEI PENG, MANG HE, AND NUERMAIMAIJIANG KULAIXI

7 Dimensions of Eldercare and Quality of Life of Elderly
  People in an Old-Age Home in Kolkata 124
  SAHELI GUHA NEOGI GHATAK

SECTION IV
Care Issues of Marginalized Elder Groups in
China and India 143

8 Successfully Aging Alone: Long-Term Singlehood
  and Care during COVID-19 in India 145
  KETAKI CHOWKHANI

9 Loss of the Only Child and Caregiving for Grandchildren
  among Older Adults—A Qualitative Case Study in China 155
  JI WU AND XUE QIU

SECTION V
Eldercare Research in China and India 171

10 Does India Have Sufficient Data to Understand the Need
   for Eldercare? 173
   DONA GHOSH

11 Conclusion: Future Research Directions for Eldercare
   Issues in China and India 219
   JAGRITI GANGOPADHYAY

Index 230

Figures

4.1 PRISMA flow diagram of the article selection process 59
9.1 Resilience: Three-stage caregiver identity construction among
the older adults 159

Tables

3.1	Background Details of the Sample Population	39
4.1	Search Strategy	57
4.2	Characteristics of Included Articles	60
4.3	Quality Appraisal Results	69
4.4	Quotations from Chinese Participants from the Selection of Articles to Illustrate Each Theme	71
4.5	Quotations from India Participants of the Selected Articles to Illustrate Each Theme	75
7.1	Socio-Demographic Profile of Elderly	129
7.2	Social Adjustment Scale Score of Male and Female Elderly in OAH	130
7.3	Comparison of Male and Female Elderly Boarders in Terms of Intra-Generational–Interpersonal Relationship	132
7.4	Dimensions of Receiving Care in OAH	133
7.5	Quality of Life of Elderly in OAH (WHO-QOL-BREF Scale Score)	136
9.1	Basic Information of the Interviewed Older Adults	157
9.2	Spindle Code Scoping	158
10.1	Description of Available Data Source on Health of the Elderly	179
10.2	Inclusion of Variables on Health of the Elderly	181

Contributors

Ketaki Chowkhani is a postdoctoral fellow at the Manipal Centre for Humanities. She researches and teaches singles studies and gender studies. She has a PhD in Women's Studies from Tata Institute of Social Sciences, Mumbai. Her doctoral work focused on sexuality education and adolescent masculinities in middle-class Mumbai. Her writing has appeared in the *Indian Journal of Medical Ethics, Journal of Porn Studies, New York Times*; in edited volumes published by Routledge and Cambridge University Press, In Plainspeak, Teacher Plus, DNA, Kafila.online, Roundtable India, and Ultraviolet. Dr Ketaki also has an MPhil in Cultural Studies from the English and Foreign Languages University and an MA in English from Pondicherry University.

Boye Fang is an Associate Professor in the School of Sociology and Anthropology at Sun Yat-sen University, Guangzhou, China. Her research focuses on gerontological sociology and medical sociology, with a special focus on elder abuse and dementia caregiving. She has published a series of high-impact papers in the *Trauma, Violence & Abuse, Journal of Interpersonal Violence, Journal of Gerontology (Series B), Gerontology, Journal of American Geriatrics Society, Psychosomatic Medicine, Health and Psychology*, and so on.

Jagriti Gangopadhyay is currently an Assistant Professor at the Manipal Centre for Humanities, Manipal Academy of Higher Education (MAHE). She is also the faculty coordinator for the Center for Women's Studies. She did her PhD from the Indian Institute of Technology Gandhinagar. For her research, she has received funding from the Indian Council of Social Science Research, India, National Commission for Women, India, Center for Southeast Asian Studies, Kyoto University, Japan, and the University of Saskatchewan, Canada. Recently she was also awarded the Shastri Publication Grant by Shastri Indo Canadian Institute for her published monograph, *Culture, Context and Aging of Older Indians: Narratives from India and Beyond*, published by Springer. She has published in journals of international and national repute such as *Journal of Cross-Cultural Gerontology* (Springer), *Adoption Quarterly* (Taylor and Francis), *Ageing International* (Springer), *Indian Journal of Medical Ethics and Contributions to Indian Sociology* (Sage).

Saheli Guha Neogi Ghatak is an Assistant Professor at the Department of Sociology, School of Liberal Arts and Culture Studies, Adamas University, Kolkata, India. She did her PhD at the University of Calcutta.

Dona Ghosh is currently an Assistant Professor at the Thiagarajar School of Management, Tamil Nadu, India. She did her PhD at the Indian Institute of Technology, Kharagpur. She has published her work in the *International Journal of Community and Social Development*, *The International Journal of Health Planning and Management*, and *Comparative Employment Relations in the Global Economy*.

Longtao He is an Associate Professor in the Research Institute of Social Development at Southwestern University of Finance and Economics, Chengdu, China. His research interests focus on qualitative health research, medical social work, and social work ethics. He has published a sole-authored book titled *Care Work, Migrant Peasant Families and Discourse of Filial Piety in China* with Springer Nature. His articles appear in *Qualitative Health Research*, *Journal of Religion & Health*, *British Journal of Social Work*, *European Journal of Ageing*, *BMJ Open*, *Journal of Ageing and Social Policy*, and so on.

Mang He is an Associate Professor and Deputy Dean of Tourism Management at the Sun Yat-Sen University, China. His research interests lie in wellness tourism and big data, pro-poor tourism and rural revitalization, leisure and sports management. His publications appear in *Tourism Management*, *Annals of Tourism Research*, *Journal of Hospitality and Tourism Management*, *International Journal of Tourism Research*, *Tourism Tribune*, and more. Dr He's research has attracted more than ten research grants, including fundings from the National Social Science Foundation.

Nuermaimaijiang Kulaixi is a lecturer in the Tourism Institute of Xinjiang University. He teaches courses such as tour guide business, travel agency management, tourism enterprise simulation, etc. Now he is a PhD candidate in School of Tourism Management, Sun Yat-Sen University. His research interests focus on wellness tourism and active aging. He participated in many projects such as Humanities and Social Science Fund of the Ministry of Education.

Marius Meinhof works as a research fellow at the Institute for Sociology at Bielefeld University in Germany. His research interests revolve around postcolonialism, governmentality, and notions of modernity and backwardness in China, primarily in the areas of consumption and of intergenerational relations. He has authored the award-winning monography *Shopping in China* (2018) in the German language and co-edited the special issue, *Postcolonialism and China* (2017) in English. He is currently the primary investigator for the project "civilized families" that researches projects to promote filial piety in China.

Fei Peng is a distinguished associate researcher of tourism management at the Sun Yat-Sen University, China. Her research interests focus on health and wellness tourism, active aging, leisure, and health. She is the associate editor of the *Blue Book on Health and Wellness* series. And her publications appear in *Journal of Transport & Health, Tourism Tribune, Journal of Social Science of Zhejiang, Aesthetic Education*, and more. Dr Peng's research has attracted more than ten research grants, including fundings from National Natural Science Foundation of China and Humanities and Social Sciences of the Ministry of Education.

Xue Qiu is a postgraduate student in the College of Humanities and Social Sciences at Harbin Engineering University, Harbin, China. Her research focuses on health social work.

Han Wu is a Master of Social Work student in the Research Institute of Social Development at Southwestern University of Finance and Economics, Chengdu, China. His research interests focus on health social work, medical sociology, and evidence-based social work. His articles appear in *Chinese General Practice*.

Ji Wu is an Associate Professor in the College of Humanities and Social Sciences at Harbin Engineering University, Harbin, China. Her research interests focus on health social work, veterans social work. Her articles appear in *Children and Youth Services Review, Chinese Mental Health Journal, Journal of Anhui Normal University (Hum. & Soc. Sci.)*, and so on.

Zhuopeng Yu is a senior undergraduate student in the School of Sociology and Anthropology at Sun Yat-sen University, Guangzhou, China. His research interests focus on medical sociology and social gerontology.

Yiming Zhang is a PhD candidate in sociology at Bielefeld Graduate School for History and Sociology. Her research interests include urban sociology, culture, and spatial governance, and practices of "tradition" in China. She simultaneously works as a research assistant for the project "civilized families" that researches projects to promote filial piety in China.

Acknowledgment

Longtao He: It was a PhD colleague and good friend, originally from India, who introduced me to Dr Jagriti Gangopadhyay, knowing we had shared research interests. Since then, we have been engaged in a marvelous research conversation and collaboration, culminating in this edited volume, with me editing the Chinese chapters (and also coordinating the whole project) and her editing the Indian ones. It has been a great pleasure to work with Jagriti, and I trust this fruitful collaboration will not end here. I also cannot thank all the chapter contributors enough. Without their diligent endeavors and support, this book would not have evolved into the rich tome you now hold in your hands. I would also like to thank editor Simon Bates from Routledge, for his belief in this edited volume and also support throughout the project.

I would like to thank my parents, Haiyang He (何海洋) and Junfang He (何俊芳), and my three-year-old son, Xuanhan He (何轩翰), for always being my rock; my friends Chia Pan and Junjian Han accompanying me in this work; my PhD supervisor, Prof Kate van Heugten, my post-doc supervisor, Prof Huamin Peng (彭华民), Dr Xiangshu Deng (邓湘树), Dr Yangu Pan (潘彦古), Prof Fang Zhao (赵芳), my PhD colleague Dr Chandan Bose, and Mona-Lynn Courteau for their support and encouragement; and my MA students, Han Wu (吴汉) and Menghua Li (李孟华), for their administrative support throughout the project and their help in organizing the online conference themed on this edited volume.

Jagriti Gangopadhyay: I would like to begin by thanking my former colleague, Dr Chandan Bose, currently an Assistant Professor at the Indian Institute of Technology, Hyderabad, for introducing me to Dr Longtao He, who is nothing short of a brilliant collaborator. It was a very rewarding and enriching experience to work with Dr He. My intellectual exchanges with him, enabled me to grow both academically as well as professionally. I also hope that this collaboration is only the beginning of our academic journey together and we continue to collaborate in the future as well.

This book also would not have been possible without the support of my family. My parents, Dr Tamonas Gangopadhyay, who is an academic himself and continues to inspire my research even today and my mother, Mrs Sonali Gangopadhyay, is my source of strength for all my academic endeavors. My husband, Dr Srijan Sengupta, has to be thanked for constantly motivating me to chase my many academic pursuits. My three-year-old son, Atmadeep Sengupta, for keeping my spirits high all the time. I would also like to thank my colleagues at Manipal Center for Humanities (MCH), Dr Nikhil Govind and Dr Gayathri Prabhu, for their encouragement and support and for creating a space such as MCH, which provides immense creative liberties for upcoming academics.

Finally, I would like to thank Routledge editor Mr Simon Bates for having faith in our edited volume and I would also like to thank all the contributors from China and India for making this edited volume possible.

1 Introduction: Eldercare Issues in Contemporary Chinese and Indian Societies

Longtao He

Fast population aging and the increasing disease burden for the elderly are evident in both China and India, albeit on different scales. In China, due to a substantial increase in life expectancy, a fall in fertility rates, and the one-child policy, fast population aging has become one of the most significant demographic trends (Nie, 2016). According to a 2018 report from the China National Health and Fitness Commission, there were 249 million elderly people aged 60+ (about 17.6% of the total population), among whom more than 40 million have disabilities and more than 180 million have some sort of non-communicable disease. In India, though on a much smaller scale, population aging has also become an important demographic trend, with 8% of the total population aged 60+ in 2010 (Ugargol & Bailey, 2018). Ganguly and Kadam (2020) reported that the disease burden associated with population aging in India is dramatically increasing, especially for type 2 diabetes, cardiovascular diseases, chronic respiratory disease, mental disorders, muscular fitness, and colon, prostate, and breast cancer. These demographic shifts place huge pressure on the pension system and generate a great burden of eldercare (Bai & Lei, 2020). Population aging itself is neither a bad nor a good thing: it is the unbalanced age structure, disease burden, and insufficient institutional arrangements that are not friendly to the elderly (Peng, 2020; Biswas et al., 2020).

Efforts to build a comprehensive social security net for the elderly remain a work at progress in both countries. China has established its pension systems, though their development remains in progress (Zhang et al., 2019). According to China's Ministry of Human Resources and Social Security (2021), by the end of 2020, 450 million (about 31.9% of the population) were enrolled in the Basic Insurance Scheme for Urban Employees (with the government, employer, and employee co-paying for the insurance) with a total funding pool of 4,530 billion RMB, and 542 million (about 38.4% of the population) were enrolled for Basic Old-Age Insurance for Urban and Rural Residents (for any rural or urban residents without an employer willing to purchase the insurance, co-paid by the government) with a total funding pool of 975.9 billion RMB. Over 70% China's population is covered by at least one type of National Pension System (NPS). Rural contributors pay a much lower premium than the urban employed, thereby entitling them to lower reimbursements (Peng, 2020). The median monthly payout for the

DOI: 10.4324/9781003254256-1

urban employed is 2,300 RMB (about 350 USD; about one month's basic salary for an ordinary restaurant server in a first-tier city, except the four biggest cities in China-Beijing, Shanghai, Guangzhou, and Shenzhen) and for urban residents 1,071 RMB (about 160 USD) in late 2014 (Zhang et al., 2019). The huge gap between the urban employed and rural residents (including unemployed urban residents or urban residents who are not enrolled in the Basic Insurance Scheme for Urban Employees) poses extra challenges for the provision of care for the rural elderly and for marginalized urban residents. Even for the urban employed, the payouts are only just sufficient to cover daily necessities; they are not enough to support long-term care or other health care services (Z. Wang et al., 2020). There are also tangible regional differences in urban pension systems, as the developed eastern provinces have better public funding than the underdeveloped western provinces for investment into pension schemes (Peng, 2020).

Additionally, China has mostly built up its universal health insurance coverage since its health reform started in 2009, with more than 95% coverage of the whole population (Diao et al., 2021). The national health insurance system is built upon three pillars: the urban employed program, the urban resident program, and the rural resident program (He, 2021). The urban employed program can cover a greater proportion of health expenditure as contributors pay a fixed portion of their salary every month, compared to the other two programs, which only require very small contributions from residents and the government investment is much higher (Diao et al., 2021). However, many families still fall into poverty because of health expenses, as health insurance schemes cannot cover all types of medicines, and there is also a threshold fee to pay for inpatient services; for instance, the threshold fee for the rural resident program in Chengdu is 11,301 RMB (about 1,748 USD), with the threshold fee deducted from reimbursements according to a fixed ratio (50% for 0–5,000 RMB; 60% for 5,000–20,000 RMB; 76% for 20,000–50,000 RMB; 91% for 50,000+ RMB) (He, 2021).

In India, the building of the social security system for the elderly has been much more limited. The central government initiated the NPS in January 2004 and made it available for all Indian citizens in 2009 (Murari, 2020). However, its subscribers are mainly civil servants and government-affiliated employees. More than 90% of all workers are in the unorganized and informal sectors, which do not have access to any type of pension scheme (Dreze & Khera, 2017). There is another relevant pension scheme—the National Social Assistance Programme with components for widows, the elderly, and disabled persons, initiated in 1995 (Bhattacharya et al., 2015). However, only families below the poverty line can participate in this scheme, which, according to Indian data from the 61st (2004–2005) round of the Household Consumer Expenditure Survey (HCES), only approximately 1% of the population falls under (Dimri & Maniquet, 2020). Moreover, the pension for the elderly stagnated at 200 rupees per month in 2006, enough for about 10 kg of rice in 2017 (Dreze & Khera, 2017). Additionally, only 32% of Indians are covered by any kind of health insurance scheme, government-sponsored or private (Thomas, 2016). For many Indian families, it takes only one medical treatment to fall under the poverty line (Pugazhenthi &

Sunitha, 2015). India thus has a much longer way to go in terms of establishing a comprehensive social security system for the elderly in comparison with China. Overall in China and India, an increasingly unbalanced age structure, a growing disease burden, and insufficient socioeconomic institutional arrangements have imposed many challenges for eldercare. However, due to the different forms and scales in those aspects mentioned above, their bond to be divergences in relevant eldercare issues too.

This book aims to elucidate several key challenge areas associated with eldercare in China and India, respectively. The book tells the story of gaps in eldercare in the two countries through five sections, each with two chapters, one for each country: eldercare and filial piety, family care, institutionalized and formal care, care for the marginalized elderly, and eldercare research. Chapter authors come from a variety of backgrounds, including health sociology, medical social work, social gerontology, gender studies, anthropology, health tourism, and health statistics. As eldercare issues are multidimensional and involve many social, economic, political, cultural, and spiritual factors, they are best examined from an interdisciplinary perspective. China and India—as the world's two most populous countries, both important global players and two "ancient" countries—have significant economic, political, and social relevance at a global level. They both also evince great adherence to cultural norms in relation to eldercare (He & van Heugten, 2021; Ugargol & Bailey, 2018). Many of these issues are captured in this book.

So far, no book has combined well-researched perspectives on eldercare issues in China and India. With its focus on several key eldercare issues in both countries, this book presents an overall picture of convergence rather than a direct cultural comparison. In doing so, we hope to open the door for future comparative studies and, more importantly, further deepen understandings of eldercare in China and India through ongoing dialogue between researchers and practitioners in the two countries.

Eldercare and Filial Piety in China and India

It is a cultural imperative in both China and India that the elderly be cared for by their family (He, 2021; Brijnath, 2012). According to He et al. (2021), filial piety broadly refers to the cultural norm that dictates that adult children respect, care for, and obey their parents and also to properly mourn their parents upon their death. In India, the concept of *seva* conveys a similar philosophy and practice (Sharma & Kemp, 2012). The implications of strong traditions of filial piety on eldercare are significant, but examinations and comparisons of filial care in China and India are scarce. To begin addressing this, the first two sections in this book present recent research findings on key eldercare issues, with a particular focus on filial piety, in contemporary Chinese and Indian societies. The comparative framework between countries that have similar cultural ideals of filial piety toward older people in their country is set out. This comparison brings about a nuanced understanding of challenges faced by older people in these societies.

For instance, it leads us to question the assumption that older people are always treated with care and reverence in these societies: Chapter 4, for example, discusses negative societal perceptions about older people and highlights agism in Chinese society, despite it being known for glorifying virtues of filial piety.

Chapter 2 analyzes discourses aiming to promote *xiao* (filial piety) and create filial subjects in contemporary China. Many Chinese governmentality studies focus on China's attempts to modernize the country and its people. However, these studies often overlook discourses on traditional culture, which stress the importance of remodeling individuals into subjects that are modern but that also remain traditional in order to preserve, promote, or restore traditional Chinese virtues. In this chapter, Marius Meinhof and Yiming Zhang present their initial results of a discourse analysis of central and local government reports and popular WeChat articles (people's comments/posts directly on WeChat) on the topic of *xiao* in order to show how different actors understand the essence of *xiao* and of traditional family values. The authors also propose a framework for remodeling of *xiao* culture and discuss what interventions are suggested or used in order to remodel or promote *xiao* in society. They then lay the initial groundwork for a theory on the governmentality of *xiao*.

Chapter 3 points out that there are also legal and cultural foundations for filial practices in India. The literature on eldercare in India lacks engagement with the concept of filial piety. Dr. Jagriti Gangopadhyay found that adopting a cultural conceptual lens is very useful in exploring how the elderly in joint families experience their independence and dependence on their adult children. Gangopadhyay also investigates the sociocultural context and the modern development of filial piety in both China and India, a novel approach that begs further exploration.

Family Care for Elders in Chinese and Indian Societies

Due to the lack of a comprehensive social security system and still-prevalent cultural norms of filial piety in both China and India, family members are still the main source of care for the elderly. According to the 2015 Fourth Survey on the Living Conditions of the Elderly in Urban and Rural China (第四次中国城乡老年人生活状况抽样调查), 90% of urban elderly and 95% of rural elderly still rely on family caregivers (in general, 43.48% are spouses, 28.64% sons, 10.08% daughters-in-law, and 10.35% daughters) (Li, 2018). In India, family caregivers also remain the main source of care for elderly people (Ugargol & Bailey, 2018). However, perceptions of family care and its practice have been challenged in recent years due to many contextual changes such as increasing population aging, family nuclearization, urbanization, neoliberal marketization, and consumerist individualism (He, 2021; Ugargol & Bailey, 2018). The two chapters in this section examine family care experiences and patterns in Chinese society and inIndian society, respectively, striving to gain a clear picture of what perceptions of family care and its practice currently stand for in both countries and what the key differences are.

Chapter 4 uses a qualitative meta-synthesis approach to examine family caregivers for elderly cancer patients in both countries. This approach allows readers to easily gain a deeper understanding of not only the family caregivers' common care experiences in both countries but also the unique textures of caregiving experiences in each society. For instance, Indian family caregivers are more concerned with the access and quality of hospital services compared to their Chinese counterparts due to the lower level of development of India's health care system. Indian family caregivers are also more focused on religious resources and the Chinese more on philosophical precepts. Caregiver gender concerns are also more evident in India than in China. Longtao He and Han Wu's novel analysis provides fertile ground for understanding family caregiving experiences for elderly cancer patients from a global viewpoint and how family caregivers could better support elderly cancer patients in engaging in active aging.

In Chapter 5, Zhuopeng Yu and Boye Fang review changes in filial piety in overseas Chinese societies. They focus on a comparative analysis of Hong Kong and US Chinese societies and find a moderate decline in filial practice in Hong Kong and adjustment in older Chinese Americans' traditional values. The chapter concludes that despite variation in overseas Chinese societies, overall filial piety still continues to play a vital role in family care for the elderly.

Institutionalized and Formal Eldercare in China and India

In both countries, family care is becoming less sustainable, and as a result, institutional care is becoming increasingly important. In recent years, due to the prolonged life expectancy, urbanization, family nuclearization, low fertility, increasing care expenses, and other relevant factors, the care needs of the Chinese elderly have become a societal issue rather than remaining exclusively within the family. Bai and Lei (2020), drawing from the 2019 data from the World Bank's Population Estimates and Projections database, found that the total dependency ratio, which is the ratio of dependent age groups (ages 0–14 and 65+) to the independent age group (age 15–64), declined from 79.0 to 69.8 in China from 1960 to 2017 (Bai & Lei, 2020). In India, there are demographic shifts resulting from shrinking families and prolonged life expectancy (Ugargol & Bailey, 2018). It is clear that institutionalized care will have to fulfill the care needs of the elderly in both countries in the future. However, as mentioned above, both countries lack a comprehensive pension and health insurance system for proper eldercare services. Zhang et al. (2019) found that access to social insurance and security has very strong positive effects on urban residents' choice of institutionalized care or self-care, while many rural residents tend to resort to family care due to a lack of sufficient pension protection. Without a sufficient social security system that provides both affordable and high-quality long-term care services and professional personnel, elderly people that are financially deprived or who live with disabilities cannot afford to enroll, while at the same time, those who can afford institutionalized care will not be willing to enroll (Li, 2018; Mishra, 2020). Moreover, filial piety that continues to prevail in both countries has also posed many challenges for the development of institutionalized eldercare (Wang et al., 2020; Ugargol & Bailey, 2018). Additionally, rising ageism may also impede the development of institutionalized eldercare (Iversen et al., 2009).

In Chapter 6, Fei Peng, Mang He, and Kulaixi Nuermaimaijiang focus on the relation between stigmatization of the elderly and the influence of "nimbyism" on community-based eldercare institutions. Such facilities have become more common in an era of population aging in China. However, agism toward the elderly and the nimbyism (from NIMBY, or "not in my backyard") these entail, have placed many obstacles in front of such developments. The authors undertook interviews with sixteen respondents including one public servant and one community leader focused on eldercare institutions, eight middle and senior managers from eldercare institutions, and six people resident in neighborhoods near such institutions. They uncovered stigmatized perceptions of older adults that related aging with decline, death, and misery, amplified by a lack of familiarity of death-related issues among Chinese people. Their analysis shows that nimbyist attitudes are directed not only toward eldercare facilities but also toward elderly people themselves. This leads the authors to propose a new social governance framework incorporating their findings.

In Chapter 7, Saheli Guha Neogi Ghatak applies a mixed-methods approach to examine Indian elderly men's and women's perceptions about their quality of life in their homes. She found that women adjust better socially than men being cared for at home, that positive intergenerational relationships are crucial for both elderly men and women in enhancing their perceived quality of life, and that the quality of their informal and formal care are both important factors in these perceptions. This chapter provides a clear understanding of how elderly residents living at home view their subjective quality of life in the Indian cultural context.

Care Issues around Marginalized Elder Groups in China and India

The elderly do not comprise a homogeneous group (Kalavar & Jamuna, 2011), and in the section of the book focusing on marginalized elder groups, care issues around two such groups are explored: the single elderly in India and the elderly in China who have lost their only child. As family size continues to shrink, the number of elderly people living alone in China has increased substantially (Bai & Lei, 2020). Some even choose to be single for the long term or permanently. This leads to care challenges and health hazard issues simply because of the lack of a person in close proximity to care for them (Gangopadhyay, 2021). Chapter 8 opens with the question, "Who will look after you when you are old and sick?" Taking a scholarly approach to this question, Ketaki Chowkhani conducted in-depth interviews with five single, middle-class women and men in May and June of 2020. She found that they constructed their own strategies of self-care during the COVID-19 lockdown. By adopting a resilience perspective, she constructs a comprehensive narrative about self-care and also enlightens other investigations on other demographic groups, such as those with low education and in older groups.

The other marginalized group examined in this section the elderly who lost their only child in China. Due to China's one-child policy, this group has become a very important social issue (Xu & Zhang, 2020). According to Mu (2016), losing one's only child imposes many physical, mental, and spiritual burdens on the elderly. In Chapter 9, Ji Wu and Xue Qiu talk about another form of the burden they carry, that of raising their grandchildren, but which also turns out to be a resource on which the grieving elderly can draw. Wu and Qiu adopt qualitative grounded theory to investigate the experiences of 12 such older adults in rearing their grandchildren and adapting to their new situation. They found that the participants went through several stages: self-healing after their child's death, raising their grandchildren, and reconstructing their identity as caregivers. These three stages shed light on the adaptation experiences of this bereaved group.

Eldercare Research in China and India

These emerging issues provide scholars with broad scope for research. The last section begins by asking whether sufficient data is available for meaningful research on eldercare issues in India. Population aging is an emerging and challenging phenomenon in Indian society (Biswas et al., 2020). In Chapter 10, Dona Ghosh reviewed the few available databases that include relevant data about the elderly population in India and determined that macro-level heterogeneity among this group is understated and detailed information on subgroups is insufficient.

Chapter 11, the concluding chapter, reviews and synthesizes what has been discussed in the book and offers recommendations for future research and for policymaking. This chapter advances an argument in favor of bringing together Chinese and Indian views on issues of eldercare relevant to both countries. This novel sense of convergence can help scholars, policymakers, social workers, and caregivers in both countries and beyond gain a deeper understanding of the challenges faced by eldercare systems in China and India that have arisen from population aging, shifting cultural norms around care, and relatively limited public resources. This understanding, it is hoped, will prompt new considerations and further study.

In this book, we decided to focus on these five key issues as they are crucially important in both Chinese and Indian societies. Many other issues of eldercare also need to be addressed. For instance, elderly women in both countries tend to be disadvantaged in terms of obtaining the care they need, as they tend to substantially outlive their husbands (Chen et al., 2018). As such, if their adult children are not able or willing to provide for their care or do not have a clear awareness of their care needs, these elderly women cannot have their care needs met (Kalavar & Jamuna, 2011). Gendered eldercare issues are explored in this book only peripherally and not as an independent theme. This book aims to broaden the arena for the comparative analysis of eldercare issues in China and in India, offering substantial insights into five key areas of eldercare systems.

References

Bai, C., & Lei, X. Y. (2020). New trends in population aging and challenges for China's sustainable development. *China Economic Journal*, *13*(1), 3–23. https://doi.org/10.1080/17538963.2019.1700608

Bhattacharya, S., Jos, M. M., Mehta, S. K., & Murgai, R. (2015). From policy to practice: How should social pensions be scaled up? *Economic and Political Weekly*, *50*(14), 60–67. https://www.jstor.org/stable/24481859

Biswas, U. N., Dellve, L., Bhattacharjee, A., & Wolmesjö, M. (2020). Ageing and values in the developments of home-based eldercare: Perspectives from India and Sweden. *Psychology and Developing Societies*, *32*(2), 224–253. https://doi.org/10.1177/0971333620937373

Brijnath, B. (2012). Why does institutionalised care not appeal to Indian families? Legislative and social answers from urban India. *Ageing & Society*, *32*, 697–717. https://doi.org/10.1017/S0144686X11000584

Chen, X. X. Giles, J., Wang, Y. F., & Zhao, Y. H. (2018). Gender patterns of eldercare in China. *Feminist Economics*, *24*(2), 54–76. https://doi.org/10.1080/13545701.2018.1438639

Diao, Y. F., Lin, M. B., Xu, K., Xu, K., Huang, J., Wu, X. W., Li, M. S., Sun, J., & Li, H. (2021). How government health insurance coverage of novel anti-cancer medicines benefited patients in China—a retrospective analysis of hospital clinical data. *BMC Health Services Research*, *21*(1), 856. https://doi.org/10.1186/s12913-021-06840-3

Dimri, A., & Maniquet, F. (2020). Income poverty measurement in India: Defining group-specific poverty lines or taking preferences into account? *Journal of Economic Inequality*, *18*(2), 137–156. https://doi.org/10.1007/s10888-019-09434-6

Dreze, J., & Khera, R. (2017). Recent social security initiatives in India. *World Development*, *98*, 555–572. https://doi.org/10.1016/j.worlddev.2017.05.035

Gangopadhyay, J. (2021). Ageing and self-care in India: Examining the role of the market in determining a new course of growing old among middle class older adults in urban India. *Ageing International*. https://doi.org/10.1007/s12126-021-09461-7

Ganguly, B. B., & Kadam, N. N. (2020). Age-related disease burden in Indian population. *Journal of the National Medical Association*, *112*(1), 57–73. https://doi.org/10.1016/j.jnma.2019.10.001

He, L. T. (2021). *Care Work, Migrant Peasant Families and Discourse of Filial Piety*. Palgrave Macmillan. https://doi.org/10.1007/978-981-16-1880-2

He, L. T., & van Heugten, K. (2021). An implementable conversation between Foucault and Chinese virtue ethics in the context of Chinese youth social work. *British Journal of Social Work*, *51*(4), 1221–1237. https://doi.org/10.1093/bjsw/bcab034

He, L. T., van Heugten, K., & Zheng, Y. (2021). Issues of elder care among migrant peasant workers in contemporary rural China: Filial piety redefined from a Foucauldian perspective. *Journal of Aging & Social Policy*, 1–21. https://doi.org/10.1080/08959420.2021.1926203

Iversen, T. N., Larsen, L., & Solem, P. E. (2009). A conceptual analysis of ageism. *Nordic Psychology*, *61*(3), 4–22. https://doi.org/10.1027/1901-2276.61.3.4

Kalavar, J. M., & Jamuna, D. (2011). Aging of Indian women in India: The experience of older women in formal care homes. *Journal of Women & Aging*, *23*(3), 203–215. https://doi.org/10.1080/08952841.2011.587730

Li, Z. (2018). Thoughts and suggestions on improving the elderly care service and long-term care system [关于完善老年服务和长期护理制度的思考与建议]. *Chinese Journal of Health Policy* [中国卫生政策研究], *11*(8), 1–7.

Ministry of Human Resources and Social Security of the People's Republic of China. (2021, July 13). The multilevel old-age insurance system will be consolidated [健全多层次养老保险体系]. *People's Daily* [人民日报]. http://www.mohrss.gov.cn/SYrlzyhshbzb/dongtaixinwen/buneiyaowen/rsxw/202107/t20210713_418346.html

Mishra, V. (2020). India's projected aged population (65+), projected life expectancy at birth and insecurities faced by aged population. *Ageing International, 45*(1), 72–84. https://doi.org/10.1007/s12126-019-09350-0

Mu, G. Z. (2016). On the national responsibilities and the civil rights of the people who lost their only child [论失独者养老的国家责任和公民权利]. *Dongyue Tribune* [东岳论丛], *37*(08), 5–9. https://doi.org/10.15981/j.cnki.dongyueluncong.2016.08.001

Murari, K. (2020). Risk-adjusted performance evaluation of pension fund managers under social security schemes (National Pension System) of India. *Journal of Sustainable Finance & Investment*. https://doi.org/10.1080/20430795.2020.1857635

Nie, J. B. (2016). Erosion of eldercare in China: A socio-ethical inquiry in aging, elderly suicide and the government's responsibilities in the context of the one-child policy. *Ageing International, 41*(4), 350–365. https://doi.org/10.1007/s12126-016-9261-7

Peng, X. Z. (2020). Coping with population ageing in mainland China. *Asian Population Studies, 17*(1), 1–6. https://doi.org/10.1080/17441730.2020.1834197

Pugazhenthi, V., & Sunitha, C. (2015). The government-sponsored health insurance schemes for the gross domestic healthiness. *Journal of Health Management, 17*(4), 438–445. https://doi.org/10.1177/0972063415606276

Sharma, K., & Kemp, C. L. (2012). "One should follow the wind": Individualized filial piety and support exchanges in Indian immigrant families in the United States. *Journal of Aging Studies, 26*(2), 129–139. https://doi.org/10.1016/j.jaging.2011.10.003

Thomas, T. K. (2016). Role of health insurance in enabling universal health coverage in India: A critical review. *Health Services Management Research, 29*(4), 99–106. https://doi.org/10.1177/0951484816670191

Ugargol, A. P., & Bailey, A. (2018). Family caregiving for older adults: Gendered roles and caregiver burden in emigrant households of Kerala, India. *Asian Population Studies, 14*(2), 194–210. https://doi.org/10.1080/17441730.2017.1412593

Wang, Z. Q., Xing, Y. A., Yan, W. X., Sun, X. R., Zhang, X. Y., Huang, S., & Li, L. (2020). Effects of individual, family and community factors on the willingness of institutional elder care: A cross-sectional survey of the elderly in China. *BMJ Open, 10*(2), e032478. https://doi.org/10.1136/bmjopen-2019-032478

Wang, J., Zhu, H., Liu, H., Wu, K., Zhang, X., Zhao, M., Yin, H., Qi, X., Hao, Y., Li, Y., Liang, L., Jiao, M., Xu, J., Liu, B., Wu, Q., & Shan, L. (2020). Can the reform of integrating health insurance reduce inequity in catastrophic health expenditure? Evidence from China. *International Journal for Equity in Health, 19*(1), 49. https://doi.org/10.1186/s12939-020-1145-5

Xu, X. J., & Zhang, N. N. (2020). "Psychological–structural" pathway of social marginalization—An empirical study of people who lost their only child in contemporary China [社会边缘化的"心理—结构"路径——基于当代中国失独人群的经验研究]. *Sociological Studies* [社会学研究], *35*(03), 145–168, 245. https://doi.org/10.19934/j.cnki.shxyj.2020.03.007

Zhang, L., Ding, Z. H., & Qiu, L. Y. (2019). Old age care preferences among Chinese middle-aged single-child parents and the related policy implications. *Journal of Aging & Social Policy, 31*(5), 393–414. https://doi.org/10.1080/08959420.2019.1578606

Section I
Eldercare and Filial Piety in China and India

2 The Extension of Xiao[1]

Marius Meinhof and Yiming Zhang

The concept of filial piety *xiao* (孝) plays an important role in studies of Chinese family life and studies on relations between parents and children. As an important sensemaking concept in contemporary China, xiao is at the core of intergenerational negotiations about the obligations of children toward their parents (Gui & Koropeckyj-Cox, 2016; Liu, 2008). Although xiao has been mentioned—and contested—in Chinese sources for thousands of years (Hu, 2009; Zhu, 2011), the existing literature on xiao in contemporary China shows a complex process of social change, in which xiao is transformed and re-negotiated between parents and their only children. Practices of xiao have been debated, especially in the context of the one-child policy (Gui & Koropeckyj-Cox, 2016) and of the aging society (Liu et al., 2017; Zhai & Qiu, 2007), where xiao continues to inform feelings of obligation, but is also transforming in the face of increased social pressures.

In English literature, xiao has so far been mainly discussed as a Chinese family value. While this focus is certainly justified—xiao is first of all a filial piety toward one's parents—it ignores the fact that many authors who call for a promotion of xiao in contemporary society tend to depict an extension of xiao from the family to a wider scope of social relations. This extension of xiao is argued in reference to similar ideas in classic Confucianist texts. But in the context of contemporary China, it links xiao to a larger concern of transforming and civilizing the population, which is one of the core population policy projects in contemporary China.

In this chapter, we will focus on this often-overlooked aspect in the discourse of xiao by showing how state discourses in China depict the promotion of xiao as part of a larger civilizational project, and in course of this extend xiao from a family value to a principle that organizes various relationships within society. We will argue that state discourses extend xiao so that the intra-family relation of xiao is depicted as a source of relations between citizens and the state, relations between younger and elder generations in the overall society, and as a basis for civil behavior in public. Based on this extension of xiao, an appellation of xiao as a principle organizing care and respect for the elderly in general, beyond support in kinship networks, takes place. However, we do not imply that xiao was historically limited to the family in the past and is now extended to wider circles.

DOI: 10.4324/9781003254256-3

Rather, we argue that an idea of xiao as a model for social relations beyond the family has regained popularity and is rearticulated in the context of social engineering projects. In this chapter, we will first look at how xiao is included in civilizational projects in China, and then describe three dimensions in which xiao is extended beyond the scope of the family. With a case study based on a discourse analysis of 300 texts from various state sources as well as from WeChat, we examine the role that the extension of xiao plays in discourses on volunteering in China. Due to the type of data we have collected so far, our argument will focus entirely on the logic of discourse, omitting the question of how these discourses influence everyday practice, or to which degree people use the extension of xiao as a concept to make sense of their everyday life.

By doing this, we will contribute to the literature on xiao in a twofold way. Firstly, we raise attention to the fact that xiao is in many discourses imagined to extend beyond the boundaries of the family, and that a discussion on xiao should therefore not automatically confine itself to the sociology of the family, but should situate itself in the context of research on high modernist civilizational projects. Secondly, by doing so, we allow the sociology of family and the debate on xiao to be connected to debates on Governmentality in China, and consequentially to debates on the ongoing history of projects to reshape the Chinese population.

Xiao in Literature

In empiric studies on contemporary Chinese society, xiao is usually depicted as a value informing obligations toward the parents (Liu & Bern-Klug, 2016; Xiao, 2001, 2013; Zhan & Montgomery, 2003; Zhou, 2019). Many studies have stressed the dynamic changes of xiao and tried to depict how family life and intergenerational relations have been subjected to deep change: Some studies have identified an increasing individualization of family relations (Feng, 2014; Shen, 2013; Yan, 2016), or diagnosed a decline of xiao in China (Chen & Qing, 2019; Cheung & Kwan, 2009; Liu, 2012). Others, however, have pointed out that xiao transformed rather than disappeared, for example, by pointing at ongoing negotiations about filial obligations in Chinese families (Chen & Qing, 2019; Liu, 2008, 2016), and especially at the change of the role of daughters in enacting xiao (Shen, 2016; Shi, 2009; Wei, 2017). Feelings of filial obligation continue to influence the care work of children as well as expectations of elders to be cared for by their children, which may lead to feelings of obligation or pressure among Children (Liu & Bern-Klug, 2016; Wang & Wang, 2014; Yang & Ouyang, 2013; Zhan & Montgomery, 2003).

However, throughout these studies, xiao and the transformation of xiao are depicted to take place within families, even though these families in turn are described as affected by population policy such as the one-child policy (Gui & Koropeckyj-Cox, 2016; Yi, 2018). The only recent works that seem to go beyond the boundaries of the family are works that look at new institutional forms of eldercare, for example, in care homes (Liu et al., 2017), and works that focus on state attempts to secure xiao within families, e.g. through laws and contracts (Chou, 2011; Wang, 2020). However, even these works have depicted xiao as being bound within the family and describe institutional care and state programs as forms of support for these families. An exception to this is Vanessa Fong's article on filial nationalism, which compares nationalist feelings of young Chinese to the idea of filial obligations and thus implies an extension of xiao toward the nation, although she does not theorize on the idea of an extension of xiao (Fong, 2004).

Existing historic literature, however, shows that historic notions of xiao have often been related to statehood and public governance. A range of works is addressing the "family-state isomorphism" (家国同构) in ancient China, which connects family authority and political authority and thus extends xiao to a political sphere (Shih, 2010; Wang, 2015; Yang, 2017). According to Shih (Shih, 2010), the Chinese family-state isomorphism is based on a system of families fulfilling functions of political authority, which emerged from the enfeoffment system of the Zhou but continued to influence Chinese political culture even after the abolishment of this system under Qin. Wang (2015) argues that filial piety was often accompanied by the interpretation of "transferring filial piety to loyalty" (移孝作忠) and "serving the king with filial piety" (以孝事君). Several works point out that Confucianist and neo-Confucianist thought in imperial China codified this relation of xiao to loyalty and its extension as a model for the relationship between ruler and ruled (Li, 2003; Xu, 2011; Zhai, 2019).[2]

Yet, literature on contemporary China rarely focuses on these ideas. One likely reason for this is that xiao started to disappear from state discourse over the history of the PRC. Already before the founding of the PRC, xiao was heavily criticized in the New Culture Movement and May Fourth Movement (Zhao, 2018). After the founding of the PRC, the state emphasized a critique on Confucianism and older family norms (Zhou, 2016), and various works point out the anti-traditionalist campaigns directed against Confucianism especially during the cultural revolution (Yan, 1999; Yang, 2011), even though ethnographic accounts raise doubts on how successful these projects ultimately were (Huang, 1998). However, Meinhof (Meinhof, 2017) has argued that this was not consistently anti-traditionalist but rather directed against all practices labeled as "backward." Indeed, some works indicate that Mao may have strategically referred to xiao and traditional family values reinterpreted as nationalist or collective values in a few situations (Xu, 2003; Zhou, 2017). However, xiao disappeared as an explicitly referenced political concept in state discourse. This continued in the reform era: in the collected speeches of state leaders Deng, Jiang, and even Hu, xiao does not play an important role and, in most cases, is not mentioned at all. Hence it seems that xiao has lost the immediate political functions it had in imperial China (see also: Chen, 2021; Shih, 2010). Indeed, Ikels (2006) argues that reform-era economic restructuring and the effects of the one-child policy have contributed to a diminishing of xiao. However, rather than a linear decline of xiao, there seem to be ups and downs of the role of xiao in state discourse. In recent years, the idea of xiao extending to public governance functions seems to have returned, albeit transformed into state discourse.

Method and Sample

In this text, we analyze statements that depict xiao as extending from family to wider social relations. Our analysis is based on the approach of Critical Discourse Analysis (Fairclough, 1992), which attempts to develop a systematic method for analyzing texts based on Foucault's discourse theory (Foucault, 1993). Fairclough asks how discourse, in some cases, fosters social change, and in some other cases, supports power relations so that change appears futile or bad (Fairclough, 1992, p. 67). Based on Fairclough's approach, we investigate how statements extend xiao so that a nostalgia for authentic family relations can be used as the foundation for civilizational projects that reshape the moral behavior of subjects.

To get ahold of the diversity of discourse on xiao, we have analyzed texts from various levels of government, as well as popular texts on xiao. To understand the government discourse, we analyzed (1) all available speeches and quote collections of Xi Jinping on family values (18 documents); (2) drawn from the website wenming wang, all available texts on moral models published by the central government since 2009 (90 documents); (3) a sample of the 20 first hits on the keyword search "xiao" on the website wenming wang; (4) all available text documents on the keyword "xiao" on the xuexi qiangguo app (81 documents).[3]

This sample allows us to get an impression on the variety of the xiao discourse. Aside from the speeches by Xi Jinping, texts from wenmingwang indicate central government positions, since the website, which is jointly organized by the Political Bureau of the CPC Central Committee and the Central Civilization Office (中央文明办) of the publicity department of the Communist Party of China is one of the key websites for nation-wide propaganda work. From the perspective of local governments, xuexi qiangguo is a mandatory app for many local officials, which are demanded to read it on a weekly or even daily basis at many places. Xuexi qiangguo is operated by the Publicity Department of the Central Committee of the Communist Party (中共中央宣传部). The publicity department of each province and city are responsible for operating branches of the xuexi qiangguo platform in their own regions, which is mainly handed over to the uniform media center (融媒体中心).

In our overall sample, we also included 89 texts from WeChat on xiao and we are currently raising and analyzing data from online discussions as well as interviews with people from different generations, that we collect through a process of theoretical sampling (Corbin & Strauss, 2008), in order to get ahold of the popular discourse on xiao. In this chapter, however, we limit our analysis to texts produced by state institutions.

Xiao as Part of a Civilizational Project

The texts on xiao in our sample are highly diverse and express a wide variety of definitions of xiao. Yet, many government texts share the notion that xiao needs to be actively inherited and promoted, and that it can be used to improve the morality of the citizens. Some texts criticize a loss or decline of xiao, but even more texts simply point at the efforts of local governments to promote xiao culture, including activities as diverse as promoting moral models, creating festivals or shows to promote xiao, installing programs to teach xiao or to promote xiao via volunteering activities, and even installing scoring systems where people would get points for xiao-related good deeds such as a virtue bank (道德银行) in a village in Shanxi or a virtue green card (道德绿卡) in a city in Zhejiang.

In these texts, xiao is frequently imagined solving various social problems and problems of governance. Especially three functions of xiao frequently appear in our sources: Firstly, xiao is assumed to be able to increase patriotism. Secondly, xiao is seen as an important value in China's "aging society" and is seen as a solution for problems of eldercare and inclusion of the elderly. Thirdly, xiao is seen to be employed to improve the morality of the people, e.g. honesty in public behavior. All three functions are in turn related to an idea of xiao increasing a sense of Chineseness and cultural self-confidence.

This idea of xiao as a solution to the problems of society makes it relevant for programs to improve public morals. Hence, promoting xiao has become an important aim for the government. The idea of promoting xiao has been part of the central government's white paper "outline for moral construction of the citizens" (公民道德建设实施纲要), which informs policies to remodel the moral behavior of the population. The first version of this outline, published in 2001, did not mention xiao, but it already placed an emphasis on traditional virtues (传统美德) and on family atmosphere (家风). The newer version, the "outline for moral construction of the citizens in the new era" (新时代公民道德建设实施纲要) does explicitly mention xiao as one of the traditional virtues that need to be strengthened.

Through this, the texts connect xiao not only to the older genealogy of Confucian ideas of xiao as part of public governance, but also to a more recent genealogical line of state attempts to shape or improve spiritual civilization. Such projects to improve Chinese society had appeared from the early twentieth century, when ideas emerged to transform a perceived "backward" Chinese culture in order to strengthen China against the colonial powers (Meinhof, 2021). In the reform era, various discourses and projects of social engineering aimed to modernize the country, the people, and individual subjects. For example, Greenhalgh (2003) has shown that the one-child policy adopted in 1979 was justified as a means to help China develop based on models that were, at that time, shared with Western development studies. Zhang (2006) has shown how big projects of urban reconstruction have been aiming at transforming Chinese urban space in order to create a modern city. A large number of works have described various social engineering projects to create a modern, consuming urban middle class and increase its share of the population (Elfick, 2011; Meinhof, 2018; Tomba, 2004). Programs to improve the Chinese population's *suzhi* (素质), which might be translated either as "quality" or "education," have been widely described and controversially debated in China Studies (Anagnost, 2004; Kipnis, 2007; Yan, 2003a; Yi, 2011).

Within these modernization projects, attempts to change public morals have played a role from early on. Since the reform and opening up, the Chinese government has gradually emphasized the policy of improving "spiritual civilization" (精神文明). The construction of spiritual civilization in the reform era was first implemented in ideological education program of "Five Concerns, Four Beauties" (五讲四美), which was promoted as one of ten points of the program for "socialist modernization" in the paper on "Resolutions on several historical issues of the party since the founding of the People's Republic of China" (关于建国以来党的若干历史问题的决议), published in 1981 by the communist party central committee, and extended by "Three Loves" (三热爱) in 1983. Although this program was suspended in 1985, the central committee reintroduced the idea to promote "spiritual civilization construction" in the "resolution of the CCCPC on the guidelines for the construction of socialist spiritual civilization" (中共中央关于社会主义精神文明建设指导方针的决议) in 1986. Subsequently, programs to create civilized cities, villages, and towns, and activities to construct a spiritual civilization were introduced one after another. In 2001, the concept of "civic moral construction" was formally introduced in the above-mentioned "outline of the moral construction of citizens." From 2006 on, the central government put forward the concept of "eight honors and eight shames" (八荣八耻荣辱观) as well as the 20-word basic moral code "Keep patriotic and law-abiding, courteous and honest, united and friendly, diligent and thrifty, self-improving and dedicated to work" (爱国守法、明礼诚信、团结友善、勤俭自强、敬业奉献). Since the 18th National Congress in 2012, the central government has defined socialist core values (社会主义核心价值观) and put them at the center of campaigns for constructing spiritual civilization.

Other than most of the modernization projects described in the China Studies literature, the moral construction projects of the twenty-first century refer not solely to the need for *modernization*, but to the importance of strengthening Chinese *tradition* in service of improving public morals. While texts on spiritual civilization in 1981 and 1986 did refer to communist or socialist morality (共产主义道德, 社会主义道德) or revolutionary tradition (革命传统), the first "outline for moral construction of the citizens" in 2001 is instead based on the notion of strengthening the "traditional virtues of the Chinese people formed over thousands of years" (中华民族几千年形成的传统美德). The second version published in 2019 makes even stronger references to tradition and raises the topic of xiao specifically as one example of the "traditional virtues of the Chinese people" (中华民族传统美德) and "fine traditional culture" (优秀传统文化). This continues older concerns about the transformation of public morals but shifts their theoretical foundation from a modernist to a traditionalist foundation.

This shift is aligned to what Perry (2017) calls a "re-Orientation" of discourses legitimating state power. Perry argues that, under Hu Jintao, state discourse began to merge nationalism with depictions of a glorious ancient Chinese tradition that the contemporary Chinese state claims to inherit and revive. The emerging references to traditional virtues as the foundation of public morals fit into this in content, although the outline for moral construction precedes the Hu

Jintao Era. Rather than a sudden shift, this seems to have been a gradual change, with state discourse picking up the slogan of Chinese people's great rejuvenation (中华民族的伟大复兴) as a key term from 1997. At least from 2001 on ideas of traditional virtues emerged, even though xiao only slowly gained in importance, starting with texts on moral models at least from 2004 on, and becoming a frequent part of state leaders' speeches only under Xi Jinping. Furthermore, in this gradual reorientation toward "tradition," the state seems to have picked up and inserted into its civilizational projects concerns about Chineseness and Confucianism that have been articulated in popular discourses and especially by intellectuals already from the 1990ies on (e.g. Du, 1997).

Hence there is, in respect to *xiao*, not entirely a re-Orientation of state discourse, but rather a merging of a continuity of concern with spiritual civilization with a discontinuity of the means through which this is achieved. Since long before the Hu-Era, the idea of moral construction has been present while its core justification has changed from a modernist one, as signified in ideas to create a socialist morality, to a traditionalist one, that depicts moral construction as a revitalization of tradition. Correspondingly, an idea of a spiritual deficiency in the population continues from the earlier texts until today, but it shifts from an idea of insufficiently modern (socialist) and progressive (revolutionary) people to an idea of a decline or loss of tradition and Chineseness. Thus, appeals to traditional virtues seem to constitute a new approach to a much older concern for improving public morals and the spiritual qualities of the population.

Extension of Xiao

The idea to employ xiao in projects of spiritual construction is closely related to an idea of "extension," which implies that xiao may originate in the family but subsequently extend to a principle organizing wider social relations, so that children's xiao toward their parents becomes a model or source for public morals. This extension of xiao is in many texts closely entangled with demands to promote xiao and depictions of xiao as a traditional virtue that needs to be re-awakened in order to exercise its beneficial effects in society. For example, the above-mentioned outline for moral construction (State Council, 2019) depicts xiao in the following way:

> 自觉传承中华孝道, 感念父母养育之恩、感念长辈关爱之情, 养成孝敬父母、尊敬长辈的良好品质; 倡导忠诚、责任、亲情、学习、公益的理念, 让家庭成员相互影响、共同提高, 在为家庭谋幸福、为他人送温暖、为社会作贡献过程中提高精神境界、培育文明风尚。

> We shall nurture the Chinese culture of xiao, gratitude for the parents' grace of nurturing the Children, gratitude for the elders' love and care, develop good qualities of xiao and respect for parents and elders. We shall promote concepts of loyalty, responsibility, affection, learning and public welfare, so that family members can influence each other and improve together. In the process of seeking happiness for families, sending warmth to others and contributing to society, we improve our spirituality and cultivate a civilized culture.

Here, xiao is described as an attitude or behavior toward one's parents and related to a feeling of gratitude for the parents' work of raising and nurturing the children. The object of xiao is father and mother (父母) and thus its subject is, by implication, that the child shows gratitude to its parents. The notion of a happy family based on xiao is then extended to warmth for others and ultimately to a contribution to society in which spiritual qualities and civilization will improve. Hence, the text constructs a logical process of extension in which xiao in the first instance describes an attitude toward parents and elders, but then builds a foundation for extended social emotions and improvement on the level of society.

Such an extension of xiao is frequent in our sample and happens mainly with respect to three dimensions, which seem to be closely related to the aforementioned three social problems of patriotism, aging society, and civilized behavior: Firstly, xiao is extended from family to the state or the country, so that xiao starts from an attitude toward one's parents but extends to feelings and obligations toward one's country. This happens most frequently by invoking the argument of an intrinsic parallel between xiao and loyalty (忠). In drawing on the notion of family-state-isomorphism, it transforms it from a model for feudal loyalty into a model for nationalist loyalty to the nation-state and its government. In addition, when claiming a need for loyalty, many texts stress the extension of xiao toward country or government. For example, some texts on xuexi qiangguo have argued that "loyalty to the country is the greatest form of piety to the parents" (对国家的忠，就是对父母最大的孝, Anonymous, 2020), or that xiao builds a "foundation for the relation between sovereign and subject" (君臣关系的根本, Anonymous, 2019b). In a speech on the spring festival show 2019, Xi Jinping appealed to "promote the unity of love for the family and love for the nation, make every person and every family contribute to the big family of the Chinese people" (提倡爱家爱国相统一，让每个人、每个家庭都为中华民族大家庭作出贡献 (Xi, 2019a)). Such arguments make xiao appear as a resource for patriotism and loyalty to a reified Chinese nation. However, it does not collapse the difference between family and state or kinship and politics, but rather addresses the family as a resource for patriotism by drawing parallels and intrinsic connections—authorized by the notion of "Chinese tradition"—between xiao within the private family and public attitudes toward one's country.

Secondly, aside from an extension toward the country, xiao is also extended from a family value to a moral system governing intergenerational relations within overall society. Several texts in our sample argue that xiao should regulate not only the relation between parents and children within a family, but relations between younger and elderly people in overall society. In government texts, such arguments have been found mainly in respect to volunteer activities (see below), making claims such as "treat the elders as they deserve, including other people's elders" (老吾老以及人之老, Anonymous, 2019a).

In some cases, xiao is not only claimed to extend toward intergenerational relations in wider society but it is even depicted as a necessary prerequisite for a functioning relation between the generations. For example, an article from China Women's News (中国妇女报) republished on xuexi qiangguo argues, that:

> 家庭是社会的细胞,只有家庭成员孝老爱亲,才有社会的和谐安定,只有从对自家长辈的孝敬尊重开始,才能拓展为面向全社会尊老、敬老、爱老、助老。
>
> The family is the cell of society, only if the family can establish piety to the elder and love to the kin, then society can be harmonious and stable, only starting from the piety and respect to ones families elders piety can expand to respect, honor, love and help the elderly for the whole society. (Zhao, 2019)

Here, again, intra-family relations are extended without claiming that society is based on kinship. Instead, relations within the family are a starting point where a good behavior toward all elderly is exercised, so that xiao within the family will inform the treatment of the elderly overall. Stronger even than in the quotes above, the text implies a need to secure correct behavior within the family, since this behavior is depicted as the prerequisite for a society respecting the elderly. This in turn makes xiao appear as a resource for the inclusion of the elderly in general.

Thirdly, xiao is described as the foundation of public morals and civilized society, which extends xiao not only in respect to the size of the group targeted but also in respect to the scope of values and practices that are based on xiao. As mentioned above, xiao is depicted as part of, sometimes even source for, civilized society, harmonious society and, in general, individual morals. For example, an article on wenming wang argues:

> 孝是社会文明的底色,一个守孝尽孝的人,才能够拥有健全的人格,才能够问心无愧、受人尊重。
>
> Xiao is the undertone of social civilization, only a person who protects and fulfills xiao can have a fully sound personality and can entirely have a good conscience and receive respect. (Jin, 2019)

These kinds of arguments preaching the greatness of xiao are widespread without fully explaining what xiao is and how it contributes to civilization and individual morals. Although they seem rather empty phrases aimed to highlight the greatness and importance of xiao, they nevertheless also imply an extension of xiao by declaring it a root for individual morals and for the realization of a civilized society. This connects to frequent claims that depict xiao as "root of morals" (道德的根本, Yan & Zeng, 2020) or as "starting point for an individual's moral self-cultivation" (个人塑造其道德人格的起点, Li, 2017), as well as with texts that argue, that a truly filial person should behave well-mannered to honor their parents, for example, "through moral integrity [...] show the quality of the parents education" (应以高尚的德行[...]彰显父母的教导, Anonymous, 2019b). In all such texts, xiao is depicted as extending from the family to a public morality, either because child-parent relations are seen as the origin of social relations, because xiao is seen as the origin of virtues, or because parents are depicted as a generalized other that informs social consciousness. This, in turn, connects xiao to the greater state project of moral construction and the establishment of a civilized society and depicts xiao as a key element for enrolling the promotion of xiao into the project of transforming public morals.

All three extensions of xiao pull the value of filial piety from the sphere of the private "family" into the public sphere by making it a matter for patriotism, public morals, and the elderly-oriented society. By extending xiao from a principle organizing parent-child relations within the family to a public civic virtue organizing social relations in society, the importance of xiao for society is highlighted. Thus, the promotion of xiao can be enrolled into, and benefit from, government projects to remodel popular culture and the public behavior of the population.

Through this, xiao becomes a possible object of high modernist projects that aim to improve the population. Scott (1998) has introduced the term "high modernist" to describe visions of improving society by rationalized means alongside central designs. By extending xiao into the sphere of the public, and declaring it as fundamental for civilized society, elderly-oriented social behavior and state-citizen relations, xiao is imagined as an important target of such high modernist projects, despite being understood as a traditional virtue. Together with the idea that xiao will or could be lost in contemporary society, this line of argument makes it inevitable to use the means of state administration to promote xiao in order to create a civilized society.

Volunteering and Xiao

One example for the ways in which the extension of xiao interacts with civilizational projects in China is the form through which an extension of xiao toward all elderly is enacted through volunteering programs. Volunteer activities are a core activity for the program of constructing a spiritual civilization that has recently risen to new prominence. Volunteerism has been widely promoted as a basic form for the construction of civilization by the central government (General Office of the CPC Central Committee, 2018), and Xi Jinping has praised it as "important attribute of social and civilizational progress" (志愿服务是社会文明进步的重要标志, Xi, 2019b). Furthermore, it is frequently promoted by local governments as part of civilizing projects.

Texts on volunteerism by local governments usually emphasize its distinctive Chinese character by omitting references or comparisons to similar volunteering activities in other countries and instead stressing two distinctive Chinese aspects of volunteering: Firstly, they emphasize that volunteering is a part of socialist morality (General Office of the CPC Central Committee, 2021). This is most frequently emphasized by describing volunteering as an expression of the spirit of Lei Feng, a Chinese soldier who was treated as the image of a new generation of socialist men with communist morality in the Mao Era. By stressing the spirit of Lei Feng, texts connect the promoted practices of volunteering to Mao-Era socialist virtues and describe volunteering as Chinese and socialist practice.

Secondly, the promotion of volunteerism is depicted to reflect Chinese traditional virtues, especially the virtue of xiao. Many volunteer activities focus on two aspects: Social care for the elderly and for the left-behind children. Thus, the volunteering activities can be related to the promotion of xiao in the sense of love for the elderly. This, too, portrays the depicted volunteering as distinctively Chinese, and connects it with discourses on a Chinese traditional identity. The relationship between volunteering and xiao, however, is complex, and in its course, the notion of xiao is frequently extended to organize intergenerational relations in overall society.

In local government texts, xiao is extended to overall society based on an entanglement of xiao-practices with the state. For the volunteer enacting *xiao*, family responsibility for the elder parents is transformed into social responsibility and taken up by groups of volunteers. In relevant reports, almost all volunteers are responsible for regularly visiting and taking care of elderly whose Children work far away and cannot regularly visit. This, in turn, is claimed to be an activity of *xiao* which extends toward society and the elderly in general. Moreover, according to official reports, most volunteer activities are led by party members and local officials, which depict volunteer service as a reflection of the government's social service practice. This in effect extends *xiao* from an intra-family relation to a part of the public welfare system and, to a certain degree, even as an equivalent for welfare state functions.

In addition, xiao is extended to a system of cross-family reciprocity, where one person supports the elderly of another family whose younger members are unavailable and will in turn receive help from other families later. For example, in a document report on volunteering activities in Yishui (Shandong) circulated via xuexi qiangguo, one volunteer is quoted as saying: "we have elder people in my own family, too, all people will one day be old! We help other people, and once we are occupied ourselves, volunteers will also go to my family and help me care for the elderly!" (我们自己家里也有老人，人都会有老的那一天！我们帮助别人，忙的时候，志愿者也会去我家里，帮助我照顾老人呢!, Yang & Sun, 2020).

This, again, is mediated by the state who guarantees as well as monitors the cross-family reciprocity. The volunteer system includes online volunteer management systems, moral banks, and so on, with the government acting as a regulator to archive people's good deeds. For example, a news article (Ji & Yang, 2020) on the volunteering program in Yishui describes in detail social scoring systems aimed at securing a functioning reciprocity for volunteering:

"队员里有党员也有群众，我们为每位党员制作了一本红色账户，为群众制作了'爱心存折'，就像银行存钱一样，为志愿者们储蓄爱心。"依托实体商店，或是志愿服务站自主管理的爱心超市，......凝聚社会爱心力量，构建"付出、积累、回报"的志愿服务激励机制。

"There are both party members and masses in the volunteer team. We made a red account for each party member and a 'love passbook' for the masses, just like a bank deposit, to record and store love from the volunteers." Said by local official......Basing on physical stores or love supermarkets managed by volunteer station, our goal is to build an incentive mechanism for volunteerism that is "pay, accumulate and reward".

According to this text, the government guarantees that society will reciprocate through institutionalized systems, using a social scoring system to reward volunteer activities. Through the technical and social network control of the volunteer system, the government acts as an incentive, a record, and a monitor. Because a volunteer's contribution has been recorded in the volunteer system, they will be given priority to receive reverse feedback and help from the volunteer system if they need it in the future. This, again, relates xiao and the cross-family reciprocity to a high modernist vision of regulating social behavior through a rationalized system of accountability measured and administered by scores that measure the degree to which the individual subject conforms to Chinese values of volunteering.

In the course of this, reciprocity, too, is extended: it is no longer a classic dyadic relation of giving and returning favors, as described in the anthropological literature on gift-giving practices (Yan, 1996; Yang, 1994). Instead, it is a triadic relationship between (1) a specific actor (the volunteer), (2) a generalized other in the form of the collective entity of "society" and/or "volunteering" from which a reciprocal act will emerge without necessarily coming from exactly the family that the volunteer supported before, and (3) the state as an institutional guarantor that supervises the flows of reciprocal support. As a result, the relationship between the subject and the target in volunteering is also linked to the relationship between the state and the people.

In addition to this extension of xiao, volunteering and its cultural awareness-raising effects are described as somehow conducive to restoring *xiao* in the family. For example, a document on volunteering of wenming wang claims that through volunteering, "the volunteers got in close contact with the elderly and took a vivid lesson on traditional Chinese virtues" (志愿者们和老人有了近距离接触,为大家上了一节生动的中华民族传统美德教育课, (Anonymous, 2019a)). Such arguments are based on the idea that care provided by volunteers may in turn arouse in children a sense of family responsibility and lead some of them to fulfill their duty of *xiao* to their parents. For example, holding regular volunteer activities for the elderly in public spaces is assumed to create an orientation of public opinion toward *xiao*. In many reports, volunteers perform shows, host dumpling feasts for the elderly, and encourage them to share their stories on an open-air stage. Government reports claim that this would promote a sense of family through the atmosphere of friendship and harmony enacted in these events. Here, too, the state is positioned as deeply entangled with the overall society through the process of promoting xiao. For example, in the article describing the Yishui volunteering program, a party secretary is quoted arguing that "the Cuncaoxin volunteer service action builds a bridge between the village party branch and the villagers, leading to the improvement of the village and the people's morale, and playing a significant role in enhancing the people's sense of access and promoting the culture of filial piety and kindness." (寸草心志愿服务行动搭起村党支部与村民之间的"连心桥", 带动了村风民风改善, 对提升群众获得感、弘扬孝善文化起到明显推动作用, Yang & Sun, 2020). By assembling the connection of volunteering and xiao and the connection of party and people into the same list of benefits of volunteering, this quote expresses a complex image of a society made of, but transcending single families, while being inseparably entangled with the state.

The volunteer system is therefore deeply connected to the extension of *xiao*. It extends xiao on at least three levels: firstly from a family-relation to an intergenerational relation in overall society, secondly from an intra-family relation to a relation of reciprocity between families, and thirdly from an individual moral supported by tradition to a public moral backed up and guaranteed by the state through rationalized, bureaucratic means. At the same time, volunteering is understood to promote *xiao* within families. Thus, volunteer activities are described to both transport the work of *xiao* from within the family to society and reinforce the tradition of *xiao* within the family. Thus, family, society, and the state become entangled and functionally related to each other.

Conclusion

In this text, we have shown how heterogeneous discourses in China claim an extension of xiao. We have shown how government texts as well as some popular articles on WeChat extend xiao at least on three dimensions: (1) to relations between citizens and the state/country, (2) to relations between the generations in overall society, (3) to public morals in general, which in turn inform a civilized society.

The xiao these texts envision goes beyond "family" in the sense of classic sociological theory, which separates family as an area of the private from politics or economics (Luhmann, 1990). Rather than being a family value, as which xiao is depicted in the existing academic literature, xiao becomes a societal, political concept because it makes intra-family relations directly matter for behavior in the public sphere. It elevates a principle of parent-child relations to a metaphor for social relations, which in turn allows to connect family to projects of social engineering aiming to create a civilized society respectful toward the elderly. This calls for and justifies a high degree of state involvement, so that family and kinship are not imagined as somehow opposite of the public or state institutions.

This extension of xiao toward society is, however, not envisioning a society where kinship-networks fulfill governmental functions as described for the traditional family-state isomorphism in historic literature. Instead, the extension of xiao means an appellation of practices imagined to originate from the family to extend toward wider social relations. This does not delegate government functions to a partial self-rule of families, as in the traditional family-state system. Rather, the state promotes and administers the moral behavior it appeals to through a rational rule (in the sense of Weber, 1982) that sometimes mirrors high modernist ideas of social engineering through scoring systems. The high modernist vision of improving public morals is based on the assumption that traditional virtues can be revitalized and channeled into a healthy direction by using means of a state bureaucracy that can measure virtuous behavior in an objective way and can create definite, plannable effects on individual behavior. This also means that social relations and reciprocity is not left to be regulated by guanxi-based strong ties, as Bian (1997) argues for Chinese job markets, but that the state installs rationalized bureaucratic means to secure the functioning of reciprocity.

Furthermore, in contrast to traditional family-state isomorphism, the extension of xiao is certainly directed toward a nation-state, of whose national identity the acclaimed tradition of xiao is part of. Thus, xiao becomes part of the construction of an "imagined community" (Anderson, 1983) based on national cultural tradition. While the ideas of filial piety and loyalty (忠孝) and the idea of a family-state isomorphism can be found in ancient texts, the extension of xiao today requires a reinterpretation of these concepts within a nationalist discourse. For example, it requires the target of loyalty to be reinterpreted from the feudal lord to the nation-state and its government, and the family as an actual unit of governance to be reinterpreted as the family as a private, emotional place, that nevertheless provides a source for public morals.

This, however, does not justify the use of older sociological tropes on a monolithic "tradition" contrasted with a dynamic and diverse "modernity." Various works indicate that xiao was debated and transformed throughout the entire Chinese history, including ancient times (Knapp, 1995; Xie, 2021). Hence, while the extension of xiao in current sources does certainly not reflect a static Confucianist tradition, it is equally questionable to describe it in contrast to an assumed static past. Rather, it should be seen as part of both a history of constant re-imaginations of the relationship between public and private forms of xiao, and a history of projects of improving the moral or spiritual "quality" of the population. State-discourse both authorizes xiao by its status as ancient, traditional Chinese culture, and—at the same time—promotes it as part of nationalist and high modernist civilizational projects which extend xiao to a principle of civilized public behavior.

By extending xiao to the public sphere, state intervention can be depicted as not only legitimate but even necessary to create a civilized society. Thus, the family ceases to be something entirely "private," just as xiao ceases to be something entirely bound within "family." This makes family a necessary target of projects to construct public morals, which in turn challenges the trends toward a differentiated sphere of the private that has been claimed by some authors in the early 21st century (Davis, 2000; Yan, 2003b). In this sense, the extension of xiao becomes a crucial link between the processes of negotiating xiao within families and the larger civilizational projects to construct a spiritual civilization or a more civilized society. Of course, as we have argued above, the data collected so far only justify statement on the level of discourse. However, further exploration is needed to understand the degree to which the extension of xiao in discourse becomes part of everyday life sensemaking, and to which degree it informs specific state practices.

Notes

1. This research was funded by the Deutsche Forschungsgemeinschaft (DFG, German Research Foundation)—Project Number 424193223.
2. For an overview of the historic development of xiao, see also He (2021, pp. 27–50).
3. All documents were collected in October 2020.

References

Anagnost, A. (2004). The corporeal politics of quality (suzhi). *Public Culture, 16*(2), 189–208.
Anderson, B. R. O.'G. (1983). *Imagined communities: Reflections on the origin and spread of nationalism*. Verso.
Anonymous. (2019a, May 5). 温泉街道甸中村妇联开展"五一"志愿服务活动. http://ynan.wenming.cn/zyfw/201905/t20190505_3018651.shtml
Anonymous. (2019b, July 4). 孝. https://www.xuexi.cn/lgpage/detail/index.html?id=11043077955584848497
Anonymous. (2020, August 21). 中国核潜艇之父"黄旭华：一生研制核潜艇, 隐姓埋名30年. https://www.xuexi.cn/lgpage/detail/index.html?id=17330185151504753671&item_id=17330185151504753671
Bian, Y. (1997). Bringing strong ties back in: Indirect ties, network bridges, and job searches in China. *American Sociological Review, 62*, 366–385.
Chen, B. (2021). 从家国结构论孝的公共性. 船山学刊. *Chuanshan Journal, 2*, 17–25.
Chen, T., & Qing, S. (2019). 中国孝道观念的代际传递效应. 人口与经济. *Population & Economics, 2*, 55–67.
Cheung, C.-K., & Kwan, A. Y.-H. (2009). The erosion of filial piety by modernisation in Chinese cities. *Ageing and Society, 29*(2), 179–198. https://doi.org/10.1017/S0144686X08007836
Chou, R. J.-A. (2011). Filial piety by contract? the emergence, implementation, and implications of the "family support agreement" in China. *The Gerontologist, 51*(1), 3–16. https://doi.org/10.1093/geront/gnq059
Corbin, J. M., & Strauss, A. L. (2008). *Basics of qualitative research: Techniques and procedures for developing grounded theory* (3rd ed.). Sage Publications.
Davis, D. (2000). Introduction: A revolution in consumption. In D. Davis (Ed.), *The consumer revolution in urban China* (pp. 1–22). University of California Press.
Du, W. (1997). 现代精神与儒家传统. 生活·读书·新知三联书店.
Elfick, J. (2011). Class formation and consumption among middle-class professionals in Shenzhen. *Journal of Current Affairs, 40*(1), 187–211.
Fairclough, N. (1992). *Discourse and social change* (Repr). Polity Press.
Feng, L. (2014). 当代中国社会的个体化趋势及其政治意义. 社会科学. *Journal of Social Sciences, 12*, 20–27.
Fong, V. (2004). Filial nationalism among Chinese teenagers with global identities. *American Ethnologist, 31*(4), 631–648. https://doi.org/10.1525/ae.2004.31.4.631
Foucault, M. (1993). *Die Ordnung des Diskurses. Fischer-Wissenschaft: Vol. 10083*. Fischer-Taschenbuch-Verl.
General Office of the CPC Central Committee. (2018). 关于建设新时代文明实践中心建设试点工作的指导意见, *document number 78*.
General Office of the CPC Central Committee. (2021). 关于深入开展学雷锋活动的意见. http://www.moe.gov.cn/jyb_xxgk/moe_1777/moe_1778/201203/t20120314_132124.html

Greenhalgh, S. (2003). Science, modernity, and the making of China's one-child policy. *Population and Development Review*, *29*(2), 163–196.

Gui, T., & Koropeckyj-Cox, T. (2016). "I am the only child of my parents": perspectives on future elder care for parents among Chinese only-children living overseas. *Journal of Cross-Cultural Gerontology*, *31*(3), 255–275. https://doi.org/10.1007/s10823-016-9295-z

He, L. (2021). *Care work, migrant peasant families and discourse of filial piety in China*. Palgrave. https://doi.org/10.1007/978-981-16-1880-2

Hu, P. (2009). 孝经译注 (2nd ed.). 中华书局.

Huang, S.-m. (1998). *The spiral road: Change in a Chinese village through the eyes of a Communist party leader* (2nd ed.). *Conflict & Social Change*. Westview Press. http://gbv.eblib.com/patron/FullRecord.aspx?p=746865

Ikels, C. (2006). Economic reform and intergenerational relationships in china. *Oxford Development Studies*, *34*(4), 387–400. https://doi.org/10.1080/13600810601045619

Ji, W., & Yang, G. (2020, August 20). 每位党员都有一个"红色账本"‖. http://dzrb.dzng.com/paper/paperShare/id/730637

Jin, W. (2019, May 24). "孝"要慧于心敏于行—浏阳文明网. http://hnlys.wenming.cn/jieri/201905/t20190524_3026845.html

Kipnis, A. (2007). Neoliberalism reified: Suzhi discourse and tropes of neoliberalism in the people's republic of China. *The Journal of the Royal Anthropological Institute of Great Britain and Ireland*, *13*(2), 383–400.

Knapp, K. N. (1995). The ru reinterpretation of Xiao. *Early China*, *20*, 195–222. https://doi.org/10.1017/S036250280000448X

Li, J. (2003). The core of Confucian learning. *The American Psychologist*, *58*(2), 146–147; discussion 148–149. https://doi.org/10.1037/0003–066X.58.2.146

Li, J. (2017, June 19). 别让孝心只停留在朋友圈. http://ynan.wenming.cn/tcrp/201706/t20170619_2761556.shtml

Liu, F. (2008). Negotiating the filial self. *YOUNG*, *16*(4), 409–430. https://doi.org/10.1177/110330880801600404

Liu, J., & Bern-Klug, M. (2016). "I should be doing more for my parent": Chinese adult children's worry about performance in providing care for their oldest-old parents. *International Psychogeriatrics*, *28*(2), 303–315. https://doi.org/10.1017/S1041610215001726

Liu, W. (2012). 孝道衰落？成年子女支持父母的观念、行为及其影响因素. 青年研究. *Youth Studies* (2), 22–32.

Liu, W. (2016). 转型期的家庭代际情感与团结: 基于上海两类"啃老"家庭的比较. 社会学研究. *Sociological Studies* (4), 145–168+245.

Liu, X., Lu, B., & Feng, Z. (2017). Intergenerational transfers and informal care for disabled elderly persons in China: Evidences from CHARLS. *Health & Social Care in the Community*, *25*(4), 1364–1374.

Luhmann, N. (1990). Sozialsystem familie. In N. Luhmann (Ed.), *Konstruktivistische perspektiven* (pp. 196–217). Westdt.-Verl.

Meinhof, M. (2017). Colonial temporality and Chinese national modernization discourses. *Interdisciplines*, *8*(1), 51–80.

Meinhof, M. (2018). *Shopping in China: Dispositive konsumistischer Subjektivation im Alltagsleben chinesischer Studierender*. VS Verlag für Sozialwissenschaften.

Meinhof, M. (2021). Die kolonialität der moderne: Koloniale zeitlichkeit und die internalisierung der idee der ‚rückständigkeit' in China. *Zeitschrift Für Soziologie*, *50*(1), 26–41. https://doi.org/10.1515/zfsoz-2021-0004

Perry, E. J. (2017). Cultural governance in contemporary China: "re-orienting" party propaganda. In P. M. Thornton & V. Shue (Eds.), *To govern China: Evolving practices of power* (pp. 29–55). Cambridge University Press. https://doi.org/10.1017/9781108131858.002

Scott, J. C. (1998). *Seeing like a state: How certain schemes to improve the human condition have failed. Yale agrarian studies*. Yale University Press.

Shen, Y. (2013). 个体家庭 *iFamily:* 中国城市现代化进程中的个体、家庭与国家. 上海三联书店.

Shen, Y. (2016). Filial daughters? Agency and subjectivity of rural migrant women in Shanghai. *The China Quarterly, 226*, 519–537. https://doi.org/10.1017/S0305741016000357

Shi, L. (2009). "Little quilted vests to warm parents' hearts": Redefining the gendered practice of filial piety in rural north-eastern China. *The China Quarterly, 198*, 348–363. https://doi.org/10.1017/S0305741009000344

Shih, Y.-K. (2010). The isomorphism of family and state and the integration of church and state: On the differences between the Confucian political tradition and democratic politics (Dandan Chen & Adrian Thieret, trans.). In T. Y. Cao, X. Zhong, & K. Liao (Eds.), *Ideas, history, and modern China: v. 2. Culture and social transformations in reform era China* (pp. 97–118). Brill. https://doi.org/10.1163/ej.9789004175167.i-447.31

State Council. (2019, October 27). 新时代公民道德建设实施纲要. http://www.gov.cn/zhengce/2019-10/27/content_5445556.htm

Tomba, L. (2004). Creating an urban middle class: Social engineering in Beijing. *The China Journal, 51*(1), 1–25.

Wang, Q. (2020). 文化治理："以孝治村"的形成机理与运行逻辑. 南京农业大学学报（社会科学版）. *Journal of Nanjing Agricultural University (Social Sciences Edition), 20*(5), 102–108.

Wang, Z. (2015). "忠孝"与"孝忠": 中国道德史的考察. 长江师范学院学报. *Journal of Yangtze Normal University, 31*(2), 1–9.

Wang, F., & Wang, T. (2014). 家庭财富累积、代际关系与传统养老模式的变化. 老龄科学研究. *Scientific Research on Aging, 2*(1), 13–19.

Weber, M. (1982). Die drei reinen Typen der legitimen Herrschaft. In J. Winckelmann & M. Weber (Eds.), *Gesammelte Aufsätze zur Wissenschaftslehre* (5th ed., pp. 475–488). Mohr.

Wei, Y. (2017). "厚此薄彼"还是"同时兼顾"？: 农村已婚女性的代际支持研究. 妇女研究论丛. *Journal of Chinese Women's Studies, 141*(3), 16–26+39.

Xi, J. (2019a, February 4). 习近平在二〇一九年春节团拜会上的讲话. http://jhsjk.people.cn/article/30613956

Xi, J. (2019b, July 24). 习近平致中国志愿服务联合会第二届会员代表大会的贺信. http://www.xinhuanet.com/politics/leaders/2019-07/24/c_1124792815.htm

Xiao, Q. (2001). 孝与中国文化. 人民出版社.

Xiao, Q. (2013). "传统孝道的当代意义与多元对话"国际学术会议论文述评. 道德与文明. *Morality and Civilization, 6*, 149–151.

Xie, H. (2021). "家国同构"还是"家国异构"？早期中国至商鞅变法时代家国体制的变迁. 求索. *Seeker, 1*, 73–81. https://doi.org/10.16059/j.cnki.cn43-1008/c.2021.01.008

Xu, Q. (2003). 我们还要提倡父慈子孝. In Q. Xu (Ed.), 毛泽东与孔夫子 (pp. 126–131). 人民出版社.

Xu, X. (2011). 重审儒家的"家—国"观: 从乔治·莱考夫的道德政治论说起. 开放时代. *Open Times, 3*, 46–60.

Yan, H. (2003a). Neoliberal governmentality and neohumanism: Organizing suzhi/value flow through labor recruitment networks. *Cultural Anthropology, 18*(4), 493–523.

Yan, J. (1999). 评"五四," "文革"与传统文化的论争. 中外文化与文论. *Cultural Studies and Literary Theory, 1*(2), 2–13.

Yan, Y. (1996). *The flow of gifts: Reciprocity and social networks in a Chinese village*. Stanford University Press.

Yan, Y. (2003b). *Private life under socialism: Love, intimacy, and family change in a Chinese village, 1949–1999*. Stanford University Press.

Yan, Y. (2016). Intergenerational intimacy and descending familism in rural north China. *American Anthropologist, 118*(2), 244–257. https://doi.org/10.1111/aman.12527

Yan, Y., & Zeng, J. (2020, September 2). 《习近平谈治国理政》第三卷中的用典 (之三). https://www.xuexi.cn/lgpage/detail/index.html?id=11461264505408119654&item_id=1146%20%201264505408119654

Yang, H., & Ouyang, J. (2013). 阶层分化、代际剥削与农村老年人自杀: 对近年中部地区农村老年人自杀现象的分析. 管理世界. *Management World* (5), 47–63.

Yang, M. M.-h. (1994). *Gifts, favors, and banquets: The art of social relationships in China*. Cornell University Press.

Yang, M. M.-h. (2011). Postcoloniality and religiosity in modern china: the disenchantments of sovereignty. *Theory, Culture and Society, 28*(2), 3–45.

Yang, W., & Sun, X. (2020, June 12). 莫道桑榆晚人间重暖情——山东沂水志愿者帮扶特困老人见闻. https://www.xuexi.cn/lgpage/detail/index.html?id=1834375884611347969&item_id=18343%20%2075884611347969

Yang, Z. (2017). 论以孝治国与家国同构的文化模式. 船山学刊. *Chuanshan Journal 5*, 15–18.

Yi, L. (2011). Turning rurality into modernity: Suzhi education in a suburban public school of migrant children in Xiamen. *The China Quarterly, 206*, 313–330.

Yi, W. (2018). 计划生育实践中的国家、家庭与身体: 基于赣北 t 村的考察. 东南大学学报 (哲学社会科学版). *Journal of Southeast University (Philosophy and Social Science), 20*(3), 86–93+148.

Zhai, X. (2019). "孝"之道的社会学探索. 社会. *Society, 5*, 127–161.

Zhai, X., & Qiu, R. Z. (2007). Perceptions of long-term care, autonomy, and dignity, by residents, family and caregivers: the Beijing experience. *The Journal of Medicine and Philosophy, 32*(5), 425–445. https://doi.org/10.1080/03605310701631695

Zhan, H., & Montgomery, R. (2003). Gender and elder care in China. *Gender & Society, 17*(2), 209–229.

Zhang, L. (2006). Contesting spatial modernity in late-socialist China. *Current Anthropology, 47*(3), 461–484.

Zhao, Y. (2018). 近代中国非孝论反思. *Social Science Research, 1*, 177–188.

Zhao, Z. (2019, April 19). 孝老爱亲, 是家事更是国事. 中国妇女报. https://www.xuexi.cn/lgpage/detail/index.html?id=18005719056919700182

Zhou, F. (2019). 慈孝一体: 论差序格局的"核心层. 学海. *Academia Bimestrie, 2*, 11–20.

Zhou, L. (2017). 冲突与融合: 抗战时期中国共产党家庭政策的变革. 妇女研究论丛. *Journal of Chinese Women's Studies, 3*, 40–48.

Zhou, Z. (2016). 儒法斗争与"传统"重构: 以 20 世纪 70 年代评法批儒运动所提供的历史构图为中心. 开放时代. *Open Times, 3*, 83–97.

Zhu, X. (2011). 论语集注. 中华书局.

3 Eldercare, Filial Piety within the Joint Family System of Urban India

Jagriti Gangopadhyay

Filial Piety: A Cultural Backdrop

Filial piety is an important virtue associated with later-life caregiving in Chinese and other East Asian cultures. In simple terms, filial piety refers to providing physical, financial, and emotional support to one's older parents (Cheung & Kwan, 2009; Lai, 2007; Sung, 1998). Apart from looking after the emotional and material needs of their older parents, filial piety also lays stress on honoring and respecting one's parents in their twilight years (Cheng & Chan, 2006; Dai & Dimond, 1998). Breaking down the concept of filial piety, Hsueh (2001), added four components to further expand the understanding of filial piety. These four components include: looking after the health and well-being of the older parents; providing economic support; fulfilling the household responsibilities of the older parents; and having regard for ancestral and parental property. In particular, scholars have noted that the notion of filial piety is intrinsically rooted in culture. Specifically, these scholars have pointed out that filial piety is a cultural belief and social norm that emphasizes on family values and requires adult children to sacrifice and fulfill parental responsibilities (Ho, 1996; Hwang, 1999; Ikles, 2004). It is also important to note that while filial piety is a key tradition of China, other Asian countries such as Taiwan, Hong Kong, Korea, Japan, and Singapore also are influenced by the norms of filial piety. In particular, studies have demonstrated how older adults in countries such as Japan and Korea continue to hold on to filial piety norms irrespective of rapid modernization (Koyano, 1996; Sung, 1995). In addition to filial piety being a cultural construct, the Governments of different countries also lay emphasis on the practice of filial piety. For instance, Governments of Taiwan and Singapore have made care and sustenance for one's older parents a responsibility of the adult children, the Hong Kong Government provides various incentives in the form of tax benefits and reduction in waiting time for public housing for adult children opting to co-reside with their older parent/s (Chow, 2006). Likewise, the Republic of Korea and Japan also regard the concept of filial piety as a major value and ensure that the aged are treated with dignity within the family as well as in the extended society (Chow, 1991, 2006).

Regardless of modernization, filial piety continues to remain an important cultural norm as the Chinese Government also placed eldercare as the responsibility of the adult children (Zhan et al., 2008). Studies examining the intersections between modernization and filial piety have found that with rapid urbanization, adult children often may not be able to co-reside with their older parents. Nonetheless, they continue to practice the culture of filial piety by demonstrating respect, solidarity, responsibility, and sacrifice, irrespective of their physical separation (Leung et al., 2010; Sun, 2017; Sung, 1998). Similar to China, India too relies on adult children for later-life caregiving. Though both countries are witnessing the gradual rise of institutional care for the elderly (Gu et al., 2007; Samanta and Gangopadhyay, 2016; Zhan et al., 2008), cohabitation with adult children continues to remain one of the most dominant forms of living arrangement in China (Zeng et al., 2014) as well as in India (Samanta et al., 2015). Despite, joint cohabitation being the most preferred living arrangement, studies examining how filial piety is constructed within the multigenerational family in neo-liberal India have been less examined in the recent gerontological narrative of India. Against this backdrop, this study uses a cultural lens and seeks to understand how older adults shape their filial expectations from their adult children residing in a cosmopolitan town of urban India. Mapping the notion of filial piety across generations, this study explores intergenerational relationships in a globalized India.

The Law and Eldercare in India

Legally, eldercare in India is regulated through the Maintenance and Welfare of Senior Citizens Act, 2007. The provisions of this Act required biological adult children, including son, daughter, grandson, and grand-daughter to provide maintenance in the form of food, clothing, residence, medical attendance, and treatment and welfare in the form of healthcare and other amenities necessary for later-life care for their biological, adoptive and step-parents (Maintenance and Welfare of Senior Citizens Act, 2007). The definition of older parents/senior citizens includes those aged 60 and above[1]. Recently, this Act was amended and the definitions of adult children, older parents, maintenance, and welfare expanded. As per the amendment, in addition to the above definitions, adult children would now include step-children, adoptive children, children-in-law, and the legal guardian of minor children, older parents would include parents-in-law, and grandparents, maintenance would include safety and security of older parents and welfare would include housing, safety and other amenities for the physical and mental well-being of a senior citizen or parent (The Maintenance and Welfare of Parents and Senior Citizens (Amendment) Bill, 2019).

A closer analysis of the Act as well as the amendment reveals that legally it is the responsibility of the adult children, irrespective of their status (biological, adoptive, or step), need to provide maintenance and look after the welfare of their older parents and parents-in-law. By placing later-life accountability on the adult children, the Government of India is also embodying the ideology of filial piety.

The law has been critiqued for emphasizing the role of adult children as caregivers and, in the process, not taking into account childless and single older adults (Gangopadhyay, 2019). Additionally, in the wake of rising cases of elder abuse by family members (Agewell Foundation, 2019), the law continues to view adult children as the primary care providers for older adults (Gangopadhyay, 2019).

Despite the law laying stress on the duty of adult children to look after their older parents, studies have noted how different forms of eldercare are emerging in urban India. In particular, these studies have demonstrated the rise of institutionalized care among the senior citizens of India (Lamb, 2009; Kalavar & Jamuna, 2011; Gangopadhyay, 2021). On the other hand, recent studies have noted that gradually many older adults are choosing to live alone and remain employed even after they turn 60 to avoid feeling lonely (Visaria & Dommaraju, 2019) and often depend on paid caregiving for their physical needs (Gangopadhyay, 2020). Transnational caregiving is also practiced in some parts of India, where older parents receive remittances and care from their adult children through various forms of information and communication technologies (Ahlin, 2018, 2020). Though these different versions of caregiving arrangements are rising in urban India, nonetheless joint living continues to be the most popular form of eldercare in India. As per statistics, 5% of older adults live alone, 12% live only with their spouse, and 32% live with their adult children in India (Ministry of Statistics and Programme Implementation, 2016).

Filial Obligations and Son Preference in India

Filial obligations, which are similar to filial piety, have received considerable academic attention among scholars examining the Indian diaspora settled across the globe. Related to the idea of filial piety, filial obligations refer to the understanding that adult children are duty-bound to provide for the financial, physical, and emotional needs of their older parents (Albert, 1990; Finley et al., 1988; Tsutsui et al., 2014). Exploring the concept of filial obligations against the backdrop of transnationalism, several studies have demonstrated how filial expectations are shaped among older Asian Indian immigrants who chose to relocate with their adult children (Diwan et al., 2011; Gangopadhyay, 2017, 2021; Murti, 2006; Lamb, 2009; Sudha, 2014). In particular, these studies have illustrated how these older adults reimagine their notion of filial expectations in a transnational setting. For instance, Lamb (2009), in her ethnographic research, highlighted that while older Indian immigrants receive financial and physical support from their adult children, their emotional void continues to persist. Specifically, she indicated how her older research participants reinterpreted their aging processes through their everyday practices and cultural values of being American and Indian at the same time. In another study conducted by Diwan et al. (2011) among Asian older Indian immigrants living in Atlanta, the USA for the last five years shows that these older adults are constantly navigating between their desires to maintain intimate relations with their adult children versus their avoidance of becoming a burden on their adult children. Likewise, in another study administered among older adults residing in the USA, Sharma and Kemp (2012) found that older adults modify their expectations and are much more willing to adjust and adapt to the lifestyle and everyday practices of their adult children and their spouses. In a nutshell, it may be suggested that these older adults are shifting between their own traditional beliefs and the modern norms of their adult children to recreate their aging identities in a transnational backdrop.

In contrast to the older Indian immigrants, studies on older adults in India have highlighted that the traditional joint family structure mandated later-life caregiving arrangements among the adult sons and their families (Gangopadhyay, 2021; Rajan & Kumar, 2003; Shah, 1973; 1999). Additionally, the joint family system required the married daughters to leave their natal homes after they were married (Desai & Andrist, 2010; Kaur & Palriwala, 2013; Madan, 1975). As a result, the adult sons and their families have to shoulder the responsibility of their older parents. Owing to these traditional customs and cultural value systems, several studies have examined the domination of son-preference across India (Arnold et al., 1998; Kaur & Vasudev, 2019; Larsen & Kaur, 2013; Milazzo, 2018; Mitra, 2014; Robitaille, 2013). In particular, these studies have indicated that since sons are viewed as breadwinners of the family and are expected to look after their aging parents, sons are more valued and preferred as compared to daughters. In some parts of India, female feticide is also committed (Dewan & Khan, 2009; Patel, 2007) and married women are pressurized to continue having children, till they give birth to a male progeny (Dutta et al., 2015; Jha et al., 2006; Malhotra et al., 1995). Moreover, female children or girl child is considered to be an economic burden and are married off at the earliest opportunity. Consequently, child marriages among girl children continue to remain a major social problem in India (Gangopadhyay, 2021; Gupta, 2012). Based on these studies, it may be suggested that the majority of the older adults co-reside with their adult sons in India. As highlighted, adult daughters are not expected to look after their aging parents. Though older adults co-habit with their adult son/s, the primary responsibility of elderly caregiving is mostly borne by the daughter-in-law/s (Dhar, 2012; Jamuna & Ramamurti, 1999; Ugargol & Bailey, 2021; Vera-Sanso, 2005). Specifically, these studies have demonstrated how elderly caregiving often leads to conflict and the daughter-in-law/s feel overburdened with their responsibilities. On another note, recent studies have also indicated that intergenerational exchanges continue to persist in the later-life and in most of the instances, the older parents provide grandparenting duties in exchange for the caregiving support received from their adult children and their families (Gangopadhyay & Samanta, 2017; Visaria & Dommaraju, 2019). Summarizing these studies, it may be suggested that elderly caregiving, intergenerational exchange, and family dynamics among older adults and their adult children have been examined by scholars of social gerontology and family sociology in India. The contributions of these studies are significant and have truly helped in expanding the intellectual knowledge of the two disciplines. However, it is important to note that a systematic understanding of how culture intersects with intergenerational ties, filial obligations, and caregiving requires a more systematic examination. Addressing these research lacunae, this chapter aims to adopt a cultural lens and investigate how filial obligations, parent–child relationships, and later-life interpersonal experiences are shaped in modern and educated joint households of neo-liberal India. Against the backdrop of Disengagement Theory, this chapter will highlight how the older research participants chose to disengage and engage with their adult children and their families. Finally, this chapter will reflect on how external factors such as globalization and urbanization play key roles in determining later-life relationships and filial obligations in urban India.

Cultural Gerontology and the Disengagement Theory

One of the biggest challenges of gerontological scholarship in India is that it is extremely interdisciplinary. Contributions from medical professionals, policymakers, population studies, sociologists, and anthropologists have helped to expand the scope of gerontology as a discipline. Consequently, majority of the studies are quantitative or reflect the medical perspective (Agarwal et al., 2020; Ingle & Nath, 2008; Kumar & Pradhan, 2019; Shah, 2003; Singh et al., 2017). In comparison to this body of scholarship, the contributions of sociologists and anthropologists have examined aging as a complex process and highlighted the different cultural practices associated with old age in India (Cohen, 1999; Lamb, 2002, 2009; van Willigen et al., 2006). Though these studies have explored aging as a cultural phenomenon, nonetheless, how growing old intersects with the idea of a neoliberal India has not been interrogated by these studies. Building upon these studies, this chapter intends to demonstrate how factors such as globalization and neo-liberalization play a key role in determining the agency and cultural practices of older adults within a joint family set-up.

Cultural gerontology has emerged as one of the most engaging fields of gerontology in recent times. Going beyond the idea of a medical perspective, cultural gerontology seeks to address aging in a much broader sense (Twigg & Martin, 2015). One of the key influences of cultural gerontology is that it takes into account the subjective experiences of older adults. Scholars of cultural gerontology have examined the influence of the market, travel, and changing fashion goals in shaping later-life experiences. Methodologically, too these scholars have often gone beyond the usual mode of data collection and instead used autobiographies and photographs to understand processes of ageing (Featherstone & Wernick, 1995; Hyde, 2015; Lewis et al., 2011; Twigg & Martin, 2015). Relatedly, scholarship on India has also examined the aging body through a cultural lens quite extensively. In particular, the studies of India have often used the framework of disengagement to explain how older adults rely on religion to detach and disengage from their surroundings as well as to loosen their ties and attachment from their loved ones (Brijnath, 2014; Cohen, 1999; Lamb, 2009; 2017).

The Disengagement Theory is one of the first theoretical models to be established in social gerontology. This model was developed by Elaine Cumming and

William Earl Henry in the year 1961, in their book titled, *"Growing Old."* In their book, they proposed nine postulates to explain the process of disengagement. These nine postulates are as follows:

> **Postulate 1:** Death is inevitable and to accept death over time the older adults will loosen their ties with regard to their close ones.
> **Postulate 2:** The older adults will gradually reduce their interactions with others and focus more on their self-perpetuation.
> **Postulate 3:** The process of disengagement would differ between older men and women.
> **Postulate 4:** Older adults are made to retire as with age skills and knowledge gradually decline.
> **Postulate 5:** Society and the older individual disengage together.
> **Postulate 6:** Older individuals abandon their central role and disengage to avoid demoralization.
> **Postulate 7:** Older individuals disengage when they loses their energy and realizes the shortness of life span. Society allows older adults to disengage by making them retire, requirements of the nuclear family system and the differential death rates.
> **Postulate 8:** Lesser interactions result affect interpersonal relationships adversely. As a result older adults chose to disengage.
> **Postulate 9:** This theoretical model is not formed by culture, but the form it takes is shaped by culture.

Though the studies on older adults in India have used the Disengagement Theory, a detailed analysis of the nine postulates has not been done to understand the aging experiences in India. Hence, this chapter will apply a cultural gerontological framework as well as these nine postulates to examine how filial ties are navigated in contemporary India.

Neoliberal India and Cosmopolitan Manipal

In 1991, India entered into the liberalization era and allowed the functioning of free markets and investments from foreign firms. Though the decision of the Government of India to trade with foreign investors was an economic policy, nonetheless, social and cultural practices were also affected. A direct result of liberalization was the influence of Western lifestyle and education systems on the middle class of India. As foreign companies started recruiting Indians and immigrating to First World countries became easier, the middle class's agency and aspirations also were influenced by consumer culture and possession of social status (Bhandari, 2020; Jodhka & Prakash, 2016; Srivastava, 2015). Ever since India adopted liberalization and the Western First World culture emerged as an ideal type, the middle class began to follow the principles of the neoliberal model as well. The neoliberal model dominant in the USA stands on the principles of self-sufficiency, success, and discipline (Clack & Paule, 2019). Soon these principles became the stepping stones of India's middle class and "work culture" became a prominent feature of neoliberal India. In a survey conducted by Future Workplace on behalf of Kronos Incorporated in 2018, among 2,772 part-time and full-time employees in countries such as Australia, Canada, France, Germany, India, Mexico, the UK, and the USA, India emerged as the country with the longest working hours (Business Standard, 2018). In particular, this survey found that if pay remained constant, Indians would still prefer to five days a week, even if they had the option to work for fewer days. Hence, it may be suggested that work ethic is one of the core values of neoliberal India.

Set against the backdrop of neoliberal India, the town of Manipal, situated in the southern state of Karnataka (the sixth largest state of India) is known for its cosmopolitan setting. Since one of the biggest and oldest private Universities of India is located in Manipal, the town's cosmopolitan approach is reflected through its food joints, tourism, and living arrangements (Joseph, 2009). Several students live in private apartments, travel to nearby beaches, and eat at the local food hubs during their stay at Manipal. The town of Manipal has often been branded as a melting pot of cultures and the town is constantly adapting to suit the needs of the University students who come from different backgrounds (The Hindu, 2006). Manipal comes across as an intersecting point for many cultures and as a University town, it also embodies the aspirations and ambitions of the youth of neoliberal India. Though Manipal is considered to be a youth-centric town, it is also home to many multigenerational families. Apart from the University, Manipal is also known for its healthcare[2] and many older adults chose to reside with their adult children to access the affordable and efficient healthcare system of Manipal. Given Manipal's mix of cultures, availability of health services and cosmopolitan context, Manipal caters to both the older and the younger generation. Thus, this study was situated in Manipal to understand how filial obligations and family ties are shaped in one of the modern towns of India.

Methodology

The empirical data for this study was collected in one of the oldest high rises of Manipal. Qualitative and non-probability sampling techniques and interview methods were used to recruit participants and administer the interviews among the research participants. Non-probability sampling techniques such as snowball and purposive sampling were used to identify research participants for this study. Initial contact with the research participants was made through personal contacts and references, who introduced the author to the first few multigenerational families. Later, using snowball sampling, the original interlocutors, referred the author to other multigenerational families. Since the author knew and had access to the residents of this particular high rise, the interviews were administered in this high rise. The inclusion and exclusion criteria were indicated to the personal contacts of the author, to abide by the principles of purposive sampling (Campbell et al., 2020).

Inclusion criteria for the older participants of the study were as follows: (1) be 60 years of age, (2) live with their adult children at least for 5 years in Manipal, (3) have at least one grandchild, and (4) be able to speak either in English or Hindi. Exclusion criteria for the older participants were as follows: (1) to be aged above 80, (2) to be permanently disabled or suffering from a terminal illness, (3) not follow or be able to speak in Hindi or English, and (4) childless and older adults living only with their adult child were not interviewed for this study. Inclusion criteria for the adult child/children were as follows: (1) living with older parents or parent in Manipal for at least five years, (2) to be married and have at least one child, and (3) speak either Hindi or English. Exclusion criteria for the adult child/children were as follows: (1) unmarried adult child/children living with their older parents were not interviewed for this study, (2) single parents living with their older parents were also not interviewed for this study, (3) adult child/children unable to speak in Hindi or English were not interviewed for this study. Scholars of qualitative research have often stressed the role of language as a key component of data collection. In particular, these studies have indicated that often different languages spoken by the interviewer and the interviewee result in miscommunications and barriers. Additionally, these studies have noted that using translators might not always be helpful as often the meaning of the research might be misrepresented or misinterpreted by the translator as well (Lopez et al., 2008; Santos et al., 2015; van Nes et al., 2010; Young & Temple, 2014). Given the emphasis on language in qualitative research and the author was fluent only in English and Hindi and can neither understand nor speak the local dialect of the state, the language preferences were specified in the inclusion and exclusion criteria of this study.

A total of 25 older adults and their co-resident adult children were interviewed for this study. In the case of older adults living with their spouses, both the older partners were interviewed. This was done deliberately to compare the similarities and differences between older adults living with spouse and their adult children and older adults living as widows/widowers with their adult children. This study did not find any older adult/s living with two of their adult children and their families living in the same household. Post the identification of the research participants, in-depth interviews face to face interviews were conducted with both the older adult as well as the adult child. The interviews lasted for an hour each for both the older adult/s and the adult child. Interview timings were fixed as per the convenience of the research participants and the older parent and the adult child were interviewed separately to receive objective empirical data. Similarly, for the older spouses, each partner was interviewed individually to ensure that the partners did not influence each other's responses. Additionally, informed consent was taken from each of the participants before beginning the interviews.

The interview tool used was a semi-structured questionnaire, which had both open and close-ended questions. Two separate semi-structured questionnaires, one for the older adult and one for the adult child were constructed. Questions for the older participants ranged from the background of the participants to

Table 3.1 Background Details of the Sample Population

Serial no.	Feature	Sample
1	Living arrangements	15 older adults with spouse, adult child, adult child's spouse and grandchild; 5 older men with adult child, adult child' spouse and grandchild/children; 5 older women with adult child, adult child's spouse and grandchild/children
2	Occupational status of the older adults	All retired; 11 of the older women interviewed have been homemakers all their lives
3	Source of income of the older adults	Pension: 15/25 older adults; personal savings: 10/25
4	Caste[3]	10/25 (Brahmins); 4/25 (Kshatriyas); 4/25 (Vaishyas); 3/25 (Other Backward Classes); 4/25 (Scheduled Caste)
5	Religion	15/25 (Hindus); 5/25 (Muslims); 3/25 (Jains); 2/25 (Christians)
6	Educational background of the older adults	All the older adults are post-graduate (total 17 to 18 years of education)
7	Profession of the adult children	20/25 (doctors); 3/25 (business owners); 2/25 (bank employees)
9	Ethnicity	All the research participants were Kannadigas (the main ethnic population of the state of Karnataka)

their reasons for settling in Manipal to their relationships with their adult child and grandchildren and their thoughts on their caregiving arrangements in case of a medical emergency or health concern. On the other hand, questions for the adult child focused on their profession, ties with their parent, spouse, and child, their major concerns regarding their family members and their thoughts on later-life caregiving arrangements for their parents, in the instance of a health exigency. Detailed information regarding the background and socio-economic features of the research participants are indicated in Table 3.1.

Data Analysis

Once the data collection was completed, thematic analysis was applied to analyze the data. Thematic analysis as a method is one of the most commonly used methods to examine qualitative data (Swain, 2018). Though this method's roots lie in psychology (Braun & Clarke, 2021), researchers from across the field have used this method to analyze their empirical data (Jacobson et al., 2019; Vaismoradi et al., 2013). This study too relied on thematic analysis and this section highlights the step-by-step process followed to analyze the data. Firstly, the data was translated verbatim from the interviews. Next, the interviews were read multiple times and similar patterns were identified. Following the identification of the patterns, they were broken into codes. After breaking the data into codes, the codes were combined to identify common themes within these codes. Those themes that seemed to be coherent with the entire data were identified and considered as the main findings of this study. Finally, all the themes were noted and only those which appeared the most relevant and unique were added to the findings section of this chapter.

Limitations of the Study

Though the caste and religious backgrounds of the research participants were noted, an intersection between aging, filial obligations, and these social factors were not performed as they remained outside the scope of the study. Additionally, the inclusion criteria being too specific, also prevented the participation of different older cohorts residing in different living arrangements in Manipal. Finally, the sample population is not uniformly divided into the caste and religious groups that exist in India. In particular, though Manipal has been discussed as a cosmopolitan town, the diverse ethnic groups of India could not be represented adequately in this study. These limitations could be attributed to the limitation of snowball sampling.

Results and Findings

Parent–Child Relationships: Grandparenting Responsibilities and Filial Expectations

Through the in-depth interviews, this study found that all the older adults had shifted to Manipal, post the birth of their grandchild/children. To be an integral part of their grandkids was one of the key motivations for the older parents to relocate with their adult children. Since their adult child as well as the spouse of the adult child were working, the adult children also wanted their older parent/s to shift with them. This way, they could leave their kids with their parents and not be concerned over their safety and well-being. 19/25 had another child living in another city or country. However, owing to Manipal's health facilities, they chose to shift to Manipal. Though this seemed like a situation that would please both parties, in their narratives, the older parent/s revealed that they felt like mere babysitters and the adult children took them for granted.

> I came to look after my daughter when she was pregnant and stayed back ever since then. Both my daughter and her husband are working and I was not very happy with the kind of paid caregiving that my grandson was receiving. So I stayed back to supervise. Initially, I used to enjoy my role and thought it gave me a new purpose in life. But now, I have no time for myself. My grandson is four years old and highly dependent on me for all his needs. Often my daughter and her husband go out for movies and diners and I stay back babysitting. I feel emotionally drained and often feel that I am seen only as a caregiver.
>
> (Older women, widowed, aged 63).

> We started living with our son after the birth of our granddaughter. We felt the child needed attention and so my wife and I decided to relocate. Though we really enjoy our time with our granddaughter, we are often blamed if something goes wrong with child. In case, she has fever then it is our fault. If the child is not eating well, then also it is our fault. We are a little tired of this blame game and are actually reconsidering going back to our natal home.
>
> (Older adult, aged 67, lives with spouse).

This "feeling of being taken for granted" was present among all the older parents. In particular, the older parent/s felt that irrespective of their age, they were still satisfying their roles as grandparents, however, the emotional expectation they had from their adult child was not being fulfilled. All the older adults expressed that while their adult children took care of their physical and health needs, their emotional needs were fulfilled only by staying close to their grandchild. The adult children hardly shared their day-to-day activities with their older parents and most conversations revolved around the grandchild and the health of the older parent.

> I do not even try to make everyone happy. Older parents I feel continue to have expectations no matter what we do for them. Here it is a small town and very easy to navigate. I hardly have any time for myself. I have given up my hobbies. Whole day I am working. I myself grew up with my grandparents. My parents had little time for me. It all reverses when your parents become old. They have different expectations. We have way more competition than our parents did. So I cannot do better than this.
>
> (Adult daughter, aged 41, living with older parents).

> I got my mother here because after my father passed away she was lonely and depressed. I thought she would be happy here with her grandchild. I was also happy that I can take care of her because my other brother lives in the US and it is impossible for him to come here and take care of here. My mother has many complaints but I also have to balance my wife and my mother. It is very hard for me and I am a very busy man. I know my mother wants my time. But I have to divide it between her and my own family. My work takes away all my time and there is only so much I can do.
>
> (Adult son, aged 37, lives with older mother).

With regard to moving back to their natal homes, the older adults living with spouses considered this option much more strongly as opposed to the older adults living alone. In comparison to the older parents, the adult children indicated that their work demanded most of their time and they often felt sandwiched between their parents, child, and work. Specifically, the adult children complained that they hardly had time for their own selves that they could give time to their older parents. Whatever little time they had, they preferred spending it with their child. The adult children conveyed that India's neoliberal work culture was too demanding and while they were grateful to their parents for looking after their child/children, nonetheless, they also felt that co-habiting was also advantageous for the older parent/s. In particular, the adult children argued that through this living arrangement, the older parent/s get to see their grandchild/children every day and in case of a health emergency, they have their adult children near them.

Navigating Disengagement and Engagement

As discussed, the older adults felt that there was an emotional gap between them and their adult children. Though all the older adults were confident that their adult children would look after them in case of major health emergencies or permanent disabilities, they were unsure about the future of their emotional bond. As a result, all the older adults suggested that they practiced emotional detachment from their loved ones and instead focused on various other forms of engagement that suited their emotional needs and requirements.

> Though I like spending time with my grandchild, I also need to do some activities for myself that will help me feel motivated. When one is old, one often feels lack of purpose and seeing and accepting one's bodily changes is not easy. One also loses ones friends and it is very important to focus on self-reflection. Hence, I meditate and listen to music regularly. It gives me a sense of calmness and mental peace.
>
> (Older male, widowed, aged 76).

> My husband and I are lucky to have each other. We discuss and share everything. We also go for regular walks. We also listen to religious scriptures together. I honestly feel that I am not yet emotionally drained because I have my husband. I might feel mentally low, in case I survive him. It is futile to expect time from ones adult children who are so busy with their work and household chores.
>
> (Older female, lives with spouse, aged 69).

> I always loved reading. I spend a lot of time reading and I believe that books are the best companion anyone can have. In our days we used to come back home and have tea time and meal times together. My daughter and son-in-law watch television when they are eating. We hardly talk to each other. I am sure they talk to each other in their own private time, but they rarely ask me how was my day or what did I do. Though I have no complaints from them with regard to their overall care, I feel the emotional void cannot be filled so easily.
>
> (Older male, widowed, aged 73).

Echoing similar thoughts, the older adults highlighted that through music, religion, meditation, and reading, they are trying to emotionally disassociate themselves from their adult children. In the process, these older adults are also shifting their filial expectations from their adult children to other mechanisms that will be emotionally rewarding for them. Older adults living with spouses indicated that they relied on their spouses for emotional support. However, the widowed older adults chose to rely on other mechanisms to find emotional strength in their later lives. Additionally, the older adults with another child also mentioned that they did not receive any emotional support from their adult child either.

Adult Daughters Versus Adult Sons: A Cultural Shift

17/25 of the older adults lived with their adult daughters and 8/25 of the older adults lived with their adult sons. This living arrangement marks a major cultural shift in Indian customs. Traditionally, as discussed before, residing with adult sons has been the cultural norm in India. Moving away from this practice, this study found that the older research participants were quite comfortable in breaking this tradition and living with their adult daughters. 12/25 of the older adults chose to live with their adult daughters to avoid conflict with their daughters-in-law. In particular, the older adults who were living with their adult sons and their spouses highlighted how they often had several disagreements with their daughters-in-law. The conversations with the older participants revealed that the adult daughters and sons-in-law were more forthcoming regarding their suggestions and childcare support as opposed to their adult sons and daughters-in-law.

> I often consider my daughter's house as my own house. I feel I have much more freedom and agency to do what I want in this house. In my son's house, I used to feel claustrophobic. I did not feel free. Plus, I can scold my daughter. But my son would often fight with me and my wife and it ended up very badly. So we prefer to live here. There is more peace and harmony. Emotionally, of course, there is not much difference because both my children are equally busy. My daughter is a doctor and has very little time for anyone. However, I would like to add that I fight much less with my daughter, as compared to my son.
>
> (Older male, lives with spouse, aged 79).

> I live with my son and we have major fights. I know my daughter-in-law is unhappy that I live with her. At times I feel she is only tolerating me. I try not to interfere and be on my own. But we often clash with regard to childcare and food habits. My son feels sandwiched and it becomes hard for him too. However, I have many health issues and it is hard for me to live alone. So it's a situation of compromise and adjustment.
>
> (Older female, widowed, aged 68).

The other older adults who had two daughters and two sons chose to stay back in Manipal owing to the natural surroundings of the town and the town's access to healthcare. Though living with adult daughters appeared to be a common form of living arrangement among these older adults, the complaint against lack of emotional disconnect was the same for older adults living with their adult daughters as well as adult sons.

Discussion

The findings of this study revealed that cohabitation within older parents and their adult children does not necessarily lead to emotional harmony. Though the adult children provide physical and health-related support, nonetheless, their lack of emotional support continues to be a major source of discontentment among their older parents. This finding is similar to Lamb's (2009) research in Kolkata, where she also highlighted how in spite of joint living, the older adults felt their adult children had very little time for them. The other significant finding of this study is that older parents continue to hold filial expectations and often consider grandparenting more as a duty than a later-life role. Earlier studies have pointed out how older parents considered grandparenting to be an important part of their lives (Gangopadhyay & Samanta, 2017; Madan, 1975). In contrast to these studies, this study found that while the older research participants fulfilled their caregiving responsibilities, however, they also viewed this role as a caregiver and often felt they were "being taken for granted." Relatedly, the adult children expressed that their demanding work schedules often prevented them from providing their older parents any personal time. Adding to the literature on intergenerational studies (Gangopadhyay & Samanta, 2017; Lamb, 2009; Verma & Satyanarayana; 2013), this study illustrated how the hectic work ethics of a neoliberal India impact the family ties in joint households.

To cope with their emotional lacunae, this study also found that the older adults chose to emotionally disconnect from their adult children. By relying on religion, music, and spirituality, these older adults opted to disengage from their adult children. This disengagement also helped them to come to terms with their age-related issues and attain peace of mind. Drawing from the postulates of the Disengagement Theory, it may be suggested that lack of emotional support from their adult children, coerced these older adults to disengage deliberately. This disengagement gave the older adults a sense of gratification and assisted them in becoming emotionally self-reliant and self-reflective as well. This finding adds to the existing literature on disengagement and aging in India (Cohen, 1999; Lamb, 2017) and suggests that going beyond the cultural norms of relying on adult children for all forms of support, these older adults are choosing independent ways to detach and loosen their kin ties.

Finally, this study found that a majority of the older adults prefer to co-reside with their adult daughters to avoid conflict with their daughter-in-law. Several studies in India have indicated how married daughters are considered to be *"paraya dhan"* (wealth that doesn't belong to you) and the responsibility of later-life caregiving rests on the adult sons (Gangopadhyay, 2021; Kaur and Palriwala, 2013; Vera-Sanso, 2005). Diverging from these studies, this study found that flouting traditional norms, these modern and educated older adults are making their choices concerning their later-life living arrangements.

Conclusion and Policy Implications

This chapter, through empirical data, illustrated how filial obligations are constructed within joint households in neoliberal India. The findings of the study discussed in this chapter showed how co-residence with adult children does not warrant emotional satisfaction. As the narratives of the older adults indicated that the work schedules of their adult children prevented them from spending time with their older parents. Hence, though the older parents were ensured of maintenance and health provisions, their need for emotional sustenance remained unfulfilled. Consequently, the older adults had emotionally disconnected from their adult children and relied on other sources such as music, yoga, religious texts, and meditation to derive self-fulfillment. The Disengagement Theory seemed relevant in this context, as all the older adults opted to disengage from their kin members. Finally, this study found that going beyond cultural traditions, many of the older adults were living with their adult daughters and going against the normative order of depending on their adult sons for later-life support.

Despite, the rise of various other forms of caregiving arrangements, such as paid and institutional caregiving, cohabitation with adult children continues to be the most dominant form of living arrangement in India. Though cohabitation emerged as the most dominant living arrangement, nonetheless, this study illustrated that cohabitation does not necessarily guarantee emotional dependency and satisfaction. With regard to policy, there is very little attention paid to the mental health of senior citizens in the country. Policymakers, NGO personals, and the state need to recognize this as a major policy gap and address this with urgency. Since financially stable older adults are relying on other modes for self-gratification, the State needs to channelize these modes for better access and availability to senior citizens of all income backgrounds.

This study focused only on those older adults who were living with their adult children. Older adults living alone and childless older adults have received little academic attention in India. Future studies could examine caregiving arrangements among these groups of older adults and expand the gerontological scholarship of India.

Acknowledgment

This chapter would not have been possible without my research participants. I extend my gratitude to them and thank them for sharing their personal stories with me.

Notes

1. The official retirement age of India is 60 in most places.
2. https://www.mediainfoline.com/awards/manipal-hospitals-conferred-prestigious-porter-prize-for-value-based-healthcare-delivery-award
3. The caste system unique to India draws from the Varna system (Srinivas, 1978). The Varna system was divided into four categories: the Brahmins (the priests), the Kshatriyas (the warriors), the Vaishyas (the traders), and the Shudras (laborers and

service providers). Outside the Varna system were the Untouchables who were considered as outcastes owing to their eating habits) (Bayly, 2001). To alleviate the social mobility and access of the lower castes in India, post-independence, caste-based reservations were introduced. Hence, Other Backward Classes and Scheduled Castes are modern constructions of a post-colonial India.

References

Agarwal A., Lubet A., Mitgang E., Mohanty S., & Bloom D.E. (2020). Population Aging in India: Facts, Issues, and Options. In: Poot J., Roskruge M. (eds) *Population Change and Impacts in Asia and the Pacific. New Frontiers in Regional Science: Asian Perspectives*, vol. 30. Singapore: Springer.

Agewell Foundation Annual Report (2019–2020). Accessed at https://www.agewellfoundation.org/wp-content/uploads/2021/01/ANNUAL-REPORT-2019-20-New_compressed.pdf.

Ahlin, T. (2018). Only near is dear? Doing elderly care with everyday ICTs in Indian transnational families. *Medical Anthropology Quarterly* 32(1):85–102. https://doi.org/10.1111/maq.12404.

Ahlin, T. (2020). Frequent callers: "good care" with ICTs in Indian transnational families. *Medical Anthropology*. https://doi.org/10.1080/01459740.2018.1532424.

Albert, S.M. (1990). Caregiving as a cultural system: Conceptions of filial obligation and parental dependency in urban America. *American Anthropologist* 92(2):319–331. https://doi.org/10.1525/aa.1990.92.2.02a00040.

Arnold, F., Choe, M. K., & Roy, T. (1998). Son preference, the family-building process and child mortality in India. *Population Studies* 52:301–315. https://doi.org/10.1080/0032472031000150486.

Bayly, S. (2001). *Caste, Society and Politics in India from the Eighteenth Century to the Modern Age*. New Delhi: Cambridge University Press.

Bhandari, P. (2020). *Matchmaking in Middle Class India: Beyond Arranged and Love Marriage*. Singapore: Springer.

Braun, V., & Clarke, V. (2021). Conceptual and design thinking for thematic analysis. *Qualitative Psychology*. Advance online publication. https://doi.org/10.1037/qup0000196.

Brijnath, B. (2014). *Unforgotten: Love and the Culture of Dementia Care in India*. Oxford: Berghahn Books.

Business Standard. (2018). Indians work hardest, happy with working 5 days a week, says study. Accessed at https://www.business-standard.com/article/economy-policy/indians-work-hardest-happy-with-working-5-days-a-week-says-study-118091100775_1.html.

Campbell, S., Greenwood, M., Prior, S., Shearer, T., Walkem, K., Young, S., & Walker, K. (2020). Purposive sampling: Complex or simple? Research case examples. *Journal of Research in Nursing* 25(8):652–661. https://doi.org/10.1177/1744987120927206.

Cheng, S-T., & Chan, A.C-M. (2006). Filial piety and psychological well-being in well older Chinese. *The Journals of Gerontology: Series B* 61(5):262–269. https://doi.org/10.1093/geronb/61.5.P262.

Cheung, C-K., & Kwan, A.Y-H. (2009). The erosion of filial piety by modernisation in Chinese cities. *Ageing and Society* 29(2):17–198. https://doi.org/10.1017/S0144686X08007836.

Chow, N. (1991). Does filial piety exist under Chinese Communism? *Journal of Aging and Social Policy* 3(1–2):209–225. https://doi.org/10.1300/J031v03n01_14.

Chow, N. (2006). The practice of filial piety and its impact on long-term care policies for elderly people in Asian Chinese communities. *Asian Journal of Gerontology and Geriatrics* 1:31–35.

Clack, B., & Paule, M. (eds). (2019). *Interrogating the Neoliberal Lifecycle: The Limits of Success.* Switzerland: Palgrave Macmillan.

Cohen, L. (1999). *No Ageing in India: Alzheimer's, the Bad Family, and Other Modern Things.* Berkeley: University of California Press.

Dai, Y. T., & Dimond, M. F. (1998). Filial piety. A cross-cultural comparison and its implications for the well-being of older parents. *Journal of Gerontological Nursing* 24(3): 13–18. https://doi.org/10.3928/0098-9134-19980301-05.

Desai, S., & Andrist, L. (2010). Gender scripts and age at marriage in India. *Demography* 47:667–687. https://doi.org/10.1353/dem.0.0118.

Dewan, B.S., & Khan. A.M. (2009). Socio-cultural determinants of female foeticide. *Social Change* 39(3):388–405. https://doi.org/10.1177/004908570903900304.

Dhar, R. L. (2012). Caregiving for elderly parents: A study from the Indian perspective. *Home Health Care Management & Practice* 24(5):242e254. https://doi.org/10.1177/1084822312439466.

Diwan, S., Lee, S. E., & Sen, S. (2011). Expectations of filial obligation and their impact on preferences for future living arrangements of middle-aged and older Asian Indian immigrants. *Journal of Cross-Cultural Gerontology* 26:55–69. https://doi.org/10.1007/s10823-010-9134-6.

Dutta, M., Shekhar, C., & Prashad, L. (2015). Level, trend and correlates of mistimed and unwanted pregnancies among currently pregnant ever married women in India. *PLoS ONE* 10(12):e0144400. https://doi.org/10.1371/journal.pone.0144400.

Featherstone, M. & Wernick, A. (eds). (1995). *Images of Ageing.* London: SAGE.

Finley, N. J., Roberts, D., Benjamin, P.H., & Banahan, F. (1988). Motivators and inhibitors of attitudes of filial obligation toward aging parents. *The Gerontologist* 28(1):73–78. https://doi.org/10.1093/geront/28.1.73

Gangopadhyay, J. (2017). Aging across worlds: Examining intergenerational relationships among older adults in two cities in transition. *Ageing International* 42(4):504–521. https://doi.org/10.1007/s12126-016-9271-5.

Gangopadhyay, J. (2019). Senior Citizens Bill will fail to provide India's elderly the "life of dignity" it claims to. *Scroll.* Accessed at https://scroll.in/article/946898/senior-citizens-bill-will-fail-to-provide-indias-elderly-the-life-of-dignity-it-claims-to.

Gangopadhyay, J. (2020) Examining the Lived Experiences of Ageing Among Older Adults Living Alone in India. In: Shankardass, M. (eds) *Ageing Issues and Responses in India* (pp. 207–219). Springer, Singapore.

Gangopadhyay, J. (2021). *Culture, Context and Aging of Older Indians: Narratives from India and Beyond.* Springer: Singapore.

Gangopadhyay, J. (2021). Does an increase in the legal age of marriage for women guarantee equality for women in India? *Journal of Indian Law and Society* 12(1):23–34.

Gangopadhyay, J., & Samanta. T. (2017). "Family matters": Aging and intergenerational social contract in urban Ahmedabad, Gujarat. *Contributions to Indian Sociology* 51(3):338–360. doi: 10.1177/0069966717720962.

Gupta, P. (2012). Child marriages and the law: Contemporary concerns. *Economic and Political Weekly* 47(43):49–55.

Gu, D., Dupre, M.E., & Liu, G. (2007). Characteristics of the institutionalized and community-residing oldest old in China. *Social Science and Medicine* 64(4):871–883. https://doi.org/10.1016/j.socscimed.2006.10.026.

Ho, D.Y.F. (1996). Filial Piety and Its Psychological Consequences. In Bond, M.H. (ed.) *The Handbook of Chinese Psychology* (pp. 155–165). Hong Kong, People's Republic of China: Oxford University Press.

Hsueh, K.H. (2001). Family Caregiving Experience and Health Status among Chinese in the United States. PhD dissertation. Ann Arbor, MI: *UMI Dissertation Services*, ProQuest Information and Learning.

Hwang, K. K. (1999). Filial piety and loyalty: Two types of social identification in Confucianism. *Asian Journal of Social Psychology* 2:163–183. https://doi.org/10.1111/1467-839X.00031.

Hyde, M. (2015). Tourism. In Twigg J., & Martin W. (eds) *The Routledge Handbook of Cultural Gerontology*. London: Routledge.

Ikles, C. (ed). (2004). *Filial Piety: Practice and Discourse in Contemporary East Asia*. California: Stanford University Press.

Ingle, G.K., & Nath, A. (2008). Geriatric health in India: Concerns and solutions. *Indian Journal of Community Medicine: Official Publication of Indian Association of Preventive & Social Medicine* 33(4):214–218. https://doi.org/10.4103/0970-0218.43225.

Jacobson, J., Ju, A., Baumgart, A., et al. (2019). Patient perspectives on the meaning and impact of fatigue in hemodialysis: A systematic review and thematic analysis of qualitative studies. *American Journal of Kidney Diseases* 74(2):179–192. https://doi.org/10.1053/j.ajkd.2019.01.034.

Jamuna, D., & Ramamurti, P.V. (1999). Contributants to good care giving: An analysis of dyadic relationships. *Social Change* 29(1 and 2):138–144. https://doi.org/10.1177/004908579902900210.

Jha, P., Kumar, R., Vasa, P., Dhingra, N., Thiruchelvam, D., & Moineddin R. (2006). Low female-to-male sex ratio of children born in India: National survey of 1.1 million households. *Lancet* 367:211–218. https://doi.org/10.1016/S0140-6736(06)67930-0.

Jodhka, S.S., & Prakash, A. (2016). *The Indian Middle Class*. New Delhi: Oxford University Press.

Joseph, T.M. (2009). Mangalore a melting pot. *The Times of India*. Accessed at https://timesofindia.indiatimes.com/city/bengaluru/Mangalore-a-melting-pot/articleshow/4044055.cms?.

Kalavar, J.M., & Jamuna, D. (2011). Ageing of Indian women in India: The experience of older women in formal care homes. *Journal of Women & Ageing* 23(3):203–215. https://doi.org/10.1080/08952841.2011.587730.

Kaur, R., & Palriwala, R. (eds). (2013). *Marrying in South Asia: Shifting Concepts, Changing Practices in a Globalising World*. New Delhi: Orient Blackswan.

Kaur, R., & Vasudev, C. (2019). Son preference and daughter aversion in two villages of Jammu. *Economic and Political Weekly* 54(13):13–16.

Koyano, W. (1996). Filial piety and intergenerational solidarity in Japan. *Australian Journal on Ageing* 15(2):51–56. https://doi.org/10.1111/j.1741-6612.1996.tb00203.x.

Kumar, S., & Pradhan, M.R. (2019). Self-rated health status and its correlates among the elderly in India. *Journal of Public Health* 27:291–299. https://doi.org/10.1007/s10389-018-0960-2.

Lai, D.W. (2007). Cultural predictors of caregiving burden of Chinese-Canadian family caregivers. *Canadian Journal on Aging* 26(1):133–147. https://doi.org/10.3138/cja.26.suppl_1.133.

Lamb, S. (2002). *White Saris and Sweet Mangoes: Ageing, Gender, and Body in North India*. Berkeley: University of California Press.

Lamb, S. (ed.) (2009). *Ageing and the Indian Diaspora: Cosmopolitan Families in India and Abroad.* Bloomington: Indiana University Press.

Lamb, S. (2017). *Successful Ageing as a Contemporary Obsession: Global Perspectives.* New Jersey: Rutgers University Press.

Larsen, M., & Kaur, R. (2013). Signs of change? Sex ratio imbalance and shifting social practices in Northern India. *Economic and Political Weekly* 47(35):45–52.

Leung, A.N-M., Wong, S.S-F., Wong, I.W-Y., & McBride-Chang, C. (2010). Filial piety and psychological adjustment in Hong Kong Chinese early adolescents. *Journal of Early Adolescence* 30(5):651–667. https://doi.org/10.1177/0272431609341046.

Lewis, D, Medvedev, K., & Seponski, D. (2011). Awakening to the desires of older women: Deconstructing ageism within fashion magazines. *Journal of Aging Studies* 25:101–109. https://doi.org/10.1016/j.jaging.2010.08.016.

Lopez, G.I., Figueroa, M., Connor, S.E., & Maliski, S.L. (2008). Translation barriers in conducting qualitative research with Spanish speakers. *Qualitative Health Research* 18(12):1729–1737. https://doi.org/10.1177/1049732308325857.

Maintenance of Welfare and Senior Citizens Act. (2007). Accessed at https://socialjustice.nic.in/writereaddata/UploadFile/Annexure-X635996104030434742.pdf.

Madan, T.N. (1975). Structural implications of marriage in north India: Wife-givers and wife-takers among the Pandits of Kashmir. *Contributions to Indian Sociology* 9(2): 217–243. https://doi.org/10.1177/006996677500900204.

Malhotra A., Vanneman, R., & Kishor, S. (1995). Fertility, dimensions of patriarchy, and development in India. *Population and Development Review* 21(2):281–305. https://doi.org/10.2307/2137495.

Milazzo, A. (2018). Why are adult women missing? Son preference and maternal survival in India. *Journal of Development Economics* 134:467–484. https://doi.org/10.1016/j.jdeveco.2018.06.009.

Ministry of Statistics and Programme Implementation. (2016). Elderly in India. Accessed at http://mospi.nic.in/sites/default/files/publication_reports/ElderlyinIndia_2016.pdf.

Mitra, A. (2014). Son Preference in India: Implications for Gender Development. *Journal of Economic Issues* 48(4):1021–1037. DOI: 10.2753/JEI0021-3624480408.

Murti, L. (2006). At both ends of care: South Indian Hindu widows living with daughters and daughters-in-law in Southern California. *Globalizations* 3(3):361–376. https://doi.org/10.1080/14747730600870191.

Patel, T. (2007). Informal social networks, sonography and female foeticide in India. *Sociological Bulletin* 56(2):243–262. doi/pdf/10.1177/0038022920070204.

Rajan, S. I., & Kumar, S. (2003). Living arrangements among Indian elderly: New evidence from national family health survey. *Economic and Political Weekly* 38(1): 75–80.

Robitaille, M-C. (2013). Determinants of stated son preference in India: Are men and women different? *The Journal of Development Studies* 49:657–669. https://doi.org/10.1080/00220388.2012.682986.

Samanta, T., Chen, F., & Vanneman, R. (2015). Living arrangements and health of older adults in India. *The Journal of Gerontology: Series B* 70(6):937–947. https://doi.org/10.1093/geronb/gbu164.

Samanta, T., & Gangopadhyay, J. (2016). Social Capital, Interrupted: Sociological Reflections from Old Age Homes in Ahmedabad, India. In: Tannistha Samanta (ed.) *Cross-cultural and Cross-disciplinary Perspectives in Social Gerontology* (pp. 109–124). Singapore: Springer.

Santos, H.P., Jr, Black, A.M., & Sandelowski, M. (2015). Timing of translation in cross-language qualitative research. *Qualitative Health Research* 25(1):134–144. https://doi.org/10.1177/1049732314549603.

Shah, A.M. (1973). *The Household Dimension of the Family in India.* New Delhi: Orient Longman.

Shah, A. M. (1999). Changes in the family and the elderly. *Economic and Political Weekly,* 34(20), 1179–1182.

Shah, N. (2003). Gender issues and oral health in elderly Indians. *International Dental Journal* 53(6):475–484. https://doi.org/10.1002/j.1875-595X.2003.tb00890.x.

Sharma, K., & Kemp, C.L. (2012). "One should follow the wind": Individualized filial piety and support exchanges in Indian immigrant families in the United States. *Journal of Aging Studies* 26:129–139. https://doi.org/10.1016/j.jaging.2011.10.003.

Singh, P., Govil, D., Kumar, V. et al. (2017). Cognitive impairment and quality of life among elderly in India. *Applied Research Quality Life* 12:963–979. https://doi.org/10.1007/s11482-016-9499-y.

Srinivas, M.N. (1978). *The remembered village.* New Delhi: Oxford University Press.

Srivastava, S. (2015). Modi-masculinity: Media, manhood, and "traditions" in a time of consumerism. *Television & New Media* 16(4):331–338. https://doi.org/10.1177/1527476415575498.

Sudha, S. (2014). Intergenerational relations and elder care preferences of Asian Indians in North Carolina. *Journal of Cross-Cultural Gerontology* 29(1):87–107. https://doi.org/10.1007/s10823-013-9220-7.

Sun, Y. (2017). Among a hundred good virtues, filial piety is the first: Contemporary moral discourses on filial piety in urban China. *Anthropological Quarterly* 90(3): 771–799. https://doi.org/10.1353/anq.2017.0043.

Sung, K-T. (1995). Measures and dimensions of filial piety in Korea. *The Gerontologist* 35(2):240–247. https://doi.org/10.1093/geront/35.2.240.

Sung, K-T. (1998). An exploration of actions of filial piety. *Journal of Aging Studies* 12(4):369–386. https://doi.org/10.1016/S0890-4065(98)90025-1.

Swain. J. (2018). A hybrid approach to thematic analysis in qualitative research: Using a practical example. *Sage Research Methods.* https://dx.doi.org/10.4135/9781526435477.

The Hindu. (2006). A cool crowd. Accessed at https://web.archive.org/web/20071001061015/http://www.hindu.com/mp/2006/12/23/stories/2006122300740100.htm.

The Maintenance and Welfare of Parents and Senior Citizens (Amendment) Bill, 2019. Accessed at https://prsindia.org/files/bills_acts/bills_parliament/Maintenance%20and%20Welfare%20of%20Parents%20and%20Senior%20Citizens%20(Amendment)%20Bill,%202019.pdf.

Tsutsui, T., Muramatsu, N., & Higashino, S. (2014). Changes in perceived filial obligation norms among co-resident family caregivers in Japan. *The Gerontologist* 54(5):797–807. https://doi.org/10.1093/geront/gnt093.

Twigg, J., & Martin, W. (2015). The challenge of cultural gerontology. *The Gerontologist* 55(3):353–359. https://doi.org/10.1093/geront/gnu061.

Ugargol, A.P., & Bailey, A. (2021). Reciprocity between older adults and their care-givers in emigrant households of Kerala, India. *Ageing and Society* 41(8):1699–1725. https://doi.org/10.1017/S0144686X19001685.

Vaismoradi, M., Turunen, H., & Bondas, T. (2013). Content analysis and thematic analysis: Implications for conducting a qualitative descriptive study. *Nursing & Health Sciences* 15(3):398–405.

van Nes, F., Abma, T., Jonsson, H. et al. (2010). Language differences in qualitative research: Is meaning lost in translation? *European Journal of Ageing* 7:313–316. https://doi.org/10.1007/s10433-010-0168-y.

van Willigen, J., Lewis, D. C., Yoon, H., & Hendricks, J. (2006). The cultural context of aging. In *Handbook on Asian Aging*. New York: Baywood.

Vera-Sanso P. (2005). "They don't need it, and I can't give it": Filial support in South India. In: Kreager P, Schröder-Butterfill E (eds) *Aging without Children: European and Asian Perspectives on Elderly Access to Support Networks* (pp. 77–105). Oxford: Berghahn Books.

Verma, S.K., & Satayanarayana, A. (2013). Process of intergenerational ambivalence: A qualitative inquiry. *Marriage & Family Review* 49(8):737–753.

Visaria, A., & Dommaraju, P. (2019). Productive aging in India. *Social Science Medicine* 229:14–21. https://doi.org/10.1016/j.socscimed.2018.07.029.

Young, A., & Temple, B. (2014). *Approaches to Social Research: The Case of Deaf Studies*. New York: Oxford University Press.

Zeng, Y., Land, K.C., Gu, D., & Wang, Z. (2014) Household and Living Arrangement Projections in China at the National Level. In: Household and Living Arrangement Projections. *The Springer Series on Demographic Methods and Population Analysis*, vol. 36. Dordrecht: Springer.

Zhan, H.J., Feng, X., & Luo, B. (2008). Placing elderly parents in institutions in urban China: A reinterpretation of filial piety. *Research on Aging* 30(5):543–571. https://doi.org/10.1177/0164027508319471.

Section II
Family Care for Elders in Chinese and Indian Societies

4 A Comparative Study of Caregiving Experiences between Family Caregivers of Elderly Cancer Patients in China and India

A Qualitative Meta-synthesis

Longtao He and Han Wu

Introduction

In recent years, due to accelerations in population aging and the rate of cancer incidence, the need for cancer care is increasing exponentially (He & van Heugten, 2020). According to a worldwide survey on cancer by the World Health Organization (WHO) and International Agency for Research on Cancer (IARC), in 2020 alone, there were more than 19.29 million new cancer patients and over 9.95 million cancer deaths (Sung et al., 2021). China and India, as the world's first and second most populous countries, respectively, have huge population bases for elderly people and cancer patients. In China, in 2020, there were 4.56 million new cancer patients and over 3.0 million cancer deaths, while in India, these figures were 1.32 million and over 850,000, respectively (International Agency for Research on Cancer, 2021a, 2021b). Cancer has become the leading cause of death in both China and India (Smith & Mallath, 2019; Zhou et al., 2019).

Family caregivers are crucially important as the quality of life (QOL) of patients depends greatly on them (World Health Organization, 2018). In addition, Lin et al. (2020) investigated 641 cancer patients and their family caregivers and found that the QOL of family caregivers was positively correlated to cancer patients' QOL. This suggests that family caregivers play a vital role in supporting cancer patients (Ahn et al., 2020; Institute of Medicine of the National Academies, 2015), as even though most cancer patients are treated in the hospital, most care is still provided by the family caregivers, be it within or outside the hospital (Li et al., 2016; Shaffer et al., 2017). Compared with the developed western countries, both China and India have limited formal eldercare services (Martin et al., 2016). In these countries, caregiving tasks are mainly undertaken by their family members, such as changing clothes, bathing, feeding, and monitoring medical machines (Liu et al., 2020), due to the low ratio of medical staff to patients, the lack of a comprehensive social security system for cancer patients (especially in

DOI: 10.4324/9781003254256-6

India), and the lack of professional caregivers with adequate knowledge and skills (Ugargol et al., 2016; Xu et al., 2016). Moreover, both China and India have long histories of and cultural imperatives for valuing family care practice for elders, especially those with a terminal illness (Lamb, 2013; Liu et al., 2012).

Thus in both China and India, family caregivers play a vital role in supporting cancer patients. However, a considerable body of literature has shown that caring for cancer patients can also bring about physical, psychological, financial, social, spiritual, and cultural burdens for family caregivers (Burke et al., 2014; Lukhmana et al., 2015; Zhang et al., 2014). In particular, some types of cancer have a high recurrence rate and a long duration, which may result in huge care pressure on the caregivers, especially family caregivers (Li et al., 2014). At the same time, caregiving can also induce positive experiences (Sánchez-Izquierdo et al., 2015; Thombre et al., 2010), such as personal growth (Mehrotra & Sukumar, 2007; Tang, 2018), and strengthening bonds with patients and other family members (Chittem et al., 2018; Chung et al., 2017). A comprehensive understanding of family caregivers' care experiences is a topic of current scholarly interest.

In recent years, the number of studies on family caregivers has risen significantly. Although there has been a significant increase in qualitative analysis, most studies remain predominantly quantitative. Yet quantitative methods may overlook deeper experiences of family caregivers (Peacock, 2011), and for this reason, it is important to also study the caregiving experiences of family caregivers using qualitative approaches. A meta-synthesis of high-quality qualitative research articles can provide a more systematic and in-depth understanding of the caregiving experience of family caregivers for cancer patients, than a singular qualitative study. While several such qualitative meta-syntheses have been carried out on the experiences of Chinese family caregivers, none have been found for Indian family caregivers. Moreover, there have been no direct comparative studies between two countries adopting the method of qualitative meta-synthesis or any other method on this topic. This study, which carried out a meta-synthesis to directly compare the caregiving experiences of family caregivers of cancer patients in China and India, allows both common and unique factors between the two countries to be explored while breaking new ground in the literature. Study results can help provide an understanding of the issues from an international perspective, which can enable more effective support for cancer patients and their family caregivers across cultures.

Methodology

Search Strategy

The article search was conducted in the Web of Science, PubMed, Embase, MEDLINE, Cochrane Library, Grew Literature in the Health Sciences, CNKI, Wanfang Data, and VIP databases. The articles searched included those from database inception to May 23, 2021, and the language was restricted to English and Chinese. In English, we used "China" or "Chinese" or "India" or "Indian"

Table 4.1 Search Strategy

Search rows	Search items	Filter
Row 1 (and)	China or Chinese	Title/Abstract/Keywords
Row 2 (and)	India or Indian	Title/Abstract/Keywords
Row 3 (and)	Neoplasia or neoplasias or neoplasm or tumors or tumor or cancer or cancers or malignancy or malignancies or malignant neoplasms or malignant neoplasm or neoplasm, malignant or neoplasms, malignant or benign neoplasms or neoplasms, benign or benign neoplasm or neoplasm, benign	Title/Abstract/Keywords
Row 4 (and)	Caregiving or care or caregiver or caregivers or carer or carers or care giver or care givers or informal caregiver or informal caregivers or informal carer or informal carers or spouse caregiver or spouse caregivers or spouse or relative or relatives or parent or parents or grandparent or grandparents or grandson or granddaughter or grandchildren or family or family member or family members or adult child or adult children or family carer or family carers or family caregiver or family caregivers	Title/Abstract/Keywords
Row 5	Qualitative	Title/Abstract/Keywords

+ "cancer" or "tumors" or "malignancy" or neoplasm" (and other Medical Subject Headings [MeSH] words) + "caregiver" or "informal caregiver" or "family caregiver" (and other related words) + "qualitative," and their respective synonyms, as the keywords. In Chinese, we used *Zhongguo* (中国, China), *Yindu* (印度, India), *aizheng* (癌症, cancer), *jiating zhaohuzhe* (家庭照护者, caregiver), *zhixing* (质性, qualitative), and their related synonyms and other MeSH words as the keywords (see Table 4.1). Additionally, reference lists of studies selected for qualitative meta-synthesis were also searched to assess eligibility.

Inclusion and Exclusion Criteria

Inclusion Criteria

1 The study must have used qualitative methodologies or mixed methods that include qualitative elements;
2 Some or all of the patients in the study had been diagnosed with some type of cancer;
3 Family caregivers were family members who take on care tasks without actual remuneration and were over 18 years old; and
4 The research objectives were to reveal the experiences of family caregivers, and the physical, psychological, financial, social, and spiritual impacts of caregiving on the caregivers.

Exclusion Criteria

1 Studies in languages other than English or Chinese;
2 Studies with only abstracts available;
3 Studies that used qualitative methodologies incorrectly; and
4 Studies of repetitive publications.

Selection and Extraction Process

Article screening and data extraction were conducted by the two authors. The second author first screened the articles by selecting their title and abstract to exclude those not in line with the research theme. Then, two authors read the articles critically and selected the eligible ones according to the inclusion and exclusion criteria. Third-party professionals were invited to make the final decision where disagreement persisted between the two authors.

Quality Assessment

There have been many quality assessment criteria (e.g. COREQ, CASP, JBI). We chose the Joanna Briggs Institute's (JBI) critical appraisal tools, specifically the Checklist for Systematic Reviews and the Checklist for Qualitative Research (Joanna Briggs Institute, 2021), because it is one of the most commonly used tools for critical appraisal in qualitative health research. For each article, ten assessment questions were asked, each with four options: yes, no, unclear, and not applicable. The scoring system adopted attributed 1 point for "yes" and 0 points for other answers, with an article's score equal to the sum of its points. The articles were then divided into three groups according to their score: 8–10 was given a rating of A, 5–7 of B, and 0–4 of C. A-rated articles have a low risk of bias and were included in the sample directly, and C-rated articles have a high risk of bias and were directly excluded. B-rated articles carry a medium-level of risk of bias, and the decision of whether to include them or not was done by both authors on a case-by-case basis. In making the judgment, the main criterion was the logic of how findings were arrived at and how information-saturated the findings were.

Results

Selected Articles

The selection process is shown in Figure 4.1. The initial search identified 4,702 studies on the caregiving experiences of family caregivers of cancer patients in China (1,981 from the Chinese-language database and 2,721 from the English) and 762 in India. After the removal of duplicates, 3,487 Chinese and 584 Indian articles were obtained. By reading titles and abstracts, 175 Chinese articles and 47 Indian articles related to this study were chosen. The articles were then fully read and the quality evaluation applied, yielding 32 studies—21 from China and 11 from India—selected for the qualitative meta-synthesis.

Family Caregivers of Elderly Cancer Patients 59

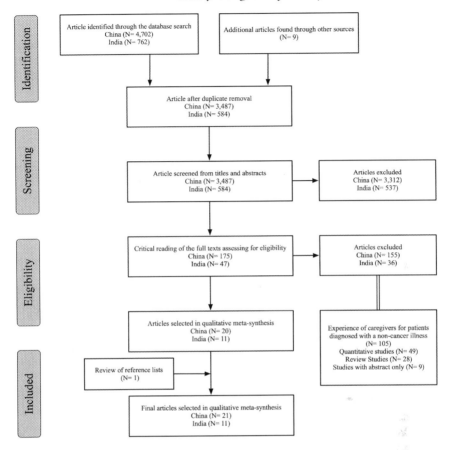

Figure 4.1 PRISMA flow diagram of the article selection process.

Characteristics of the Articles

As Table 4.2 shows, in the 21 qualitative studies on the experiences of family caregivers of cancer patients in China, 7 articles used phenomenological analysis, 4 used thematic content analysis, 2 used grounded theory, 2 used interpretive phenomenological analysis, 2 were qualitative descriptive studies, 1 used empirical phenomenology, 1 was a multiple embedded-case study, 1 used qualitative interpretive description, and 1 used Foucauldian discourse analysis. There are 331 family caregivers who participated in these studies, the majority female (200, versus 109 male; 2 studies did not specify gender), and most spouses or adult children. All articles analyzed the family caregivers' experience of care. Only 4 articles (Simpson, 2005; Li et al., 2014; Chen et al., 2015; Si et al., 2018) included both family caregivers' and patients' experiences; we included only findings about the family caregivers. In the 11 articles about Indian family caregivers, 4 articles used qualitative content analysis, 2 used thematic analysis,

Table 4.2 Characteristics of Included Articles

Article	Methodology	Research objective	Main themes	Data collection	Sample characteristics
Chen et al. (2015)	Embedded multiple case study	To explore participants' constructions of hope.	1 Hope for the best and prepare for the worst 2 "Hope for the best" and interpersonal connectedness 3 "Hope for the best" and hope to work 4 Sociocultural influences of "hope for the best"	In-depth interviews	5 family caregivers (gender not specified) 10 patients
Chung et al. (2017)	Qualitative interpretive description	To explore the Chinese spousal experience with their dying loved ones suffering from terminal cancer.	1 The "we" experience of confronting mortality 2 Balancing the end-of-life tension between cure and comfort 3 Prioritizing the family's goals and concerns 4 De-medicalizing caregiving 5 Working for mutuality 6 Creating a legacy of love	Semi-structured interviews (8 months)	15 family caregivers (female = 8, male = 7)
Fu et al. (2018)	Thematic content analysis	To explore the perception of hope that family caregivers hold during patients' different treatment stages.	1 From diagnosis to the first phase of treatment 2 After two courses of chemotherapy 3 After four courses of chemotherapy	Semi-structured interviews	16 family caregivers (female = 8, male = 8)
He & van Heugten (2020)	Foucauldian discourse analysis	To build a comprehensive explanatory theoretical model for mediating the role of filial piety in caregivers' lived experiences.	1 Care burden 2 Discourse of *tianjingdiyi* 3 Filial piety as a resource 4 Filial piety as a hindrance	In-depth interviews (5 months)	24 family caregivers (female = 12, male = 12)

(Continued)

Table 4.2 Characteristics of Included Articles (Continued)

Article	Methodology	Research objective	Main themes	Data collection	Sample characteristics
Li et al. (2015)	Thematic content analysis	To understand the experiences, concerns, and needs of couples living with cancer	1 Communication dynamics 2 Living with change 3 Negative and positive impacts 4 Network of support	Focus group (90–120 min)	17 family caregivers (female = 9, male = 8) 11 patients
Li et al. (2017)	Qualitative descriptive study	To explore the mutual support of couples in their journey of coping together with cancer.	1 Support and reciprocity 2 Challenges encountered in the provision of support 3 Experiencing adjustments/outcomes	In-depth interviews (60–90 min)	11 family caregivers (female = 6, male = 5)
Li et al. (2018)	Phenomenological analysis (Colaizzi analysis)	To explore the psychological experiences of family caregivers with hepatocellular carcinoma with the hepatitis B virus.	1 Stress over the diagnosis 2 Indebtedness and self-blame 3 Fear and sadness over the possibility of losing the loved ones 4 Anxieties 5 Joint stigma	Semi-structured interview (30–60 min) + 1 follow-up interview	12 family caregivers (female = 8, male = 4)
Lin et al. (2020)	Qualitative content analysis	To explore the experience of care burden of spouses of cancer patients.	1 Coping with changes from assuming the caregiver role 2 Meeting the care needs of cancer patients 3 Communication challenges 4 Accessibility of diversified support	Focus group (90–120 min)	24 elderly spousal caregivers of cancer patients (female = 11, male = 13)
Liu et al. (2012)	Interpretative phenomenological analysis (Colaizzi analysis)	To understand the experiences of family caregivers of cancer patients.	1 Complicated psychological reactions to cancer diagnosis 2 Changes in role and social functions 3 Care experiences	In-depth interviews (20–30 min)	11 primary caregivers (female = 8, male = 3)
Mok et al. (2003)	Grounded theory	To describe the caregiving process and the impact of being the main caregiver for a terminally ill patient.	1 Precondition: commitment in caring 2 The process of caregiving 3 Consequences 4 Influential factors in the process of caregiving	Semi-structured interviews (75–135 min)	24 family caregivers (female = 21, male = 3)

(Continued)

Table 4.2 Characteristics of Included Articles (Continued)

Article	Methodology	Research objective	Main themes	Data collection	Sample characteristics
Si et al. (2018)	Descriptive qualitative analysis (Colaizzi analysis)	To examine the feelings of family caregivers, the multiple roles in care, and the support needed.	1 Fatigue 2 Anxiety 3 Pressure 4 Feelings of alienation 5 Desire 6 Helplessness	Semi-structured interviews (20–30 min)	10 family caregivers (female = 8, male = 2) 10 patients
Simpson (2005)	Analytical, interpretive phenomenology	To identify family beliefs about breast cancer.	1 Beliefs about the cause of cancer 2 Balancing strategies	Minimally structured interviews	39 family caregivers (female = 19, male = 17, gender not specified = 3) 20 patients (female = 20)
Tang (2018)	Grounded theory	To obtain a deeper understanding of the experiences of family caregivers of terminally ill cancer patients in Shenzhen, Southern China.	1 Challenges 2 Personal growth 3 Social support	Semi-structured interviews (90 min)	20 family caregivers (female = 13, male = 7)
Tang (2019)	Thematic content analysis	To identify the main elements of caring and bereavement experiences for family caregivers of patients diagnosed with terminal cancer.	1 Illness symptoms 2 Negative influence of caregiving on the bereavement process 3 Attitudes toward death 4 The truth-telling process 5 The color of death 6 Informal and formal social support 7 Moment of death 8 Caregiving experiences and views of death	Semi-structured interviews (90 min)	20 family caregivers (female = 12, male = 8)

(Continued)

Table 4.2 Characteristics of Included Articles (Continued)

Article	Methodology	Research objective	Main themes	Data collection	Sample characteristics
Wang et al. (2010)	Phenomenological analysis (Colaizzi analysis)	To articulate the experience and care needs of family caregivers for dying elderly patients.	1 Meeting the physiological needs of patients 2 Need for communication technology 3 Spiritual need for reducing the fear and pain of patients 4 Need for hospice 5 Need for professional medical management 6 Breath support	Semi-structured interview (40–60 min)	8 family caregivers (female = 8, male = 0)
Wang et al. (2016)	Phenomenological analysis (Colaizzi analysis)	To understand the experiences of immediate family members as caregivers of cancer patients.	1 Family members' reactions after the patients were diagnosed 2 Patients' tremendous physical and psychological burden 3 Mutual support during the post-treatment period	Intensive interview (30 min–2 h)	14 family caregivers (gender not specified)
Wong & Chan (2007)	Phenomenological analysis	To describe the experiences of Chinese family members of terminally ill patients during the end-of-life process in a palliative care unit.	1 Grief reactions 2 Commitment to care 3 Being with the patient in the last moment	Semi-structured interviews (60–90 min)	20 family caregivers (female = 16, male = 4)
Wu et al. (2016)	Phenomenological analysis (Colaizzi analysis)	To identify the care experiences of family caregivers for hospitalized senile patients.	1 Heavy care tasks 2 Shattered daily life 3 Eager for professional care knowledge 4 Role change 5 Financial burden	Semi-structured interview (40–60 min)	10 family caregivers (female = 8, male = 2)

(Continued)

Table 4.2 Characteristics of Included Articles (Continued)

Article	Methodology	Research objective	Main themes	Data collection	Sample characteristics
Xu et al. (2016)	Phenomenological analysis (content analysis method)	To understand the current status and needs of caregivers for terminal cancer patients.	1 Huge stress from caregiving 2 Role change for caregivers 3 Various levels of acceptance of new knowledge and skills 4 Need to improve patients' quality of life 5 Need for caregiving knowledge and skills 6 Need for social support for patients and caregivers 7 Need for emotional communication 8 Need for end-of-life counseling	Semi-structured interview (20 min–2 h)	10 family caregivers (female = 8, male = 2)
Zeng et al. (2014)	Empirical phenomenology	To explore the experiences of seniors' family caregivers in Shanghai with regards to responsibility, burden, and support needs.	1 It is so hard 2 It is my responsibility 3 Support is never enough	Semi-structured interviews (45–80 min)	11 family caregivers (female = 9, male = 2)
Zhang et al. (2013)	Phenomenological analysis (Colaizzi analysis)	To illuminate the perceived burden of family caregivers of osteosarcoma patients.	1 Anxiety and depression 2 Lack of social support systems	In-depth interviews (30 min–1 h)	10 family caregivers (female = 8, male = 2)
Amaresha et al. (2015)		To assess the needs of women caregivers of such patients being treated in a government-run tertiary care hospital in Bangalore, Karnataka.	1 Professional service needs 2 Informational needs 3 Psychological/emotional needs 4 Personal and spiritual needs 5 Social support needs	Semi-structured interviews (30–45 min)	30 family caregivers (female = 30)

(Continued)

Table 4.2 Characteristics of Included Articles (Continued)

Article	Methodology	Research objective	Main themes	Data collection	Sample characteristics
Antony et al. (2018)	Descriptive survey, phenomenological approach	To assess stress and coping among caregivers of cancer patients on palliative care and to acquire a deeper understanding of their lived experiences.	1 Adaptation to life 2 Pillars of support 3 Trusting relationship 4 Shield of strength and courage 5 Stress and strain 6 Living with fear and uncertainty	Descriptive survey, semi-structured interviews	80 family caregivers, quantitative (female = 75, male = 5) 8 family caregivers, qualitative (female = 6, gender not specified = 2)
Chittem et al. (2018)	Qualitative content analysis	To explore Indian primary family caregivers' experiences of disclosure versus nondisclosure to patients about their cancer diagnosis.	1 Reasons for disclosing given by disclosing caregivers 2 Reasons for not disclosing given by nondisclosing caregivers	Semi-structured interviews (25 min)	15 family caregivers (female = 3, male = 12)
Datta et al. (2016)	Thematic analysis	To explore the role of family members in the communication process.	1 Importance of family for physical and psychological care 2 Balancing patient autonomy and their relative's protectiveness 3 Negotiating with family members 4 Influence of socioeconomic circumstances of both patient and family 5 Shifting responsibility from family to patient 6 Family and communication skills training	In-depth interviews	10 family caregivers (female = 5, male = 5) 10 patients 21 doctors

(Continued)

Table 4.2 Characteristics of Included Articles (Continued)

Article	Methodology	Research objective	Main themes	Data collection	Sample characteristics
Daya et al. (2018)	Exploratory, descriptive study, content analysis	To assess the medical, social, spiritual, psychological, and financial needs of the caregivers of people in need of palliative care.	1 Difficulty among caregivers in providing physical care 2 Difficulty of caregivers in coping with psychological problems of the patients 3 Physical and psychological issues of the caregivers 4 Reasons for psychological problems of the caregivers 5 Financial issues of the caregivers 6 Social issues of the caregivers 7 Spiritual issues of the caregivers 8 Bereavement and grief	Semi-structured interviews	Family caregivers (female = 14, male = 7)
Goswami et al. (2019)	Qualitative content analysis	To understand the psychosocial impact of caregivers of oral cancer patients	1 Impact on physical health and lifestyle 2 Emotional impact 3 Impact on the family and social relationships 4 Impact on financial and work status 5 Necessity of improving the services provided in the health facilities 6 Spiritual concerns 7 Acceptance of the disease	In-depth interviews (40–60 min)	24 family caregivers (female = 14, male = 10)
Joad et al. (2011)		To assess the needs of informal caregivers of terminally ill cancer patients.	1 Medical needs 2 Psychological domain 3 Financial needs 4 Information needs 5 Social needs 6 Unmet needs	Semi-structured interviews (45–60 min)	56 family caregivers (gender not specified)

(Continued)

Table 4.2 Characteristics of Included Articles (Continued)

Article	Methodology	Research objective	Main themes	Data collection	Sample characteristics
Kumar et al. (2017)	Analytical framework approach	To understand family caregivers' perceptions of what ICU care meant to them.	1 Understanding about ICU 2 Decision-making concerning ongoing treatment 3 Relationship with healthcare providers	Semi-structured interviews (30–40 min)	20 family caregivers (female = 5, male = 15)
Mehrotra & Sukumar (2007)	Qualitative content analysis	To explore sources of strength in the process of caregiving from the perspectives of Indian women caring for relatives suffering from cancer.	1 Religious beliefs and practices 2 Appraisal of caregiver role 3 Prior experience of caregiving	Semi-structured interviews (30–90 min)	20 family caregivers (female = 20)
Parsekar et al. (2020)	Thematic analysis	To examine the perceptions and practices of psychological caregiving among caregivers and care recipients of breast cancer in India.	1 Caregiver's understandings of care provision and perceptions on their role 2 Care recipient's understanding of mental health care 3 Caregiver's psychological needs	Semi-structured interviews (20–90 min)	39 family caregivers (gender not specified) 35 patients
Paul & Fernandes (2020)		To identify and comprehend the challenges that caregivers face while taking care of a terminally ill patient in a home-based palliative care setting and the mechanisms that facilitated their coping.	1 Referral to home-based palliative care 2 Interface with home-based palliative care team 3 Patient's insights 4 Support systems 5 Bereavement	3 focus group discussions, 4 in-depth interviews	27 family caregivers (female = 10, male = 17)

1 used a phenomenological approach, 1 used an analytical framework approach, and 3 did not specify the methodology. There are 268 family caregivers included in the Indian studies, the majority also female (108, versus 66 male; 2 studies did not specify gender), and most were spouses or adult children of cancer patients. In the 11 articles about Indian family caregivers, 2 (Datta et al., 2016, Parsekar, 2020) included both family caregivers' and patients' experiences; we only included findings about family caregivers. In addition, 1 article used mixed-methods research; we only included the qualitative elements.

Quality Assessment

The results of the quality assessment on the studies included, done using the 2021 Joanna Briggs Institute's (JBI) critical appraisal tools, specifically the Checklist for Systematic Reviews and the Checklist for Qualitative Research, are shown in Table 4.3. All articles have "Yes" as answers for at least six of the questions. The quality evaluation yielded 14 studies rated as A and the others as B. The two authors agreed that the risk of bias for all B articles was insufficient to meet the exclusion criteria, and therefore, all were included in this study.

Themes of Chinese Caregiving Experiences of Family Caregivers of Cancer Patients

From the analysis of the 21 articles about China included in the study, a total of 89 research themes were extracted. These were systematically evaluated, integrated, and summarized into three principal themes encompassing a total of 16 sub-themes, as shown in Table 4.4.

Patient-Centered Caregiving Skills and Care Needs

The principal theme of patient-centered caregiving skills and needs includes the sub-themes of care skills, medical information, spiritual support, financial support, and social support. The studies show that caregivers are in great need of disease-related caregiving skills and medical knowledge, such as appropriate meal planning and wound-cleaning skills. In the caregiving process, family caregivers also require financial, social, and spiritual support.

Care Burden

The principal theme of care burden comprises physical, psychological, emotional, finances and work, social, stigma-related, and cultural burdens. Cancer is one of the most serious diseases, some types of which have a long disease cycle and lead to the poor patient ability for self-care; caregivers are thus essential to provide comprehensive and intense care, and they are susceptible to various types of burden.

Table 4.3 Quality Appraisal Results

Article	Q1	Q2	Q3	Q4	Q5	Q6	Q7	Q8	Q9	Q10[1]	Quality
Chen et al. (2015)	Yes	Yes	Yes	Yes	Yes	No	Yes	Yes	Yes	Yes	A (9 "Yes")
Chung et al. (2017)	Unclear	Yes	Yes	Yes	Yes	No	Yes	Unclear	Yes	Yes	B (7 "Yes")
Fu et al. (2018)	Yes	Yes	Yes	Yes	Yes	No	Yes	Yes	Yes	Yes	A (9 "Yes")
He & van Heugten (2020)	Yes	Yes	Yes	Yes	Yes	Yes	Yes	Yes	Yes	Yes	A (10 "Yes")
Li et al. (2015)	Yes	Yes	Yes	Yes	Yes	Yes	Yes	Yes	Yes	Yes	A (10 "Yes")
Li et al. (2017)	Yes	Yes	Yes	Yes	Yes	Yes	Yes	Yes	Yes	Yes	A (10 "Yes")
Li et al. (2018)	Yes	Yes	Yes	Yes	Yes	No	No	Yes	Yes	Yes	A (8 "Yes")
Lin et al. (2020)	Yes	Yes	Yes	Yes	Unclear	No	No	Yes	Yes	Yes	B (7 "Yes")
Liu et al. (2012)	Yes	Yes	Yes	Yes	Yes	No	No	No	Yes	Yes	B (6 "Yes")
Mok et al. (2003)	Unclear	Yes	Yes	Yes	Yes	No	Yes	Yes	Yes	Yes	A (8 "Yes")
Si et al. (2018)	Unclear	Yes	Yes	Yes	Yes	No	No	Yes	Yes	Yes	B (7 "Yes")
Simpson (2005)	Yes	Yes	Yes	Yes	Yes	Yes	Yes	Yes	Yes	Yes	A (10 "Yes")
Tang (2018)	Yes	Yes	Yes	Yes	Yes	Yes	Yes	Yes	Yes	Yes	A (10 "Yes")
Tang (2019)	Yes	Yes	Yes	Yes	Yes	Yes	Yes	Yes	Yes	Yes	A (10 "Yes")
Wang et al. (2010)	Yes	Yes	Yes	Yes	Yes	No	Yes	Yes	Yes	Yes	A (9 "Yes")
Wang et al. (2016)	Yes	Yes	Yes	Yes	Yes	No	No	Yes	No	Yes	B (7 "Yes")
Wong & Chan (2007)	No	Yes	Yes	No	Yes	No	Yes	Yes	Yes	Yes	B (7 "Yes")
Wu et al. (2016)	Yes	Yes	Yes	Yes	Yes	Yes	Yes	Yes	Yes	Yes	A (10 "Yes")
Xu et al. (2014)	Yes	Yes	Yes	Yes	Yes	No	Yes	No	No	Yes	B (7 "Yes")
Zeng et al. (2014)	Yes	Yes	Yes	Yes	Yes	No	No	Unclear	Yes	Yes	B (7 "Yes")
Zhang et al. (2013)	Unclear	Yes	Yes	Yes	Yes	No	No	Yes	Yes	Yes	B (7 "Yes")
Amaresha et al. (2015)	Unclear	Yes	Yes	Yes	Yes	No	No	Yes	No	Yes	B (6 "Yes")
Antony et al. (2018)	Unclear	Yes	Yes	Yes	Yes	No	No	Yes	Yes	Yes	B (7 "Yes")
Chittem et al. (2018)	Unclear	Yes	Yes	Yes	Yes	Yes	No	Yes	Yes	Yes	A (9 "Yes")
Datta et al. (2016)	Yes	Yes	Yes	Yes	Yes	Yes	No	Yes	Yes	Yes	A (9 "Yes")
Daya et al. (2018)	Yes	Yes	Yes	Unclear	Yes	No	No	Yes	No	Yes	B (6 "Yes")
Goswami et al. (2019)	No	Yes	Yes	Yes	Unclear	No	No	Yes	Yes	Yes	B (6 "Yes")

(Continued)

Table 4.3 Quality Appraisal Results (*Continued*)

Article	Q1	Q2	Q3	Q4	Q5	Q6	Q7	Q8	Q9	Q10[1]	Quality
Joad et al. (2011)	Yes	Yes	Yes	Unclear	Yes	No	No	Yes	Yes	Yes	B (7 "Yes")
Kumar et al. (2017)	Unclear	Yes	Yes	Yes	Yes	No	No	Yes	No	Yes	B (6 "Yes")
Mehrotra & Sukumar (2007)	Unclear	Yes	Yes	Yes	Yes	No	No	Unclear	Yes	Yes	B (6 "Yes")
Parsekar et al. (2020)	No	Yes	Yes	Yes	Yes	No	No	Unclear	Yes	Yes	B (6 "Yes")
Paul & Fernandes (2020)	No	Yes	Yes	Yes	Yes	No	No	Unclear	Yes	Yes	B (6 "Yes")

1. Is there congruity between the stated philosophical perspective and the research methodology?
2. Is there congruity between the research methodology and the research question or objectives?
3. Is there congruity between the research methodology and the methods used to collect data?
4. Is there congruity between the research methodology and the representation and analysis of data?
5. Is there congruity between the research methodology and the interpretation of results?
6. Is there a statement locating the researcher culturally or theoretically?
7. Is the influence of the researcher on the research, and vice-versa, addressed?
8. Are participants, and their voices, adequately represented?
9. Is the research ethical according to current criteria or, for recent studies, and is there evidence of ethical approval by an appropriate body?
10. Do the conclusions drawn in the research report flow from the analysis, or interpretation, of the data?

Table 4.4 Quotations from Chinese Participants from the Selection of Articles to Illustrate Each Theme

Theme	Sub-theme	Quotations from family caregivers in primary studies
Patient-centered caregiving skills and needs	Care skills	I don't have the time to take part in programmes teaching caregiving skills (Zeng et al., 2014). I would have liked the nurse to teach me how to take care of his oral hygiene… turn him in bed… do exercises, etc. We would have liked to take care of him ourselves, but we did not know how to carry out basic care. We worried that we might hurt him (Wong & Chan, 2007). I feel that nutrition and food are very important for the cause of cancer and for its treatment. But everyone seems to have a different opinion on what one should eat after chemotherapy. I think this is the biggest problem (Li et al., 2015).
	Medical information	If medical professionals or the hospital could provide a brochure to patients with relevant information on cancer and instructions, we would like to follow the instructions. This would protect us from being misled by other unauthorized information (Li et al., 2015). I hope doctors can provide more information about the survival rate of this type of cancer and, more specifically, show some confidence in his treatment so we can know more about the disease, its treatment, and its effect (Fu et al., 2018).
	Spiritual support	We shared our experiences and supported each other spiritually (Li et al., 2017). I wanted the nurses to care about us more, to come and show their concern for us… to support us so as to reduce our feeling of helplessness (Wong & Chan, 2007).
	Financial support	Because my son suffered from liver cancer, it led to financial tension in the family. An oncology social worker helped me apply for government subsidies to alleviate financial pressure (Tang, 2019). We need financial support. Our children are good, and they can offer us financial support for the time being, which has greatly lessened my burden. However, this is not a permanent solution. I hope that the government can pay more attention to cancer patients and offer us financial support (Li et al., 2015).
	Social support	All of the support that we receive from the people around us is essential to be able to continue treatment. For instance, nutritional guidance from the professionals and the suggestions from other patients in the ward, particularly those who were suffering from the same type of cancer, helped a lot during the period of ongoing chemotherapy (Li et al., 2015). Sometimes you can't talk with the patient; it can be very relaxing and freeing to talk with someone else, like today (Lin et al., 2015).

(Continued)

Table 4.4 Quotations from Chinese Participants from the Selection of Articles to Illustrate Each Theme (Continued)

Theme	Sub-theme	Quotations from family caregivers in primary studies
Care burden	Physical	I'm old too, and my health status is declining. At this age others should be taking care of me, but he needs to be cared for more than I do, sometimes I feel tired, powerless… I am too old to provide him with better care (Zeng et al., 2014).
	Psychological and emotional	My life is bitter, stuffy, and damned hard. My personal life is completely paralyzed… I am living a life of bondage. I can't go anywhere… life is like this day after day. We don't have any fun… we are suffering (Zeng et al., 2014). When he is not around, the pain and fear of losing him is almost unbearable. I often cry with my mom in his absence (He & van Heugten, 2020).
	Finances and work	Our family planned to try our best, even if we had to sell our house, to pay for the cost of treatment for my wife [their mother] if it could extend her life. However, my wife decided to give up treatment… It was really a tough experience for the whole family (Li et al., 2017). My company also has strict rules about requests for leave. Usually, we only get to go back home for the spring festival. I have no choice. I wanted to find work at home, but I couldn't. When this [my parent's illness] happens, even if I might be fined or lose my job, I will still come back (He & van Heugten, 2020).
	Social	I get almost no chance to see my old friends… even when there is a party I don't have time to attend. // I used to dance and travel, but after he fell ill, I had to give those up (Zeng et al., 2014). Because I have to take care of her, I don't have time to do relaxing things like other older people do, such as take a walk in the park or play Chinese chess (Wu et al., 2016).
	Stigma-related	I did not tell many people because they might think it is contagious. Would they still want to be around me if they knew? (Li et al., 2018).
	Cultural	You can always squeeze in time even if you are super busy… You should not ask for help from others. Why? Because it is our filial responsibility! (He & van Heugten, 2020). My father was suffering from lung cancer with systemic metastasis, and he insisted on giving up the intrusive treatment… I think as long as he breathes another day, we should keep on with the treatment. My father threatens me with suicide, so I cannot keep him out of my sight now (Wang & Fei, 2010). I didn't tell my son that he had colon cancer. We held a family conference that included my wife, my daughter, and other relatives. We decided that he'd be better off not knowing his true condition (Chung et al., 2017). Truth telling in China may also be influenced by cultural and ethical factors. The reason why I didn't tell the truth about cancer was I worried that my mother could not take the emotional impact (Tang, 2019).

(Continued)

Family Caregivers of Elderly Cancer Patients 73

Table 4.4 Quotations from Chinese Participants from the Selection of Articles to Illustrate Each Theme (Continued)

Theme	Sub-theme	Quotations from family caregivers in primary studies
Care gains	Enhancement of status	Everybody in my village knows how much I have on my shoulders. I still paid for my mother's surgery even if I had to borrow a lot of money from people. They all know how filial I am [smiling with apparent pride] … There was one guy in the exact same situation from my village last year, he did not fulfil his [filial responsibilities] [with a disapproving look] (He & van Heugten, 2020). I think taking care of mother is one of my responsibilities. It will also serve as a good example for my children (Tang, 2018).
	Spiritual gain	To be able to care for Mom during the last journey of her life gave me satisfaction…. While we were young, she worked very hard to bring us up. We felt glad to have the opportunity to pay her back for what she had done for us (Mok et al., 2003). I should do this because he is my father, and it is my filial duty. I feel pride in myself (Wang et al., 2016).
	Personal growth	Of course, my mother was a huge part of that, of my changing attitudes and the way I thought and the way I lived. It made me go on my journey too to get myself in order and to repair damage that had been done within family and so on (Tang, 2018). I did not know anything before the diagnosis… Now I feel motivated to learn about cancer from the TV, doctors, and nurses (Wu et al., 2016).
	Improved intimacy	Before, all I wanted was money. Now I treasure the relationship with my family. Since my wife cared very much for the children, I spend much more time with the kids to fulfil her wishes (Mok et al., 2003). We had kisses and held each other tight, we watched movies and listened to music while lying on bed, just like what we did at home.… if we didn't do it today, we might not be able to do it tomorrow. We have to learn to live together in the moment (Chung et al., 2017).
	Improved understanding of love	Simply being together with my husband can make both of us feel happy and loved, and to treasure the time we have left (Li et al., 2017). I was there to share and lighten her burden. This love is the essence of our marriage… It is an homage to our love. It was me as her husband who helped her to get through the stage of being an object overwhelmed by pain and suffering, to regain control and again be a subject connected with me with joy and love but also sadness and sorrow (Chung et al., 2017).

Care Gains

The principal theme of care gains for caregivers includes enhancement of their status, spiritual gain, personal growth, improved intimacy, and improved understanding of love. Care experiences can be two-sided as even in the face of terrible illness, caregiving can lead to positive experiences.

Themes of Indian Caregiving Experiences of Family Caregivers of Cancer Patients

From the analysis of the 11 articles about Indian family caregivers included in the study, a total of 56 research themes were extracted. These were systematically evaluated, integrated, and summarized into three principal themes encompassing a total of 16 sub-themes, as shown in Table 4.5.

Patient-Centered Caregiving Skills and Needs

The principal theme of patient-centered caregiving skills and needs includes medical information, psychological support, religious support, need for better hospital services, financial support, and social support. Indian caregivers require medical knowledge and various kinds of support similar to their Chinese counterparts, but also have different needs in terms of hospital improvement and religious support.

Care Burden

The principal theme of the care burden includes the sub-themes of physical well-being and lifestyle, psychological and emotional, family and social, finances and work, practice of nondisclosure, gender as a burden, and religion. It should be noted that gender stands out as a major factor in the care burden in India. Although female caregivers appear to provide most care in both countries, gender as a burden tends to be manifested in Indian participants' quotes than in those of their Chinese counterparts.

Care Gains

The principal theme of care gains comprises the sub-themes of improved understanding of love, improved intimacy, sense of hope, personal growth, and fulfillment of responsibility toward God; this latter sub-theme is the point of difference from those applying to the Chinese family caregivers.

Discussion

The aim of this study was to systematically evaluate and integrate the caregiving experiences of family caregivers of cancer patients in China and India and to explore both their common and unique features. Three broad principal themes of the caregiving experiences of family caregivers of cancer patients in China and India emerged from the synthesis: patient-centered caregiving skills and care

Table 4.5 Quotations from India Participants of the Selected Articles to Illustrate Each Theme

Theme	Sub-theme	Quotations from family caregivers in primary studies
Patient-centered caregiving skills and needs	Medical information	My husband had tracheostomy done and it often gets blocked and needs to be cleared almost every second day. As I am not an expert in doing that, I lack confidence in cleaning the tube (Goswami et al., 2019). No, I didn't ask the doctor anything much about her condition. After all, who am I to ask the doctor? I do not feel it right in asking questions; he may not like it (Kumar et al., 2017).
	Psychological support	If I was alone, it would have been difficult. Because I have family [siblings and in-laws] here [native place] it is better for me. I can ask them anything or share my feelings (Parsekar et al., 2020). The fellow caregivers contributed in facilitating management of emotions (sharing their experiences and coping), sharing burden and providing instrumental support (buying amenities for the others, taking care of the patient in the absence of the caregiver), and sharing problem-solving strategies (resources they utilized to deal with crisis, knowledge of available means to deal with difficulties) (Mehrotra & Sukumar, 2007).
	Religious support	Being tested by God (Mehrotra & Sukumar, 2007). Need to "accept what God gives" (Mehrotra & Sukumar, 2007). My husband was taken to the ICU in the morning, at 6 a.m. They said he had no pulse; he was alive because of artificial respiration. They told us to pray to God, pray to Jesus. I prayed that I would get him back. Now also I believe Jesus. My husband was in a serious condition, but Jesus saved him. Without God there is no doctor and without doctors there is no God. Both of them should be there (Kumar et al., 2017).
	Need for better hospital services	Patient's relatives are concerned about the patient. If the doctor speaks in a good tone and spends [some] time with them, they will be happy. If they [doctors] speak rudely, it will add to their [relatives'] tension (Kumar et al., 2017). Doctors should follow professional ethics and should be qualified enough to consider if the person should go to the intensive care unit. They should have the ability to discuss [the issues]. I can understand few of the technical terms. Some may not understand anything at all. So, doctors should use language that the patient/caregivers understand (Kumar et al., 2017). Nobody is telling us the condition of the patient at other times. If we ask them [doctors and nurses], they say, "please wait we will ask and tell [you]," but then they never tell [anything] (Kumar et al., 2017). I have to spend the whole day in the hospital for his [father's] follow-up. Moreover, we have to go from one place to other for check-ups and investigations (Goswami et al., 2019). Long waiting hours in the hospital make me think more into the disease condition of my brother. That increases the emotional stress as a result of the disease (Goswami et al., 2019). For minor illnesses, such as cough and cold, fever or loose stools, many a time the PHC doctor avoids treating my father and advises me to take him to the cancer hospital (Mehrotra & Sukumar, 2007). But in the hospital, we were only asked to get more money, do this treatment, but they didn't tell us anything about what would happen (Paul & Fernandes, 2020).

(Continued)

Table 4.5 Quotations from India Participants of the Selected Articles to Illustrate Each Theme (*Continued*)

Theme	Sub-theme	Quotations from family caregivers in primary studies
Care burden	*Financial support*	We don't have enough money to employ someone to look after him... even if we employ nobody can adjust to him... he used to drink alcohol and speak badly (Daya et al., 2018).
	Social support	Friends provided similar forms of emotional, instrumental, informational, and spiritual support as the family. Another form of support from friends came in terms of unexpected help (arranging for donations of blood, finances) (Mehrotra & Sukumar, 2007).
	Physical well-being and lifestyle	Apart from taking care of my father-in-law, I have to do the regular household chores, like cooking, cleaning, sweeping, etc., in the house. That makes me very tired at the end of the day (Mehrotra & Sukumar, 2007).
		As my mother's condition is worsening day by day, I started feeling hopeless and most days I have disturbed sleep. Mid-sleep I used to wake up and sit up. I don't know what more I can do (romba manakavalaya irukku...enakku ena panrathune theriyala) (Daya et al., 2018).
		I do not have time to care for myself. It has been ages since I looked into the mirror. I do not care for myself before, such as putting henna to my hair, polishing my nails, or wearing new clothes. I spend most of my time with him—why should I care about my appearance? I do not care about myself as much as my son's well-being (Antony et al., 2018).
	Psychological and emotional	I always keep thinking about the health of my father (Goswami et al., 2019).
		I do not understand what to do when he [her husband] cries out in agony and pain, and I sometimes think of dying rather than standing helpless (Goswami et al., 2019).
		When he is well, I feel all right. But, when he deteriorates or is in pain, I feel disturbed. The worst thing is to see him suffering with pain (Antony et al., 2018).
	Family and social	I can't spend enough time with my children these days, because after returning back from work I have to manage all the household chores and I have to provide care for her also. By the time I finish all these jobs I feel so tired, and my children have fallen asleep by that time (Daya et al., 2018).
		I am not attending any family functions because.... I used to feel so bad, so nowadays I started to avoid functions (Daya et al., 2018).
		Could not participate in other activities because cancer patients needed a lot of assistance (Goswami et al., 2019).
		After the illness of their family members, the neighbors were not visiting their homes like before (Goswami et al., 2019).
		They [the caregivers] remained busy in caretaking; they seldom could take out time to attend any social event (Goswami et al., 2019).
		I do not have time for other leisure activities. A person caring for a palliative patient is always busy taking care of the ill person. It has been ages since I have gone out. I spend most of the time with her (Antony et al., 2018).

(*Continued*)

Family Caregivers of Elderly Cancer Patients 77

Table 4.5 Quotations from India Participants of the Selected Articles to Illustrate Each Theme (Continued)

Theme	Sub-theme	Quotations from family caregivers in primary studies
	Finances and work	I had to shift the schooling of my children from English medium to the Marathi medium government school, as it was not possible on my part to meet the expenses of that private school (Goswami et al., 2019). I had to sell the livestock like cattle, goats to arrange money for continuing treatment (Goswami et al., 2019). I quit the job to take care of my mother, and a few of her cancer drugs I am getting from private facilities. I don't have enough money and we are dependent on my brother and other relatives… I am having debts all around (Daya et al., 2018).
	Practice of nondisclosure	Frankly, we are scared that she'll get very scared. How am I supposed to tell her when I myself am so scared? (Chittem et al., 2018). The patient is already unstable because of pain. Why should I worsen it for them [by telling them about the illness]? (Chittem et al., 2018). If you tell the patient, then you have to tell everyone. Telling no one is beneficial. If too many know… especially ladies… they will appear sad in front of the patient. This will make the patient depressed even further (Chittem et al., 2018). I hid it from the patient that he was in the last stage (Paul & Fernandes, 2020).
	Gender as a burden	We three [the participant and her two brothers] discussed who should stay back to look after [the mother]. Then I suggested that I would stay, as I am the daughter…. Women should look after the sick family member…. Women may be shy to express their problems to men… Men don't know how to look after. So only women can be a caregiver (Parsekar et al., 2020). In our case, my husband goes to work. Then children only, that two daughters take care. Will the sons be the caregivers? No, they will not. I have one son—he is also outside (Parsekar et al., 2020). Often the psychosocial needs of women caregivers are unmet. Their primary concern is for the patient's treatment. Hence, caring for their own psychological and emotional needs is neglected (Amaresha et al., 2015). I find it so difficult to take care of him… he is suffering a lot… I can't take him to any good hospitals to provide treatment. I don't have any support from anybody… being a woman what I will do alone…. (Daya et al., 2018).
	Religion	I lost faith in God… previously I used to pray every day and used to go to temples every Thursday, but nothing I got out of that… people who are bad and make others suffer are happier and we people who have never thought of doing anything bad to others are suffering for the whole life, then why should we believe in God and other things? Everything is happening as per our fate only… nobody can change anything (Daya et al., 2018).

(Continued)

Table 4.5 Quotations from India Participants of the Selected Articles to Illustrate Each Theme (*Continued*)

Theme	Sub-theme	Quotations from family caregivers in primary studies
Care gains	*Improved understanding of love*	To whom they [care recipient] love more, provide accompany and care, then they can cure earlier.... For me, if my husband is there along with me then I get courage compared to other people (Parsekar et al., 2020).
	Improved intimacy	Now, we don't have that depression—we can face anything together, we have become very attached [to each other] (Chittem et al., 2018).
	Sense of hope	We have taken him [the patient] to the best hospitals, and he is undergoing the best treatment available. We are confident that he will be cured (Goswami et al., 2019).
		We always have hope, and we always pray for miracles to happen. Like, they'll improve. It's the human tendency to think that way (Kumar et al., 2017).
	Personal growth	Learning to tolerate minor irritations/hassles (Mehrotra & Sukumar, 2007).
		Experiencing a perspective shift in terms of being more accepting of each day and also being able to prioritize my life issues (Mehrotra & Sukumar, 2007).
		We [the patient and family] mature from the experience (Chittem et al., 2018).
	Fulfillment of responsibility toward God	Experience of feeling closer to God, of being "cared for and supported by Him" while being "tested by Him" at the same time (Mehrotra & Sukumar, 2007).
		The recurrent expression of strong hope [that the patient would recover] often occurred, along with expression of faith in God (Mehrotra & Sukumar, 2007).
		I became stronger in mind, because I didn't have any other choice. I just grew a lot. I learned to pray a lot. I learned to put myself in God's hands, especially when he was going through what he was going through. I am just praying to God to give us strength and guide us through these hurdles in life (Antony et al., 2018).

needs, care burden, and care gains. Both Chinese and Indian family caregivers are in great need of medical knowledge, training in caregiving skills, and various forms of support; both groups face physical, psychological, financial, social, and cultural forms of burden as well as various forms of positive experiences such as personal growth, sense of hope, improved intimacy, and improved understanding of love. However, due to contextual differences in relation to the health service system, religious beliefs, gender issues, and perceptions and practices around filial piety, each principal theme might have different connotations in the two countries.

Upon comparison of the caregiving experiences of family caregivers of cancer patients in China and India, four broad differences can be identified. First, China has a more developed health system than India in several aspects. In regard to the medical facilities, China has built a three-tier system of basic medical services (Meng et al., 2004), aiming to provide efficient and affordable medical services to all Chinese citizens. This system was established in China's most recent medical reform in 2009 and reached a certain degree of success, especially in terms of the service coverage of the whole population (Ma et al., 2018; Yu et al., 2013). Although India has also established a three-tier basic medical service system (Chakraborty & Chakraborti, 2015), the government's expenditure on health care, the number of medical professionals, and the medical coverage are far lower than in China (Karan et al., 2021; Kedia et al., 2020; Younger, 2016). As of 2020, China has over 1 million health institutions and around 911 million hospital beds (National Bureau of Statistics, 2021), while in 2019, there were 69,265 hospitals and close to 2 million hospital beds in India (Center for Disease Dynamics, Economics & Policy, 2020). China had around 13.46 million health professionals (doctors, nurses, pharmacists, dentists, and other medical practitioners) in 2020 (National Bureau of Statistics, 2021), while India had 5.76 million health professionals in the year of 2018 (World Health Organization, 2018). For two countries with similar population sizes, this is a direct reflection of the development level of their respective medical systems. Moreover, China has been establishing equitable health insurance and social security for all Chinese. Since the 1990s, the Chinese central government has launched three national insurance schemes to address access issues to health services: the Urban Employee Basic Medical Insurance (UEBMI) for urban employees, Urban Resident Basic Medical Insurance (URBMI) for the urban unemployed, and the New Cooperative Medical System (NCMS) for rural residents (Barber & Yao, 2011; Meng & Tang, 2013). By 2011, these three health schemes covered around 95% of Chinese residents, compared to a few years earlier in 2003, when these figures were 55.9% and 21.4%, respectively (Lee et al., 2018). This greatly reduced the financial burden on patients and their families, even if health expenses remain a major reason for Chinese to fall into poverty (He, 2021). In the meanwhile, 7% of Indians fall into poverty each year because of unaffordable health care (Reddy, 2018), as India's social security and health insurance system has very low national coverage (Reddy, 2015; Shroff et al., 2020). Additionally, medical social work, which enables comprehensive support and helps cancer patients, has been developing for almost a decade in China (Liu, 2016), while for India, no sign was found of this in the relevant research; we can only presume medical social work is still at a preliminary development stage. As a result, family caregivers in India have more complaints about the health service than those in China and have expressed a more urgent need for better hospital services.

Second, Indian family caregivers appear to face greater care burdens compared to the Chinese family caregivers in the studies examined for this analysis. Even though most family caregivers in both countries are female (with the percentage higher in India than in China), Indian female family caregivers explicitly tied their perceived burden to their being female, whereas their Chinese counterparts focused more on their care burden as an individual or a family member. Both India and China have had a strongly patriarchal culture for a long time, in which women are considered as the main source of care and their familial and social status is inferior to that of men (Chowdhury & Al Baset, 2018; Jin, 2010). Although feminist movements have become increasingly visible in both countries in recent years, their extent and manifestations are rather different. By the end of the nineteenth century, western feminist thought was introduced into China, which sparked the awakening of female consciousness, opposition to foot-binding, striving for working rights, the creation of women's newspapers, and other independent activities (Zhou & Qin, 2017). Since the 1920s, driven by the socialist revolution led by the Communist Party, a form of state feminism has been promoted that has had a profound positive influence on the promotion of women's equal rights in China (Liao, 2020; Yin, 2021). Even though gender equality is still a major issue, China has made a lot of progress in terms of gender equality; for instance, 43.2% of the workforce in China is female (National Bureau of Statistics, 2020). In India, however, women still occupy a much more disadvantaged position in all aspects of life than in China, including political rights, economically, right to education, status in the family, marriage freedom, and so on (Bhattacharya et al., 2019); for instance, only 20.4% workforce in India is female (International Labour Organization, 2019). Indian women are taught from an early age to perform household duties and care for men, while men are taught that they are superior to women (Chaturvedi et al., 2014). Many scholars, such as Amaresha et al. (2015) and Kim et al. (2018), have found that Indian women continue to be faced with limited educational opportunities, financial difficulties, forced marriage, domestic violence, and low levels of family support, due to India's still-prevalent caste system, patriarchal system, and other cultural perceptions and practices. Therefore, Indian female family caregivers may face more care burdens induced by gender inequality than do their Chinese counterparts.

Third, Indian family caregivers of cancer patients were more likely to have recourse to the power of religion than their Chinese counterparts. Religiosity is an important factor in caregiving experiences as it can be used as a temporary escape mechanism to relieve short-term stress (Gibbs et al., 2020), as well as providing spiritual resources for inner strength to cope with the burden (Eagle et al., 2019; Gibbs et al., 2020). Chinese society is more influenced by Confucianism, and china has a recent history of restricting religious belief (Gan & Zhou, 2012; Li, 2020). Compared with other Asian countries, including India, the number of people with explicit religious belief in China is relatively low (Choi et al., 2016; Lu, 2014), although there appears to have been an increase, especially in Buddhism (among other religions), in recent years (Wei, 2018). Studies have shown that religious belief (Hindu, Muslim, Christian, and others) is widely drawn from in India to cope with stressful situations such as terminal illness and bereavement (Eagle et al., 2019). Cancer patients and their caregivers in India pray at every illness stage because they believe that prayer can relieve pain, alter the course of disease, and provide relaxation (Elsner et al., 2012; Simha et al., 2013). Overall, religion is an important source of strength for family caregivers of cancer patients in India, whereas Chinese caregivers tend to have recourse to philosophical precepts and cultural beliefs such as filial piety. It is noteworthy the conflicts some Indian caregivers experience vis-à-vis religious belief in the process of rationalizing a cancer diagnosis.

Fourth, a form of filial piety practice is seen in the caregiving experiences in both countries. For example, both Chinese and Indian family caregivers demonstrated adherence to a filial discourse of "not telling their parents about the diagnosis of cancer," identified by He & van Heugten (2020). However, the connotations and practices of filial piety in the two countries must be differentiated. In China, filial piety is understood as an "obligatory duty" and is defined as "respect, obedience, loyalty, material provision and physical care [to] parents [by their] children" (Qiu et al., 2017). Since Confucius's conceptualization of filial piety over 2,000 years ago, it has developed beyond mere cultural perception and practice to a quasi-metaphysical theoretical framework that can be used to inform other familial and social practices (He & van Heugten, 2021). Although India has a similar concept, *seva*, it has not achieved the same level of influence in Indian society (Beckerlegge, 2016). Therefore, the influence of expectations of filial piety over Chinese family caregivers is more multifaceted than for Indian family caregivers. This can be seen in the quotations from both sides. In terms of disclosure of the diagnosis, Indian family caregivers only stressed its negative consequences in terms of the patient's emotional acceptance, whereas the Chinese caregivers also took their filial responsibilities into account in opting for nondisclosure. Such practices inevitably increase the emotional pressure on the caregivers in terms of how they deal with their burdens, such as not being able to say goodbye or refusing to ask for help from outside (Si et al., 2018; Tang, 2019; Wang et al., 2016). For example, Chinese adult children attach more importance to extending their parents' life expectancy and tend to choose active intervention treatment rather than palliative care, and thereby ignore the dignity and self-determination rights of their parents at the end of life in the first place (Zhang et al., 2015). Filial piety also has positive effects on Chinese family caregivers. Studies have shown that caregivers can have gains from being filial through several mechanisms: the enhancement of their reputation in the community as a filial child, setting a good example for the next generation to practice filial piety in order to obtain future care, and facilitating a closer and mutually beneficial relationship with their parents (He & van Heugten, 2020). The positive impact of the filial practice is also consistent with some Indian studies (Kadoya & Khan, 2016). However, few scholars have studied the negative effects of filial piety on family caregivers in India. More comprehensive studies from India on filial piety and the caregiving experiences of family caregivers are needed in order to make a more accurate comparison.

Limitations

This study has two main limitations. First, the quality of our qualitative meta-synthesis is tied to the quality of the original research in the studies included in the synthesis. Our evaluation of the articles points to the quality of the China-based studies as relatively higher than that of the India-based ones (albeit still in great need of improvement). For example, the China-based studies pay more attention to methodology and richness of data analysis than the India-based ones, especially among those published in English-language journals. Therefore, knowledge of and skills in the application of qualitative research methods need to be further developed. Second, literature search we conducted was not comprehensive: grey literature that has not been formally published is not found in this study, and language is also a because this synthesis only considered studies published in Chinese and English language databases and not those published in databases that include different Indian languages including Hindi. Therefore, the overall synthesis may be limited.

Conclusion

By adopting a qualitative meta-synthesis method, we gain an understanding of not only the common but also the unique features of caregiving experiences between family caregivers in China and in India. This novel analysis provides fertile ground for understanding family caregiving experiences for elderly cancer patients from a global point of view, and how family caregivers could be better supported. We hope that further research endeavoring to investigate family caregiving issues in a more integrated or comparative perspective between China and India is put in place in the near future, as a potential way to better understand oneself is through comparison with others, especially with those similar to us.

References

Ahn, S., Romo, R. D., & Campbell, C. L. (2020). A systematic review of interventions for family caregivers who care for patients with advanced cancer at home. *Patient Education and Counseling*, *103*(8), 1518–1530. https://doi.org/10.1016/j.pec.2020.03.012

Amaresha, A. C., Reddy, N. K., Ahmed, A., Ross, D., & Arthur, J. A. J. (2015). Women caregivers of persons with brain tumour: A psychosocial needs assessment in a tertiary care hospital in Bangalore. *Indian Journal of Gender Studies*, *22*(1), 41–62. https://doi.org/10.1177/0971521514556944

Antony, L., George, L. S., & Jose, T. T. (2018). Stress, coping, and lived experiences among caregivers of cancer patients on palliative care: A mixed method research. *Indian Journal of Palliative Care*, *24*(3), 313–319. https://doi.org/10.4103/IJPC.IJPC_178_17

Barber, S. L., & Yao, L. (2011). Development and status of health insurance systems in China. *International Journal of Health Planning and Management*, *26*(4), 339–356. https://doi.org/10.1002/hpm.1109

Beckerlegge, G. (2016). Seva: The focus of a fragmented but gradually coalescing field of study. *Religions of South Asia*, *9*(2), 208–239. https://doi.org/10.1558/rosa.v9i2.31070

Bhattacharya, A., Camacho, D., Kimberly, L. L., & Lukens, E. P. (2019). Women's experiences and perceptions of depression in India: A metaethnography. *Qualitative Health Research*, 29(1), 80–95. https://doi.org/10.1177/1049732318811702

Burke, L. A., Neimeyer, R. A., Young, A. J., Bonin, E. P., & Davis, N. L. (2014). Complicated spiritual grief II: A deductive inquiry following the loss of a loved one. *Death Studies*, 38(4), 268–281. https://doi.org/10.1080/07481187.2013.829373

Center for Disease Dynamics, Economics & Policy. (2020). *COVID-19 in India: State-wise estimates of current hospital beds, intensive care unit (ICU) beds and ventilators.* https://cddep.org/wp-content/uploads/2020/04/State-wise-estimates-of-current-beds-and-ventilators_24Apr2020.pdf

Chakraborty, R., & Chakraborti, C. (2015). India, health inequities, and a fair healthcare provision: A perspective from health capability. *Journal of Human Development and Capabilities*, 16(4), 567–580. https://doi.org/10.1080/19452829.2015.1105201

Chaturvedi, S. K., Strohschein, F. J., Saraf, G., & Loiselle, C. G. (2014). Communication in cancer care: Psycho-social, interactional, and cultural issues. A general overview and the example of India. *Frontiers in Psychology*, 5, 1332. https://doi.org/10.3389/fpsyg.2014.01332

Chen, H., Komaromy, C., & Valentine, C. (2015). From hope to hope: The experience of older Chinese people with advanced cancer. *Health*, 19(2), 154–171. https://doi.org/10.1177/1363459314555238

Chittem, M., Norman, P., & Harris, P. (2018). Primary family caregivers' reasons for disclosing versus not disclosing a cancer diagnosis in India. *Cancer Nursing*, 43(2), 126–133. https://doi.org/10.1097/ncc.0000000000000669

Choi, Y. S., Hwang, S. W., Hwang, I. C., Lee, Y. J., Kim, Y. S., Kim, H. M., Youn, C. H., Ahn, H. Y., & Koh, S. J. (2016). Factors associated with quality of life among family caregivers of terminally ill cancer patients. *Psycho-Oncology*, 25(2), 217–224. https://doi.org/10.1002/pon.3904

Chowdhury, R., & Al Baset, Z. (2018). *Men and feminism in India* (1st ed.). Routledge India. https://doi.org/10.4324/9781351048248

Chung, B. P. M., Leung, D., Leung, S. M., & Loke, A. Y. (2017). Beyond death and dying: How Chinese spouses navigate the final days with their loved ones suffering from terminal cancer. *Supportive Care in Cancer*, 26(1), 261–267. https://doi.org/10.1007/s00520-017-3844-z

Datta, S. S., Tripathi, L., Varghese, R., Logan, J., Gessler, S., Chatterjee, S., Bhaumik, J., & Menon, U. (2016). Pivotal role of families in doctor-patient communication in oncology: A qualitative study of patients, their relatives and cancer clinicians. *European Journal of Cancer Care*, 26(5), 1–22. https://doi.org/10.1111/ecc.12543

Daya, A., Sarkar, S., & Kar, S. S. (2018). Needs of the caregivers of people requiring palliative care in an urban area of Pondicherry, South India. *International Journal of Community Medicine and Public Health*, 5(6), 2259–2265. http://dx.doi.org/10.18203/2394-6040.ijcmph20181973

Eagle, D. E., Kinghorn, W. A., Parnell, H., Amanya, C., Vann, V., Tzudir, S., Kaza, V. G. K., Safu, C. T., Whetten, K., & Proeschold-Bell, R. J. (2019). Religion and caregiving for orphans and vulnerable children: A qualitative study of caregivers across four religious traditions and five global contexts. *Journal of Religion and Health*, 59(3), 1666–1686. https://doi.org/10.1007/s10943-019-00955-y

Elsner, F., Schmidt, J., Rajagopal, M. R., Radbruch, L., & Pestinger, M. (2012). Psychosocial and spiritual problems of terminally ill patients in Kerala, India. *Future Oncology*, 8(9), 1183–1191. https://doi.org/10.2217/fon.12.97

Fu, F., Chen, Y. Y., Li, Q. Y., & Zhu, F. Z. (2018). Varieties of hope among family caregivers of patients with lymphoma. *Qualitative Health Research, 28*(13), 2048–2058. https://doi.org/10.1177/1049732318779051

Gan, C. S., & Zhou, Y. Q. (2012). The religious nature of Confucianism in contemporary China's "Cultural Renaissance Movement." *Contemporary Chinese Thought, 44*(2), 3–15. https://doi.org/10.2753/CSP1097-1467440200

Gibbs, L. A. L., Anderson, M. I., Simpson, G. K., Jones, K. F., & Dein, S. (2020). Spirituality and resilience among family caregivers of survivors of stroke: A scoping review. *NeuroRehabilitation, 46*(1), 41–52. https://doi.org/10.3233/NRE-192946

Goswami, S., Gupta, S. S., & Raut, A. (2019). Understanding the psychosocial impact of oral cancer on the family caregivers and their coping up mechanism: A qualitative study in Rural Wardha, Central India. *Indian Journal of Palliative Care, 25*(3), 421–427. https://doi.org/10.4103/IJPC.IJPC_9_19

He, L. T. (2021). *Care work, migrant peasant families and discourse of filial piety*. Palgrave Macmillan. https://doi.org/10.1007/978-981-16-1880-2

He, L. T., & van Heugten, K. (2020). Chinese migrant workers' care experiences: A model of the mediating roles of filial piety. *Qualitative Health Research, 30*(11), 1749–1761. https://doi.org/10.1177/1049732320925420

He, L. T., & van Heugten, K. (2021). An implementable conversation between Foucault and Chinese virtue ethics in the context of Chinese youth social work. *British Journal of Social Work*, 1–17. https://doi.org/10.1093/bjsw/bcab034

Institute of Medicine of the National Academies. (2015). *Dying in America: Improving quality and honoring individual preferences near the end of life*. The National Academies Press (US). https://doi.org/10.17226/18748

International Agency for Research on Cancer. (2021a). GLOBOCAN 2020 Population Fact Sheet: China. https://gco.iarc.fr/today/data/factsheets/populations/356-india-fact-sheets.pdf

International Agency for Research on Cancer. (2021b). GLOBOCAN 2020 Population Fact Sheet: India. https://gco.iarc.fr/today/data/factsheets/populations/160-china-fact-sheets.pdf

International Labour Organization. (2019). *Periodic Labour Force Survey*. https://ilostat.ilo.org/data/country-profiles/

Jin, Y. H. (2010). Mobile paternal authority: Change in migrant farmer families [流动的父权：流动农民家庭的变迁]. *Social Sciences in China* [中国社会科学], *4*, 151–165.

Joad, A. S. K., Mayamol, T. C., & Chaturvedi, M. (2011). What does the informal caregiver of a terminally ill cancer patient need? A study from a cancer centre. *Indian Journal of Palliative Care, 25*(1), 191–196. https://doi.org/10.4103/0973-1075.251090

Joanna Briggs Institute. (2021, April 26). *Checklist for Qualitative Research*. https://jbi.global/sites/default/files/2021-03/Checklist_for_Qualitative_Research.docx

Kadoya, Y., & Khan, M. S. R. (2016). Can concern for the long-term care of older parents explain son preference at birth in India? *Journal of Women & Aging, 29*(3), 254–266. https://doi.org/10.1080/08952841.2015.1138048

Karan, A., Negandhi, H., Hussain, S., Zapata, T., Mairembam, D., De Graeve, H., Buchan, J., & Zodpey, S. (2021). Size, composition and distribution of health workforce in India: Why, and where to invest? *Human Resources Health, 19*(1), 39. https://doi.org/10.1186/s12960-021-00575-2

Kedia, M., Wang, Z. C., & Liu, M. Q. (2020). Human resources for health development policy: A comparison between China and India. *Journal of Asian Public Policy*, 1–20. https://doi.org/10.1080/17516234.2020.1778244

Kim, Y., Mitchell, H. R., & Ting, A. (2018). Application of psychological theories on the role of gender in caregiving to psycho-oncology research. *Psycho-Oncology, 28*(2), 228–254. https://doi.org/10.1002/pon.4953

Kumar, S., Christina, J., Jagadish, A. R., Peter, J. V., Thomas, K., & Sudarsanam, T. D. (2017). Caregiver perceptions on intensive care: A qualitative study from southern India. *National Medical Journal of India, 30*(3), 131–135.

Lamb, S. (2013). In/dependence, intergenerational uncertainty, and the ambivalent state: Perceptions of Old Age Security in India. *South Asia—Journal of South Asian Studies, 36*(1), 65–78. https://doi.org/10.1080/00856401.2012.732552

Lee, Y. H., Chiang, T., Shelley, M., & Liu, C. T. (2018). Chinese resident education levels and social insurance coverage. *International Journal of Health Care Quality Assurance, 31*(7), 746–756. https://doi.org/10.1108/ijhcqa-06-2017-0098

Li, C. Y., Zhang, W., Bi, X. Y., Wang, L. M., He, F., & Li, Y. Y. (2018). Qualitative study of psychological experience of caregivers among patients with liver cancer complicated with viral hepatitis B [肝癌合并乙型病毒性肝炎患者照顾者心理体验的质性研究]. *Chinese Journal of Practical Nursing* [中国实用护理杂志], *21*, 1642–1646.

Li, L., Liang, J., Tian, Z. R., & Liu, C. F. (2014). Quality of life and related factors among family members of adolescents with head and neck cancer [青少年头颈部癌症病人家属的生活质量及影响因素分析]. *China Nursing Study* [护理研究], *28*(2), 186–188.

Li, Q. P., Lim, C. V. C., Xu, X. F., Xu, Y. H., & Loke, A. Y. (2015). The experiences of Chinese couples living with cancer: A focus group study. *Cancer Nursing, 38*(5), 383–394. https://doi.org/10.1097/NCC.0000000000000196

Li, Q. P., Lin, Y., Chen, Y., & Loke, A. Y. (2017). Mutual support and challenges among Chinese couples living with colorectal cancer. *Cancer Nursing, 41*(5), E50–E60. https://doi.org/10.1097/NCC.0000000000000553

Li, Q. P., Xu, Y. H., Zhou, H. Y., & Loke, A. Y. (2016). Factors influencing the health-related quality of life of Chinese advanced cancer patients and their spousal caregivers: A cross-sectional study. *BMC Palliative Care, 15*(72), 1–14. http://dx.doi.org/10.1186/s12904-016-0142-3

Li, S. F. (2020). Freedom in handcuffs: Religious freedom in the constitution of China. *Journal of Law and Religion, 35*(1), 113–137. https://doi.org/10.1017/jlr.2020.1

Liao, S. (2020). Feminism without guarantees: Reflections on teaching and researching feminist activism in China. *Asian Journal of Women's Studies, 26*(2), 259–267. http://dx.doi.org/10.1080/12259276.2020.1769368

Lin, Y., Hu, C. P., Xu, Y. H., Zhao, J. E., & Li, Q. P. (2020). The mutual impact and moderating factors of quality of life between advanced cancer patients and their family caregivers. *Supportive Care in Cancer, 28*(11), 5251–5262. http://dx.doi.org/10.1007/S00520-020-05351-X

Lin, Y., Xu, Y. H., Li, Q. P., & Li, J. P. (2015). The Qualitative study on the experiences of caregivers burden in spouse of elderly cancer patients [晚期癌症患者照顾者照护现状和需求的质性研究]. *PLA Nursing Journal* [解放军护理杂志], *32*(20), 1–6.

Liu, J. T. (2016). The scope of health social work practice system in China and the role of modern humanistic care social work character [中国健康社会工作实务体系范围与现代医生人文关怀型社会工作角色]. *The Journal of Humanities* [人文杂志], *4*, 94–101.

Liu, L. L., Chen, M. X., Wang, Y. J., & Zhang, X. Q. (2020). A qualitative meta-synthesis of the caregiving experiences of family caregivers of pancreas cancer patients [胰腺癌患者的家庭照护者照护体验质性研究的 Meta 整合]. *Chinese Journal of Modern Nursing* [中华现代护理杂志], *26*(31), 4345–4351.

Liu, W. Z., & She, S. T. (2011). A qualitative study of the real experience of primary caregivers of cancer patients [癌症患者主要照顾者真实体验的质性研究]. *Medical Information* [医学信息], *24*(7), 130–131.

Liu, Y., Insel, K. C., Reed, P. G., & Crist, J. D. (2012). Family caregiving of older Chinese people with dementia: Testing a model. *Nursing Research*, *61*(1), 39–50. https://doi.org/10.1097/nnr.0b013e31823bc451

Lu, Y. F. (2014). Report on contemporary Chinese religious based on data of CFPS (2012) [当代中国宗教状况报告：基于 CFPS (2012) 调查数据]. *World Religious Cultures* [世界宗教文化], *1*, 11–25.

Lukhmana, S., Bhasin, S. K., Chhabra, P., & Bhatia, M. S. (2015). Family caregivers' burden: A hospital based study in 2010 among cancer patients from Delhi. *Indian Journal of Cancer*, *52*(1), 146–151. https://doi.org/10.4103/0019-509X.175584

Ma, Z. F., Yin, S. G., Qiao, W. Y., Li, Z. J., & Wu, Q. Y. (2018). Spatial equilibrium state and its time evolution of Medical health resource supply level in China [中国医疗卫生资源供给水平的空间均衡状态及其时间演变]. *Scientia Geographica Sinica* [地理科学], *38*(6), 869–876.

Martin M. J., Olano-Lizarraga, M., & Saracibar-Razquin, M. (2016). The experience of family caregivers caring for a terminal patient at home: A research review. *International Journal of Nursing Studies*, *64*, 1–12. https://doi.org/10.1016/j.ijnurstu.2016.09.010

Mehrotra, S., & Sukumar, P. (2007). Sources of strength perceived by females caring for relatives diagnosed with cancer: An exploratory study from India. *Supportive Care in Cancer*, *15*(12), 1357–1366. https://doi.org/10.1007/s00520-007-0256-5

Meng, Q. Y., & Tang, S. L. (2013). Universal health care coverage in China: Challenges and opportunities. *Procedia—Social and Behavioral Sciences*, *77*, 330–340. https://doi.org/10.1016/j.sbspro.2013.03.091

Meng, Q., Shi, G., Yang, H., Gonzalez-Block, M., & Blas, E. (2004). *Health policy and systems research in China*. Geneva World Health Organization. https://www.who.int/tdr/publications/documents/health-research-china.pdf

Mok, E., Chan, F., Chan, V., & Yeung, E. (2003). Family experience caring for terminally ill patients with cancer in Hong Kong. *Cancer Nursing*, *26*(4), 267–275. https://doi.org/10.1097/00002820-200308000-00003

National Bureau of Statistics. (2020). *China Population and Employment Statistics Yearbook* [中国人口和就业统计年鉴]. China Statistics Press [中国统计出版社].

National Bureau of Statistics. (2021). *National Data-2020 Data* [国家数据-2020 年度数据]. https://data.stats.gov.cn/easyquery.htm?cn=C01

Parsekar, S. S., Bailey, A., Binu, V. S., & Nair, S. (2020). Exploring perceptions and practices of cancer care among caregivers and care recipients of breast cancer in India. *Psycho-Oncology*, *29*(4), 737–742. https://doi.org/10.1002/pon.5326

Paul, A., & Fernandes, E. (2020). Experiences of caregivers in a home-based palliative care model—A qualitative study. *Indian Journal of Palliative Care*, *26*(3), 306–311. https://doi.org/10.4103/IJPC.IJPC_154_19

Peacock, S. C. (2011). *The lived experience of family caregivers who provided end-of-life care to a relative with advanced dementia* (Publication No. 857080394) [Doctoral dissertation, University of Alberta (Canada)]. ProQuest Dissertations & Theses Global. http://www.pqdtcn.com/thesisDetails/F934CC68FA2825A25D7F23321071E222

Qiu, X. C. H., Sit, J. W. H., & Koo, F. K. (2017). The influence of Chinese culture on family caregivers of stroke survivors: A qualitative study. *Journal of Clinical Nursing*, *27*(1–2), E309–E319. https://doi.org/10.1111/jocn.13947

Reddy, K. S. (2015). International health care systems—India's aspirations for universal health coverage. *New England Journal of Medicine*, *373*(1), 1–5. https://doi.org/10.1056/NEJMp1414214

Reddy, K. S. (2018). Health care reforms in India. *JAMA, 319*(24), 2477–2478. https://doi.org/10.1001/jama.2018.5284

Sánchez-Izquierdo, M., Prieto-Ursúa, M., & Caperos, J. M. (2015). Positive aspects of family caregiving of dependent elderly. *Educational Gerontology, 41*(11), 745–756. https://doi.org/10.1080/03601277.2015.1033227

Shaffer, K. M., Jacobs, J. M., Nipp, R. D., Carr, A., Jackson, V. A., Park, E. R., Pirl, W. F., El-Jawahri, A., Gallagher, E. R., Greer, J. A., & Temel, J. S. (2017). Mental and physical health correlates among family caregivers of patients with newly-diagnosed incurable cancer: A hierarchical linear regression analysis. *Supportive Care in Cancer, 25*(3), 965–971. https://doi.org/10.1007/s00520-016-3488-4

Shroff, Z. C., Marten, R., Ghaffar, A., Sheikh, K., Bekedam, H., Jhalani, M., & Swaminathan, S. (2020). On the path to universal health coverage: Aligning ongoing health systems reforms in India. *BMJ Global Health, 5*(9), 1–3. https://doi.org/10.1136/bmjgh-2020-003801

Si, S. J., Shi, C. Y., Xu, S. L., Wang, H. Q., Chen, W. H., & Wan, R. (2018). A qualitative study of the experience of home-transitioned caregivers in military hospitals for retired elderly people [军队离退休老年人医院-家庭过渡期照护者体验的质性研究]. *Electronic Journal of Practical Clinical Nursing* [实用临床护理学电子杂志], *14*, 172–175.

Simha, S., Noble, S., & Chaturvedi, S. K. (2013). Spiritual concerns in Hindu cancer patients undergoing palliative care: A qualitative study. *Indian Journal of Palliative Care, 19*(2), 99–105. https://doi.org/10.4103/0973-1075.116716

Simpson, P. (2005). Hong Kong families and breast cancer: Beliefs and adaptation strategies. *Psycho-Oncology, 14*(8), 671–683. https://doi.org/10.1002/pon.893

Smith, R. D., & Mallath, M. K. (2019). History of the growing burden of cancer in India: From antiquity to the 21st century. *Journal of Global Oncology, 5*, 1–15. https://doi.org/10.1200/JGO.19.00048

Sung, H., Ferlay, J., Siegel, R. L., Laversanne, M., Soerjomataram, I., Jemal, A., & Bray, F. (2021). Global cancer statistics 2020: GLOBOCAN estimates of incidence and mortality worldwide for 36 cancers in 185 countries. *CA—A Cancer Journal for Clinicians, 71*(3), 209–249. https://doi.org/10.3322/caac.21660

Tang, Y. (2018). Challenges, personal growth and social support among family caregivers of terminally ill cancer patients in Southern China. *Qualitative Social Work, 18*(4), 638–654. https://doi.org/10.1177/1473325018755890

Tang, Y. (2019). Caregiver burden and bereavement among family caregivers who lost terminally ill cancer patients. *Palliative and Supportive Care, 17*(5), 515–522. https://doi.org/10.1017/S1478951518001025

Thombre, A., Sherman, A. C., & Simonton, S. (2010). Religious coping and posttraumatic growth among family caregivers of cancer patients in India. *Journal of Psychosocial Oncology, 28*(2), 173–188. https://doi.org/10.1080/07347330903570537

Ugargol, A. P., Hutter, I., James, K. S., & Bailey, A. (2016). Care needs and caregivers: Associations and effects of living arrangements on caregiving to older adults in India. *Ageing International, 41*(2), 193–213. https://doi.org/10.1007/s12126-016-9243-9

Wang, B. L., Pang, S. Q., Wu, Y. L., Lu, Z. Y., Zheng, L. X., Mei, Y. Y., & Zhang, H. B. (2016). A qualitative study of the care needs of family members of dying elderly patients [老年临终患者家属照护需求的质性研究]. *PLA Nursing Journal* [解放军护理杂志], *23*, 11–14+19.

Wang, X. W., & Fei, F. Y. (2010). Qualitative study on the nursing experience of immediate family members in patients with malignant tumor [恶性肿瘤患者直系亲属照护体验的质性研究]. *Chinese Journal of Modern Nursing* [中华现代护理杂志], *35*, 4277–4279.

Wei, D. D. (2018). Chinese Buddhism: From ancient to present and beyond. *Religioni e Società Rivista di scienze sociali della religione, 33*(91), 18–27. https://doi.org/10.19272/201831302003

Wong, M. S., & Chan, S. W. C. (2007). The experiences of Chinese family members of terminally ill patients—A qualitative study. *Journal of Clinical Nursing, 16*(12), 2357–2364. https://doi.org/10.1111/j.1365-2702.2007.01943.x

World Health Organization. (2018). *National Health Workforce Accounts (NHWA)* https://apps.who.int/gho/data/node.country.country-IND?lang=en

World Health Organization. (2018, January 12). *Definition of palliative care.* www.who.int/cancer/palliative/definition/en/

Wu, Z., Guan, Q. Y., & Gao, J. B. (2016). Qualitative study on the real experience of relatives of hospitalized elderly patients [住院高龄患者亲属照顾者真实体验的质性研究]. *PLA Nursing Journal* [解放军护理杂志], *33*(7), 12–15.

Xu, Y., Ye, W. Q., & Jiang, P. (2014). Qualitative study of current status and needs of caregivers of terminal cancer patient. [晚期癌症患者照顾者照护现状和需求的质性研究]. *PLA Nursing Journal* [解放军护理杂志], *31*(22), 1–4.

Xu, Y. M., Wu, Y., Zhang, Y., Ma, R. Y., & Li, X. H. (2016). Investigation of nursing human resources in Chinese hospitals [全国医院护士人力资源现状的调查]. *Chinese Journal of Nursing* [中华护理杂志], *51*(7), 819–822.

Yin, S. Y. (2021). Re-articulating feminisms: A theoretical critique of feminist struggles and discourse in historical and contemporary China. *Cultural Studies.* https://doi.org/10.1080/09502386.2021.1944242

Younger, D. S. (2016). Health care in India. *Neurologic Clinics, 34*(4), 1103–1114. https://doi.org/10.1016/j.ncl.2016.06.005

Yu, D. Z., Zhang, Z. Z., & Yang, H. W. (2013). *Research on healthcare reforms* [医改专题研究]. People's Medical Publishing House [人民卫生出版社].

Zeng, L., Zhu, X. P., Meng, X. M., Mao, Y. F., Wu, Q., Shi, Y., & Zhou, L. S. (2014). Responsibility and burden from the perspective of seniors' family caregivers: A qualitative study in Shanghai, China. *International Journal of Clinical and Experimental Medicine, 7*(7), 1818–1828.

Zhang, Q., Yao, D., Yang, J., & Zhou, Y. (2014). Factors influencing sleep disturbances among spouse caregivers of cancer patients in Northeast China. *PLoS One, 9*(10), e108614. http://dx.doi.org/10.1371/journal.pone.0108614

Zhang, X. L., Shan, C. M., & Zhang, J. J. (2013). Qualitative study on the family care burden of osteosarcoma patients [骨肉瘤病人家属照顾负荷的质性研究]. *Nursing Research* [护理研究], *23*, 2465–2466.

Zhang, Z., Chen, M. L., Gu, X. L., Liu, M. H., & Cheng, W. W. (2015). Cultural and ethical considerations for cardiopulmonary resuscitation in Chinese patients with cancer at the end of life. *The American Journal of Hospice & Palliative Care, 32*(2), 210–215. http://dx.doi.org/10.1177/1049909113520215

Zhou, J. H., & Qin, Y. Y. (2017). Feminism in China: Analysis of the plight of theory and practice [女权主义在中国：理论与实践困境]. *Journal of Hubei University of Economics* [湖北经济学院学报], *15*(4), 123–128.

Zhou, M., Wang, H., Zeng, X., Yin, P., Zhu, J., Chen, W., Li, X., Wang, L., Wang, L., Liu, Y., Liu, J., Zhang, M., Qi, J., Yu, S., Afshin, A., Gakidou, E., Glenn, S., Krish, V. S., Miller-Petrie, M. K., … Liang, X. (2019). Mortality, morbidity, and risk factors in China and its provinces, 1990–2017: A systematic analysis for the global burden of disease study 2017. *Lancet, 394*(10204), 1145–1158. https://doi.org/10.1016/S0140-6736(19)30427-1

5 Filial-Piety-Based Family Care in Chinese Societies

Zhuopeng Yu and Boye Fang

Introduction

China has the highest number of older people in the world, with its population aging at an unprecedented pace. According to the Chinese State Council, the number of people over 60 years of age in China has reached 255 million in 2020, with the number of senior citizens exceeding 29 million and the old-age dependency ratio increasing to 28%. In particular, about 118 million older Chinese adults have long-term care needs and most of them receive care in the family setting (Chen 2019; Wang et al. 2018). The family-based care pattern reflects the culture of filial piety.

Definition of Traditional Filial Piety

Traditional filial piety refers to the social norm based on Confucianism, which suggested parents should love and care for their children and the children should respect and provide care to their parents in turn (Ha et al. 2016). According to this culturally specific value, prevails in Chinese societies, was defined as the expectation for children to revere and care for their aging parents. In the time of Confucius, filial piety evolved as part of a structured social order in China and prescribed family care responsibility, which was observed for thousands of years (Li 1997). For centuries, filial piety has played an essential role in keeping family order by promoting responsibility, sacrifice, interdependence, interconnectedness, and harmony (Bengtson & Putney 2000).

Filial piety emphasizes the family-centered cultural value that affects children's attitudes and behaviors toward their aging parents, which indicates that adult children are expected to sacrifice their individual financial, physical, and social interests for the benefit of their parents and even other older family members (Kim & Kang 2015; Pan et al. 2017). It is an ideology that stipulates a series of bidirectional social practices (Lai 2010). Specifically, it prescribes how children and parents should treat each other. On the one hand, parents are expected to provide their young children with financial assistance, proper care, lessons, and wisdom from life experiences (Kim & Kang 2015). More importantly, filial piety obliges adults to respect parental authority and

DOI: 10.4324/9781003254256-7

requires children to provide their parents with daily necessities, hands-on care, and respect in their later life, during sickness, and after deaths (Ho et al. 2012; Mahoney et al. 2005).

Health Effect of Filial Piety and Filial-Piety-Based Care

Guided by the cultural norms based on filial piety, the majority of older Chinese adults heavily rely on adult-children caregivers (Yu et al. 2016). To fulfill the obliged care piety, intergenerational coresidence is common in China. Such living arrangements and caregiving patterns have complex impacts on the physical and mental health of both the adult-children caregivers and their older parents.

Some studies have suggested the positive effects of filial piety on older adults receiving care in the family. Filial piety has been associated with increased life satisfaction (Li & Dong 2018) and psychological well-being as well as a decreased risk of suicidal ideation and loneliness (Cheng & Chan, 2006; Dong & Zhang, 2016; Hsu 2017; Simon et al. 2014). Research has documented that perceived filial piety is associated with a decreased level of depression in older adults (Guo et al. 2018). Children's practice of filial responsibilities has been recognized as a result of successful parenting, which further boosts older adults' self-image and thus contributes to positive well-being (Simon et al. 2014). On the contrary, older care recipients may feel shamed and humiliated if their adult children fail to fulfill filial piety (Lai 2010). Such negative effect might further impair their psychological outcomes (Li & Dong 2018). Up to date, research on the association between filial piety and adult-children caregivers' health status has generated mixed results. Some studies suggested that caregivers' belief in traditional filial obligation is a contributor to poor health status among caregivers (Pan et al. 2017; Vitaliano et al. 2003). Plausibly, caregivers who live up to filial responsibilities while having to balance other role activities would face multiple sources of stress that can place them in the situation of burnout (Zhan 2006).

In contrast, other studies reported a significant association between filial piety and caregiver psychological well-being (Hsueh 2001; Tang 2006). For example, families that observe filial virtue are more likely to develop emotional intimacy and cohesion between adult-children caregivers and their older parents. Intergenerational affective intimacy has been found to effectively reduce the level of care burden as perceived by the caregivers (Stoller & Pugliesi 1989). Consistently, some authors argue that caregivers who believe in filial piety generally rate their care-related burden as less intensive, as they tend to internalize caregiving responsibilities as a normal part of their daily activities rather than an extra stressor and thus consider care provision as a rewarding process (Lai 2010). There is therefore not surprising that adult-children caregivers with a belief in filial piety were found to be less depressed in comparison to their counterparts without such belief, as documented in recent literature (Pan et al. 2017).

Challenges of Filial Piety in Modern Context

In recent decades, demographic and socioeconomic changes have increasingly challenged the traditional family care system in China (Feng 2017). For thousands of years, the virtue of filial piety has predominately emphasized the devotion and obligation of adult children to respect and care for aging parents. In special historical periods and social contexts, filial piety even prescribes adult children's absolute obedience to and unconditional provision of material and psychological care to parents (Yeh 2009).

The traditional values of filial piety have originated from a patriarchal tradition that promotes patrilocal residence and patrilineal transfer of assets such as houses and lands (Djundeva et al. 2018). In adherence to such tradition, in traditional Chinese society, married women are often expected to live with their husbands' families to ease care provision for their parents-in-law (Hu & Scott 2016). Related to this filial practice is the cultural expectation that the first-born son and his wife are recognized as the primary caregivers for older parents (Kim & Kang 2015). Under most circumstances, the oldest son is supposed to provide financial support, while the daughter-in-law is expected to provide hands-on care and instrumental support (Chen & Jordan 2018).

However, with the accelerated process of industrialization, urbanization, and "westernization" in Chinese societies, the sociocultural foundation of filial piety has been greatly undermined in recent decades (Cheng & Chan 2006). Influenced by such sociocultural transformation, the realization of filial piety in contemporary Chinese societies has become different from that in the traditional social context. Specifically, compared to the traditional definition that filial piety means unconditional obedience of adult children to aging parents, the practice of filial piety has largely depended on the adult children's actual condition and availability in the modern social context.

Perceptions, Desires, and Motivations

A range of economic and cultural factors have affected the foundations of traditional filial piety and people's desire to practice filial piety. These factors include but are not limited to increasingly high employment expectations, competing social values between generations, role conflicts, and role strain (Kim & Kang 2015). Significant changes in family living arrangements are an important factor directly related to the practice of filial piety. Specifically, the number of multigenerational households has decreased, while other forms of living arrangement have emerged and gradually increased, such as nuclear families, single-parent families, single-person and cohabitant households, as well as those with dual incomes but no children (Tang & Hooyman 2018). The shrinking family size and changing family structure significantly have weakened the roots of collectivism that dominates the traditional family-centered cultural value (Pan et al. 2017). Due to this transition, individuals' belief in familial collectivism has been gradually weakened, while individualism has been strengthened in modern China (Wu & Li 2012).

Practice Ability and Division

As one of the most populous countries in the world, China has experienced an enormous increase in life expectancy and decreases in fertility. In part, as a result of the one-child policy, family size is shrinking, with intergenerational families gradually replaced by nuclear families (Feng 2017). Consequently, fewer children are available to support and care for their parents. This may create an intensive care burden on adult-children caregivers with aging parents who have long-term care needs and who view family care as the "best caregiving option" (Flaherty et al. 2008). Particularly, along with significant cultural and economic transformations, women may face more challenges in practicing filial-piety-based family care as they start to take up more roles both inside and outside of the family (Jiang & Dai 2019; Mu 2020). In the past few decades, women's increasing involvement in employment markets has enabled women to pursue financial independence and to make financial contributions to the family. This emerging situation means that women can no longer provide continuous hands-on care to both their children and aging parents-in-law or their parents (Liu et al. 2020). This can be particularly serious for families with a married daughter who is the only child, where older parents generally cannot guarantee care and support in the family (Zhan & Montgomery 2003). This phenomenon has become a notable social problem that challenges the eldercare system of society.

Problems related to eroded filial piety can have a different presentation in rural areas. The outflow of the young labor force from rural to urban areas has received increasing public attention (Li et al. 2019; Zhang et al. 2019). Although older rural community-dwellers are cultivated in the culture of filial piety and may have high expectations of filial receipt, their adult children who are less adherent to the traditional meaning of filial obligation may prefer to pursue individual development in urban areas (Lui 2021). As a result, family functions that adult children can potentially fulfill such as economic support, hands-on care, and emotional support have dramatically diminished. Meanwhile, there has been a serious shortage of formal social services to compensate for the weakening family care system in rural areas (Chow 2006). Consequently, problems such as inadequate daily care, improper medical treatment, insufficient companionship are commonly seen in older empty-nesters (Jiao & Kong 2011; Jing 2011; Liu et al. 2020). These pieces of empirical evidences suggest that a decrease in filial notion and practice has brought about significant challenges to the physical and psychological well-being of older empty-nesters dwelling in rural communities, which has raised awareness of old-age policymakers.

Although Asian counties such as China and Singapore have formulated old-age policies based on filial piety, adherence to filial responsibilities has been weakening among the younger generation in China (Liu & Kendig 2000). Possibly, higher education attainment, a greater desire for individual career pursuit, decreased multigenerational households, and smaller family sizes have jointly played a part in altering adult children's decision and ability to fulfill caregiving responsibilities for their parents (Cheung & Kwan 2009b; Lum et al. 2016;).

Given this cultural transition, the development and improvement of the national social security system, infrastructure, and community institutions share the family caregiving function and have an influential impact on the family caregiving pattern in contemporary China. On the one hand, the pension system has enabled older adults in especially those living in urban areas to become increasingly financially independent. The pension system has partially replaced a family's function in economic protection and has challenged the practices and behaviors of filial piety (Du 2013). On the other hand, as a supplement to home care, the development of formal social support for old-age care has effectively reduced the burden and stress of the adult caregivers. Formal old-care services may also perform some caregiving tasks beyond the family capacity, such as professional care for dementia older adults. In this way, it has become a useful alternative or supplementary resource to compensate for inadequate family care as a result of eroded filial piety.

Filial Piety in Contemporary China

Although traditional filial piety is still widely accepted in contemporary Chinese societies, the practice of which has been redefined in changing social contexts (Hao 2021). Partially attributed to the transition of social norms and ideologies occurring in recent decades, as we mentioned above, changes in filial expectation and practice are observed in many studies (e.g. Sun 2017; Sung 1998; Wang et al. 2009; Yeh et al. 2013). Contrary to the traditional filial value that requires children's unconditional obligation to provide material and spiritual support to their old parents (Bell & Pei 2020), caregiving responsibilities in the contemporary social context have become increasingly conditional and dependent on the children's ability and socioeconomic situation (Yeh 2009). Multigenerational cohabitation as an essential filial element that promotes support between generations (Laidlaw et al. 2010) has also become less common. Perhaps, higher education attainment, a greater desire for individual career pursuit, and decreased familial collectivism have jointly reshaped young people's definition and practice of filial piety (Cheung & Kwan 2009a; Lum et al. 2016).

Current studies indicate that the redefined meaning of filial piety in the modern context has shown a series of obvious changes. These findings generally focus on a few key questions about the definition and practice of filial piety, including: (1) How have the forms of filial piety practice changed? (2) How are filial responsibilities distributed among the children? (3) How have the intergenerational relationships implied by filial piety changed? The next section is organized to respond to these questions.

Reciprocalization of the Content

As revealed in recent research, the understanding of filial piety in contemporary China has become more egalitarian and reciprocal rather than authoritative or unilateral. Filial observance in the modern context is no longer an absolute value. Instead, it has become increasingly dependent on other factors such as the mutual exchange between older parents and children (Chow 2006). Under such changing circumstances, some older parents reported having more expectations on the larger "collectivism" of the state, other than the smaller "collectivism" of the clan or family (and thus their children) (Bedford & Yeh 2021). Such transition emphasizes not only the responsibility of children to respect and support their elderly parents, but also the importance of financial support from the social security system (Du 2013).

That is to say, the pattern that adult children's absolute obedience to and unconditional support for their parents has changed into the practice of parent-child mutual communication. With parent-child mutual communication, adult children tend to provide care and material support to their older parents according to their actual situation (Liu & Huang 2009; Yeh 2009). Meanwhile, the younger generations also expect to gain understanding and receive support from their older parents when needed (Fu & Chui 2020).

Diversification in the Ways of Fulfilling Filial Piety

As discussed above, the realization of filial responsibilities nowadays has become increasingly dependent on adult children's capacity and their actual conditions (Yeh 2009). Besides, huge variation is observed in terms of the realization of filial piety depending on different communities (Hao 2021). For example, in some communities, financial support for parents may also be considered sufficient to satisfy the filial requirement (Chow 2006). Paying for the parents' long-term care and relevant services, rather than performing hands-on caregiving tasks, has also been adopted as a form of realizing filial piety in the modern societies in which adult children and in-laws are mostly engaged with employment in the workplace (Lum et al. 2016; Yeh 2009). Correspondingly, intergenerational coresidence and unconditional obedience are no longer required by most Chinese older adults (Lee & Hong-Kin 2005; Ng et al. 2002).

Equalization of Gender Division

Another notable change in the "reconstructed" meaning of filial piety is the equalization of gender division. Affected by the one-child policy implemented in mainland China in the past few decades, sons' filial responsibilities are no longer emphasized (Djundeva et al. 2018). Instead, in families with a daughter being the only child, the daughter is expected to care for and support their aging parents. As a result, it's common that sons and daughters are assigned equal filial responsibilities (Chen & Jordan 2018).

As the first cohort of the only children entering their forties, both only son and only daughter are expected to take the responsibilities to care for their parents (Chen & Jordan 2018). Couples who are both from only-child families have to take care of four parents and four grandparents, which creates a significant care burden on the couples (Feng 2017; Hu 2017).

To conclude, although many younger Chinese adults continue to perform filial piety by respecting, supporting, and caring for their older parents, filial piety is no longer defined as absolute authority of parents and unconditional obedience of children (Laidlaw et al. 2010; Mehta & Ko 2004). However, partially due to the traditional filial obligation and the shortage of formal old-age care system in China, the family remains a central unit in which family members collaborate and share resources to meet their physical, psychological, and social needs (Cheng & Chan 2006). As Chinese parents show increasing tolerance and acceptance of their children's filial performance, the intergeneration relationship has accordingly changed from a hierarchical and authoritarian one to a reciprocal one.

Therefore, policymakers should still take the limitations and challenges faced by individual family caregivers into consideration. They need to realize that filial piety does not permanently support family caregiving. Indeed, without adequate national intervention and external assistance (Tsai et al. 2008), the virtue of filial piety has been eroded, particularly when adult children and other relatives are engaged in multiple roles and related demands (Lai 2010). Therefore, culturally appropriate support services should be provided and delivered to these family caregivers. It is also necessary to figure out influencing factors and outcomes of adult-children caregivers' well-being (Yu et al. 2016) as early as possible.

Filial Piety and Family Care in Overseas Chinese Societies: From Asia to the World

Although the term "filial piety" has originated from local Chinese culture, the virtue of familial obligation in providing parental care has universal significance for Chinese communities around the world (Lai & Fang 2019). Previous studies have suggested that traditional Confucian filial piety may have been modified and perhaps eroded, implying ongoing changes in intergenerational relationships in modern societies (Ng et al. 2002). In Taiwan, the concept of filial piety has transformed into a dual concept model, including authoritarian filial piety and reciprocal filial piety (Bedford & Yeh 2021). Reciprocal filial piety emphasizes the natural intimate affection and appreciation of children for their old parents, which includes emotional, spiritual, physical, and financial support for the parents, as well as the remembrance of the parents after their death (Chen et al. 2016). On the other hand, authoritarian filial piety emphasizes the children's obligation to their parents, which requires children to suppress their own needs, unconditionally comply with their parents' wishes, strive to honor their parents and ancestors, and produce offspring to continue the family lineage (Yeh 2003, 2006). Recent studies continue to examine the associations between the two types of filial piety and caregiver health, which generated mixed findings. For instance, Jen et al. (2019) suggested that the two types of filial piety beliefs reflect different qualities of parent-child relationships fostered in the family environments. Yan and Chen (2018) indicated that both reciprocal and authoritarian filial piety have a positive impact on caregivers' life satisfaction. According to

Chen and Ho (2012), reciprocal filial piety was found to strengthen interpersonal relationships, reduce parent-child conflicts, and help children to internalize their parents' values. On the contrary, Yeh (2006) reported that authoritarian filiation was linked to a higher level of depression, anxiety, and aggression.

Under the influence of these two types of filial piety, how to practice filial piety has become a complicated decision for adult children in Taiwan. On the one hand, children are considered unfilial when they decide to send their parents to caring institutions (Chow 2006). On the other hand, the nature of reciprocal exchange within the family may also have a significant impact on long-term care solutions for older adults (Wu et al. 1997). Similar findings were found in studies in Japan and Korea, with both Asian societies that have long been historically influenced by Chinese culture and Confucian traditions. Long-term health care in both countries is mostly provided by families, with institutional care being the last resort (Kim & Maeda 2001).

In Hong Kong, filial piety has been deeply rooted in a post-industrial context. However, the realization of filial piety in Hong Kong has become conditional, negotiable, and reciprocal commitments (Wong & Chau 2006). The notion of reciprocity between generations reflects that the emotional bond connecting parent and children remains important (Wong & Chau 2006). Specifically, Chinese parents in Hong Kong tend to embrace a declining but realistic concept of filial piety, as they recognize the challenges that their adult children face in their employment and family lives in a contemporary social context (Chong & Liu 2016). In addition, older adults in Hong Kong are mostly able to achieve higher levels of well-being by performing reciprocal filial practices. For example, they can continue to raise the younger generation (grandson and granddaughter) and witness the meaningful life and career development of their children (Chong & Liu 2016).

Another notable finding is that older parents in Hong Kong tend to have lower expectations of filial piety than younger people. This is largely due to diversified social, economic, and familial demands in a highly modernized and transformed society (Ho 1986). First, the implementation of the government's retirement policy and developed institutional care have weakened the older adults' reliance on their children for care and support (Leung et al. 2017; Woo & Chau 2009). Second, older adults have shown considerable understanding of their adult children who desire to pursue individual development (Lee & Hong-Kin 2005) and consider supporting the younger generation as an important family responsibility in their later years (Chong & Liu 2016). Additionally, some young people believe that living separately from their parents contributes to better intergenerational relationships. These social and ideological changes help to explain a general normative and structural transformation of eldercare in modern Hong Kong (Lee & Hong-kin 2005).

In Australia and the United Kingdom, filial piety still has an important impact on the relationships between parents and children, which is usually reflected in a high degree of structural, effectual, and normative solidarity between the generations (Laidlaw et al. 2010). In America, Chinese immigrants need to reconcile traditional values with sociohistorical change and caring demands (Lieber et al. 2004), which has partly led to differences in their filial piety expectation. Some older Chinese American parents still view filial piety as a key symbol of reverence and highly expect filial piety from younger generations (Dong et al. 2014). However, in some places, older adults' perception of filial piety has changed. Pang et al. (2003) found that in American, Chinese immigrant older adults have shifted their expectations of filial piety from their children to others. Specifically, they tend to rely on their friends and neighbors for support when they need help (Guo et al. 2020).

Research on Chinese American filial piety further illustrated two ways to protect the health of older adults. First, maintaining strong filial expectations is a protective factor for older immigrants' mental health (Guo et al. 2020; Simon et al. 2014). For instance, Li and Dong (2018) suggested that an increase in filial expectations was significantly linked to the remission of depression. Second, when filial expectations are not well met due to various socioeconomic conditions of immigrant families, older adults tend to utilize informal community support by turning to neighbors and friends for help as a supplement of filial receipt from the adult children (Lieber et al. 2004; Pang et al. 2003). A previous study conducted in Chicago found that community involvement was an important moderator in the relationship between perceived filial piety and depression among older Chinese immigrants, especially those with weak intergenerational ties (Kao et al. 2007).

In Canada, although filial piety has gendered nature, it generally serves to reduce the stress of caregiving (Chappell & Kusch 2007). Although older Chinese immigrants tend to lower their expectations for their adult children to fulfill filial duties, they still value and expect emotional care from their children (Zhang 2020). This is perhaps Chinese immigrants are influenced both by Confucian culture deriving from China and Western value from Canada. On the one hand, the development of long-term care facilities, old-age policies, and the old-age welfare system in Canada mean that older adults do not have to heavily rely on family care. On the other hand, affected by Chinses traditional filial culture, older Chinese immigrants still have a higher filial expectation in comparison to their Canadian counterparts (Zhang 2020).

In summary, although cross-cultural variations in terms of filial piety have been reported overseas, filial piety is deeply internalized in caregiving contexts among Chinese families. The above findings provide the following lessons. In terms of the perception of filial piety, reciprocal filial piety needs to be readjusted to accommodate the economic and cultural transformation, while protecting the health of both caregivers and care recipients at the same time. For the practice of filial piety, the government and related departments need to provide culturally appropriate health care services for older adults to cope with the erosion and transformation of filial piety in modern societies. Further, community resources should be explored and care centers should be developed to compensate for insufficient informal care in families where filial expectations are unmet.

Future Directions of Research and Policy

This chapter begins with a traditional definition of filial piety and its impact on the health of the older adults and caregivers. The challenges faced by filial piety and filial-piety-based family care in contemporary Chinese societies are described and the redefinition of filial piety is provided. In addition, transformations and readjustment of filial piety occurring in overseas Chinese societies are mentioned. Based on an in-depth review of these studies, recommendations for future academic research and government intervention are listed to help better inherit and promote filial piety in modern societies to enhance the quality of eldercare.

Academic Research

First, it is necessary to reassess the willingness and ability of the younger generation to practice filial piety in modern Chinese societies. Additionally, solutions to maintain an optimal balance between expected family care responsibilities and caregivers' abilities in contemporary social contexts should be further investigated. Considering the erosion of filial piety, it is also necessary to reflect on the boundaries between family care and institutional care and how they specifically complement each other in modern contexts.

Policy Intervention

The government should play an important role in the promotion of filial piety. Firstly, the government should strengthen the institutional safeguards for the implementation of filial piety. Measures in this regard include, but are not limited to, the inclusion of filial piety in old-age-related laws and the imposition of more detailed obligations for eldercare. Secondly, meanwhile, government and community interventions should play a role in eldercare to better meet the emerging needs of older populations in modern Chinese societies around the world. By doing so, the governments are expected to give adequate financial support for eldercare and make full use of long-term care facilities to reduce the burden on family caregivers who are usually adult children. Further, related departments are expected to provide culturally appropriate healthcare services for older adults to cope with the erosion and transformation of filial piety in modern societies.

References

Bedford, O., & Yeh, K. H. (2021). Evolution of the conceptualization of filial piety in the global context: From skin to skeleton. *Frontiers in Psychology*, 12, 995.

Bell, D., & Pei, W. (2020). Just Hierarchy between Intimates: On the Importance of Shifting Roles. In *Just Hierarchy* (pp. 29–65). Princeton University Press.

Bengtson, V. L., & Putney, N. M. (2000). Who Will Care for Tomorrow's Elderly? Consequences of Population Aging East and West. In *Aging in East & West: Families, States, & the Elderly* (pp. 263–286. Springer.

Chappell, N. L., & Kusch, K. (2007). The gendered nature of filial piety—A study among Chinese Canadians. *Journal of Cross-cultural Gerontology*, 22(1), 29–45.

Chen, W. C. (2019). *A survey of maltreatment propensity of dementia elderly caregivers in long-term care facilities & the preliminary construction of its risk assessment model* (Master's thesis, Southern Medical University).

Chen, J., & Jordan, L. P. (2018). Intergenerational support in one-and multi-child families in China: does child gender still matter?. *Research on Aging*, 40(2), 180–204.

Chen, W. W., & Ho, H. Z. (2012). The relation between perceived parental involvement and academic achievement: The roles of Taiwanese students' academic beliefs and filial piety. *International Journal of Psychology*, 47(4), 315–324.

Chen, W. W., Wu, C. W., & Yeh, K. H. (2016). How parenting and filial piety influence happiness, parent–child relationships and quality of family life in Taiwanese adult children. *Journal of Family Studies*, 22(1), 80–96.

Cheng, S. T., & Chan, A. C. (2006). Filial piety and psychological well-being in well older Chinese. *The Journals of Gerontology Series B: Psychological Sciences & Social Sciences*, 61(5), P262–P269.

Cheung, C. K., & Kwan, A. Y. H. (2009a). City-level influences on Chinese filial piety practice. *The Journal of Comparative Asian Development*, 8(1), 105–123.

Cheung, C. K., & Kwan, A. Y. H. (2009b). The erosion of filial piety by modernization in Chinese cities. *Ageing & Society*, 29(2), 179.

Chong, A. M. L., & Liu, S. (2016). Receive or give? Contemporary views among middle-aged and older Chinese adults on filial piety and well-being in Hong Kong. *Asia Pacific Journal of Social Work & Development*, 26(1), 2–14.

Chow, N. (2006). The practice of filial piety and its impact on long-term care policies for elderly people in Asian Chinese communities. *Asian Journal of Gerontology & Geriatrics*, 1(1), 31–35.

Djundeva, M., Emery, T., & Dykstra, P. A. (2018). Parenthood and depression: Is childlessness similar to sonlessness among Chinese seniors?. *Ageing & Society*, 38(10), 2097–2121.

Dong, X., Zhang, M., & Simon, M. A. (2014). The expectation and perceived receipt of filial piety among Chinese older adults in the Greater Chicago Area. *Journal of Aging Health*, 26(7), 1225–1247.

Dong, X., & Zhang, M. (2016). The association between filial piety and perceived stress among Chinese older adults in greater Chicago area. *Journal of Geriatrics & Palliative Care*, 4(1). 10.13188/2373-1133.1000015. https://doi.org/10.13188/2373-1133.1000015

Du, P. (2013). Intergenerational solidarity and old-age support for the social inclusion of elders in Mainland China: the changing roles of family and government. *Ageing & Society*, 33(1), 44–63.

Feng, Z. (2017). Filial Piety and Old-age Support in China: Tradition, Continuity, and Change. In *Handbook on the Family & Marriage in China*. Edward Elgar Publishing.

Flaherty, E. G., Sege, R. D., Griffith, J., Price, L. L., Wasserman, R., Slora, E., ... & Binns, H. J. (2008). From suspicion of physical child abuse to reporting: primary care clinician decision-making. *Pediatrics*, 122(3), 611–619.

Fu, Y. Y., & Chui, E. W. T. (2020). Determinants of patterns of need for home and community-based care services among community-dwelling older people in urban China: The role of living arrangement and filial piety. *Journal of Applied Gerontology*, 39(7), 712–721.

Guo, M., Byram, E., & Dong, X. (2020). Filial expectation among Chinese immigrants in the United States of America: A cohort comparison. *Ageing & Society*, 40(10), 2266–2286.

Guo, M., Steinberg, N. S., Dong, X., & Tiwari, A. (2018). A cross-sectional study of coping resources and mental health of Chinese older adults in the United States. *Aging & Mental Health*, 22(11), 1448–1455.

Guo, Q., Gao, X., Sun, F., & Feng, N. (2020). Filial piety and intergenerational ambivalence among mother–adult child dyads in rural China. *Ageing & Society*, 40(12), 2695–2710.

Ha, J. H., Yoon, H., Lim, Y. O., & Heo, S. Y. (2016). The effect of widowhood on parent-child relationships in Korea: Do parents' filial expectations and geographic proximity to children matter? *Journal of Cross-cultural Gerontology*, 31(1), 73–88.

Hao, H. (2021). Inheritance and innovation of Chinese filial piety culture. *Philosophy Study*, 11(2), 89–95.

Ho, D. Y. (1986). Chinese patterns of socialization: A critical review. In M. H. Bond (Ed.), *The Psychology of the Chinese People* (pp. 1–37). Oxford University Press.

Ho, D. Y., Xie, W., Liang, X., & Zeng, L. (2012). Filial piety and traditional Chinese values: A study of high and mass cultures. *PsyCh Journal*, 1(1), 40–55.

Hsu, H. C. (2017). Parent-child relationship and filial piety affect parental health and well-being. *Sociology & Anthropology*, 5(5), 404–411.

Hsueh, K. H. (2001). *Family caregiving experience and health status among Chinese in the United States* (Doctoral dissertation, The University of Arizona).

Hu, A. (2017). Providing more but receiving less: Daughters in intergenerational exchange in mainland China. *Journal of Marriage & Family*, 79(3), 739–757.

Hu, Y., & Scott, J. (2016). Family and gender values in China: Generational, geographic, and gender differences. *Journal of Family Issues*, 37(9), 1267–1293.

Huang, H. (2021). From "The moon is rounder abroad" to "bravo, my country": How China misperceives the world. *Studies in Comparative International Development*, 1–19.

Jen, C. H., Chen, W. W., & Wu, C. W. (2019). Flexible mindset in the family: Filial piety, cognitive flexibility, and general mental health. *Journal of Social & Personal Relationships*, 36(6), 1715–1730.

Jiang Q. C., & Dai, Y. P. (2019). Childcare, labor force participation, and flexible employment: How Chinese women balance family and work. *Southern Economics*, 38(12), 82–99.

Jiao, K. Y., & Kong, Q. W. (2011). The present situation, problem and outlet of the empty nester in the countryside—based on the survey in Zhuozixian in Inner Mongolia [J]. *Guangdong Agricultural Sciences*, 15.

Jing, W. E. I. (2011). Old security system research on the empty nester individuals in rural area of Gansu Province. *Journal of Gansu Lianhe University (Social Science Edition)*, 2.

Kao, H. F. S., McHugh, M. L., & Travis, S. S. (2007). Psychometric tests of expectations of filial piety scale in a Mexican-American population. *Journal of Clinical Nursing*, 16(8), 1460–1467.

Kim, I. K., & Maeda, D. (2001). A comparative study on sociodemographic changes and long-term health care needs of the elderly in Japan and South Korea. *Journal of Cross-Cultural Gerontology*, 16(3), 237–255.

Kim, Y. J., & Kang, H. J. (2015). Effect of filial piety and intimacy on caregiving stress among Chinese adult married children living with parents. *Indian Journal of Science & Technology*, 8(S1), 434–439.

Lai, D. W. (2010). Filial piety, caregiving appraisal, and caregiving burden. *Research on Aging*, 32(2), 200–223.

Lai, D. W. L., & Fang, G. B. Y. (2019). Filial Responsibility among Chinese Families. In D Gu and ME Dupre (Eds.), *Encyclopedia of Gerontology & Population Aging, Section of Informal/Family Caregiving*. Springer, Cham. https://doi.org/10.1007/978-3-319-69892-2_17-1

Laidlaw, K., Wang, D., Coelho, C., & Power, M. (2010). Attitudes to ageing and expectations for filial piety across Chinese and British cultures: A pilot exploratory evaluation. *Aging & Mental Health*, 14(3), 283–292.

Lee, W. K. M., & Hong-Kin, K. (2005). Differences in expectations and patterns of informal support for older persons in Hong Kong: Modification to filial piety. *Ageing International*, 30(2), 188–206.

Leung, M. Y., Yu, J., & Chong, M. L. (2017). Impact of facilities management on the quality of life for the elderly in care and attention homes–Cross-validation by quantitative and qualitative studies. *Indoor & Built Environment*, 26(8), 1070–1090.

Li, C. Y. (1997). Shifting perspectives: Filial morality revisited. *Philosophy East & West*, 47(2), 211–233.

Li, J., Guo, M., & Lo, K. (2019). Estimating housing vacancy rates in rural China using power consumption data. *Sustainability*, 11(20), 5722.

Li, M., & Dong, X. (2018). The association between filial piety and depressive symptoms among US Chinese older adults. *Gerontology & Geriatric Medicine*, 4, 2333721418778167.

Lieber, E., Nihira, K., & Mink, I. T. (2004). Filial piety, modernization, and the challenges of raising children for Chinese immigrants: Quantitative and qualitative evidence. *Ethos*, 32(3), 324–347.

Liu, B. S., & Huang, H. C. (2009). Family care for the elderly and the importance of filial piety. *Hu li za zhi The Journal of Nursing*, 56(4), 83–88.

Liu, W. T., & Kendig, H. (2000). Critical Issues of Caregiving: East-West Dialogue. In *Who should Care for the Elderly* (pp. 1–23). World Scientific.

Liu, Y., Qu, Z., Meng, Z., & Wang, S. (2020). Relationship between loneliness and quality of life in elderly empty nesters from the Wolong Panda Nature Reserve in Sichuan province, China, from the perspective of Rural Population and Social Sustainability. *Physica A: Statistical Mechanics & Its Applications*, 551, 124154.

Lui, L. (2021). Filial Considerations in Mate Selection: Urban and Rural Guangdong in the Post-Mao Era. *Modern China*, 47(4), 383–411.

Lum, T. Y., Yan, E. C., Ho, A. H., Shum, M. H., Wong, G. H., Lau, M. M., & Wang, J. (2016). Measuring filial piety in the 21st century: Development, factor structure, and reliability of the 10-item contemporary filial piety scale. *Journal of Applied Gerontology*, 35(11), 1235–1247.

Mahoney, D. F., Cloutterbuck, J., Neary, S., & Zhan, L. (2005). African American, Chinese, and Latino family caregivers' impressions of the onset and diagnosis of dementia: Cross-cultural similarities and differences. *The Gerontologist*, 45(6), 783–792.

Mehta, K. K., & Ko, H. (2004). Filial piety revisited in the context of modernizing Asian societies. *Geriatrics & Gerontology International*, 4, S77–S78.

Mu, Y. T. (2020). Family-work conflict and personal life well-being. *Financial Studies*, 46(10), 123–138.

Ng, A. C. Y., Phillips, D. R., & Lee, W. K. M. (2002). Persistence and challenges to filial piety and informal support of older persons in a modern Chinese society: A case study in Tuen Mun, Hong Kong. *Journal of Aging Studies*, 16(2), 135–153.

Pan, Y., Jones, P. S., & Winslow, B. W. (2017). The relationship between mutuality, filial piety, and depression in family caregivers in China. *Journal of Transcultural Nursing*, 28(5), 455–463.

Pang, E. C., Jordan-Marsh, M., Silverstein, M., & Cody, M. (2003). Health-seeking behaviors of elderly Chinese Americans: shifts in expectations. *The Gerontologist*, 43(6), 864–874.

Simon, M. A., Chen, R., Chang, E. S., & Dong, X. (2014). The association between filial piety and suicidal ideation: findings from a community-dwelling Chinese aging population. *Journals of Gerontology Series A: Biomedical Sciences & Medical Sciences*, 69(Suppl 2), S90–S97.

Stoller, E. P., & Pugliesi, K. L. (1989). Other roles of caregivers: Competing responsibilities or supportive resources. *Journal of Gerontology*, 44(6), S231–S238.

Sun, Y. (2017). Among a hundred good virtues, filial piety is the first: Contemporary moral discourses on filial piety in urban China. *Anthropological Quarterly*, 90(3), 771–799.

Sung, K. T. (1998). Filial piety in modern times: Timely adaptation and practice patterns. *Australasian Journal on Ageing*, 17, 88–92.

Tang, Y. (2006). Obligation of filial piety, adult child caregiver burden, received social support, and psychological well-being of adult caregivers for frail elderly people in Guangzhou, China. *Dissertation Abstract International: Section A. Humanities & Social Sciences*, 68(7-A), 3090.

Tang, Y., & Hooyman, N. (2018). Filial piety, living arrangements, and well-being of urban older adults in Southern China. *Asian Social Science*, 14(6), 21–29.

Tsai, H. H., Chen, M. H., & Tsai, Y. F. (2008). Perceptions of filial piety among Taiwanese university students. *Journal of Advanced Nursing*, 63(3), 284–290.

Vitaliano, P. P., Zhang, J., & Scanlan, J. M. (2003). Is caregiving hazardous to one's physical health? A meta-analysis. *Psychological Bulletin*, 129(6), 946.

Wang Z. Y., Cheng Z. Y., Ma Q. F., & Guo C. Y. (2018). Situation analysis of anxiety, depression and subjective well-being of empty nesters under different caring models. *Collection*, 4.

Wang, D., Laidlaw, K., Power, M. J., & Shen, J. (2009). Older people's belief of filial piety in China: Expectation and non-expectation. *Clinical Gerontologist*, 33(1), 21–38.

Wong, O., & Chau, B. (2006). The evolving role of filial piety in eldercare in Hong Kong. *Asian Journal of Social Science*, 34(4), 600–617.

Woo, J., & Chau, P. P. (2009). Aging in Hong Kong: The institutional population. *Journal of the American Medical Directors Association*, 10(7), 478–485.

Wu, F., & Li, J. (2012). Policy approaches to development capacity of family. *Population Research*, 4, 37–43.

Wu, S. C., Li, C. Y., & Chang, A. L. (1997). The influence of intergenerational exchange on nursing home admission in Taiwan. *Journal of Cross-Cultural Gerontology*, 12(2), 163–174.

Yan, J., & Chen, W. W. (2018). The Relationships between Filial Piety, Self-esteem, and Life Satisfaction among Emerging Adults in Taiwan. In *Close Relationships & Happiness across Cultures* (pp. 151–164). Springer.

Yeh, K. H. (2003). The beneficial and harmful effects of filial piety: An integrative analysis. *Progress in Asian Social Psychology: Conceptual & Empirical Contributions: Conceptual & Empirical Contributions*, 42, 67–82.

Yeh, K. H. (2006). The impact of filial piety on the problem behaviours of culturally Chinese adolescents. *Journal of Psychology in Chinese Societies*.

Yeh, K. H. (2009). Intergenerational exchange behaviors in Taiwan: The filial piety perspective. *Indigenous Psychological Research in Chinese Societies*, 31, 97–141.

Yeh, K. H., Yi, C. C., Tsao, W. C., & Wan, P. S. (2013). Filial piety in contemporary Chinese societies: A comparative study of Taiwan, Hong Kong, and China. *International Sociology*, 28(3), 277–296.

Yu, H., Wu, L., Chen, S., Wu, Q., Yang, Y., & Edwards, H. (2016). Caregiving burden and gain among adult-child caregivers caring for parents with dementia in China: The partial mediating role of reciprocal filial piety. *International Psychogeriatrics*, 28(11), 1845.

Zhan, H. J. (2006). Joy and sorrow: Explaining Chinese caregivers' reward and stress. *Journal of Aging Studies, 20,* 27–38.

Zhan, H. J., & Montgomery, R. J. (2003). Gender and elder care in China: The influence of filial piety and structural constraints. *Gender & Society, 17*(2), 209–229.

Zhang, R., Jiang, G., & Zhang, Q. (2019). Does urbanization always lead to rural hollowing? Assessing the spatio-temporal variations in this relationship at the county level in China 2000–2015. *Journal of Cleaner Production, 220,* 9–22.

Zhang, W. (2020). Perceptions and expectations of filial piety among older Chinese immigrants in Canada. *Ageing & Society,* 1–24.

Section III
Institutionalized and Formal Eldercare in China and India

6 Stigmatization of the Elderly and the Influence of NIMBY in Community-Based Eldercare Institutions

Fei Peng, Mang He, and Nuermaimaijiang Kulaixi

Introduction

China has become an aging society since the late 1990s. Over the next two decades, with the combined effects of declining birth rates and increasing average life expectancies, the problem of population aging has been escalating. The onset of related social problems such as aging, disablement, empty nesting, and fewer children have led to a severe weakening of the family's eldercare function. The phenomenon of "aging before getting wealth" and "becoming old before getting ready" has become essential obstacles to dealing with the aging problem in China. In 2019, the Chinese government had proposed a strategy to actively manage population aging by accelerating the construction of an aged care service system that coordinates with home and community-based institutions and this integrated system aim to combine medical care, health, and wellness. Among them, the community-based eldercare institution is an innovative senior care model that bridges the individual limitations of home, community, and institutional care and effectively integrates eldercare resources from within and around the society. It meets the mental expectations of people who would prefer returning to familiar surroundings and settling down nearby in their advanced ages, and the proximity of the eldercare institutions are often termed as "within the distance of one bowl of soup." This model is also an important initiative to deal with the aging problem in China.

However, while state and provincial governments in China actively promote community-based eldercare institutions, there are also increasing opposing voices from community residents in megacities cities such as Guangzhou, Wuhan, Shenzhen, and Shanghai (Wang, 2019). Through a study of 83 eldercare service projects to be built, Zhang and Zhao (2017) found that over 80% of the projects under construction faced resistance to varying degrees and nearly 40% were forced to suspend or abandon the projects. The phenomenon of protests, rallies, and even group incidents caused by eldercare institutions in the community is increasing. This phenomenon is colloquially known as the "Not In My Backyard" (NIMBY) effect. Despite the social benefits of these institutions, they also suffer from the dissatisfaction and protests of the neighboring residents. The latter does not want these institutions near their homes. With the increasing number of conflicts caused by community eldercare institutions appearing

DOI: 10.4324/9781003254256-9

in recent years, it marks the climax of the NIMBY movement in China, and the unresolved issues have directly led to the intensification of the NIMBY effect under the trend of an aging population.

The development of aging in China faces the dual challenges of an insufficient supply of eldercare facilities and the difficulty of implementing community-based eldercare institutions. The fact that senior care institutions are trapped in an awkward situation of the NIMBY effect also reflects, to some extent, the fragmentation between traditional Chinese filial piety values and contemporary attitudes toward the elderly. Under the moral constraints of traditional culture and the "Three Cardinal Guides and the Five Constant Virtues," filial piety has been advocated and promoted in China for over two thousand years. Chinese people have also been adhering to the concept of home care and support for their elderly family members, and such responsibility and caregiving duties are mostly interpreted as filial piety to parents, which is also regarded as a traditional virtue of the Chinese nation. Each younger generation plays important roles such as carrying on the family line and supporting their elderly in Chinese traditional culture. As a result of rapid socio-economic development, the impact of a multi-cultural collision and the concept of traditional filial piety within family units has gradually disintegrated or eroded in terms of the social system of respecting and caring for the elderly. This disintegration is embodied in the disrespect and lack of empathy for other elderly people in society. Especially under the influence of social media, the problem of discrimination and even stigmatization of the elderly (in contrast with traditional filial piety) has started to spread and ferment. Reports such as "blackmailed for helping the elderly," "old people asking for seats on the bus," and "square-dancing aunties disturbing the public" have fomented negative images of the elderly. The stigmatization of the elderly is triggered by the alienation of people from the psychological distance to the actual living distance of the elderly, and the NIMBY effect of the eldercare institutions is an important manifestation of the stigmatization toward the aging of Chinese society at present.

In this chapter, we have focused on the stigmatization of the elderly in China, as well as the discussion on the resulting NIMBY effect on eldercare institutions. It is hoped that this discussion will further explore the NIMBY effect theory and lead to a reflection on the transformation of the traditional Chinese filial culture to the stigmatization of the elderly. Our study also aims to increase awareness of exploring the construction of an elderly-friendly social environment with filial piety and respect for the elderly and a positive aging path with Chinese characteristics.

Literature Review

Aging in Place

There is a strong correlation between the aging body and place (Gao et al., 2015), especially at the final stage of the life cycle, limited mobility across regions may, to some extent, increase one's sense of loneliness and social isolation, and the living worlds of older adults gradually shrink to the confines of home and its immediate environment (Rowles, 1986). This is particularly evident in Chinese society, where aging close to home is an essential form of maintaining the dignity and security of older people, with the home and its surroundings becoming the best place to provide support and care for older people (Andrews et al., 2007).

In terms of eldercare, with the change in economic development, institutional and cultural attitudes, China's eldercare model is gradually shifting from traditional family care to institutional care (Chen, 2000), and the older elderly prefer to spend their old age in an eldercare institution (Cao et al., 2009). In some regions, such as Shenzhen city, as many as 23.38% of the elderly above 75 years old would prefer non-family care (Liu et al., 2017). And the community-based elderly institution is a crucial service facility for highly urbanized areas with a dense elderly population.

Evolution of Filial Piety Culture

Filial piety is closely related to culture (He & Heugten, 2020). As early as the Western Zhou period, it was said that "all old people ... will be raised in the township school at fifty, in the state at sixty, in the university at seventy, which is equivalent to reaching the vassal" (凡养老……五十养于乡, 六十养于国, 七十养于学, 达于诸侯) (Chen, 2002, p. 430). The virtue of filial piety has always been regarded as one of the most exemplary Chinese traditional cultures, which is not an isolated concept, but a moral socialization mechanism centered on filial piety (Ma, 2003). However, from the traditionalist perspective, respecting the elderly is seen as virtuous and the elderly have always been in the position of being supported. To a certain extent, it led to the long-held, passive concept of aging in China, such as family-oriented caregiving, serving, and respecting the elderly. As Tornstam (2006) pointed out, pitying positivity toward older adults can lead to greater dependency, which results in negative outcomes such as over-care and indebted status.

With the influx of Western liberal and democratic thoughts, especially after the May Fourth Movement in 1919, China has initiated criticisms of traditional culture, including the deconstruction of the culture of filial piety. These criticisms had mainly focused on patriarchy and paternalism, which led to a deconstructed state of filial piety and a tendency to strengthen the father's self-obligation, resulting in a reversal of the rights and obligations in parent-child relationships and an intergenerational phenomenon of injustice toward the father (Ma, 2003).

While in contemporary society, because of the market economy's reverence for productivity, the widespread culture of attaching more importance to youth, and the general fear of death in society, the older person is gradually seen as a burden consuming resources, and they have encountered social discrimination and stigmatization of varying degrees. People unconsciously labeled the elderly as "evil grannies" and "stubborn old men," coupled with negative news such as social disturbance from square-dancing aunts and younger people forced to give up their seats to elderly people on public transport. Especially in 2006, when the case of "Peng Yu who kindly helped up the fallen elderly but in turn was blackmailed as the perpetrator" was widely publicized and reported, the negative impact of this phenomenon and the fermentation of word-of-mouth has become a trigger for the outbreak of public discontent with the elderly. This has led to a series of implications that eldercare institutions in developed areas are often faced with increasing opposition and complaints during the site selection and construction processes, and therefore community NIMBY is now one of the primary considerations during the site selection process.

NIMBY Effect

The concept of NIMBY was first introduced by O'Hare in the 1970s, and usually refers to the social phenomenon that some public facilities increase the overall welfare of the society while bringing perceived risks and benefits damage to the neighboring residents, resulting in protests from the neighboring residents (O'Hare, 1977). The ridiculing statement—"chicken shit in my backyard, but eggs in someone else's house"—vividly illustrates the essence of the NIMBY effect and the dissatisfaction of neighboring residents regarding resource allocation. The NIMBY phenomenon mainly includes three aspects, the first is the NIMBY object, usually involving NIMBY facilities, NIMBY projects, NIMBY enterprises, etc.; the second reflects the residents' attitude toward NIMBY; the third is the NIMBY process, reflecting the residents' NIMBY behavior and interest negotiation throughout the event process, which is an important embodiment of the governance of the NIMBY effect.

In the production of urban space, different public facilities need to be built to meet the needs of urban development and urbanites, and these facilities are welcomed or opposed by the public depending on their service nature and externality impact. For example, parks, squares, libraries, and other facilities are called "welcome facilities" because of their positive externalities. On the other hand, facilities such as landfills and wastewater treatment plants are opposed by the surrounding residents as NIMBY facilities because of their potential adverse environmental, health, and reputational impacts on the surrounding residents. In the early years of NIMBY research, researchers mainly focused on traditional high pollution and high-risk facilities, such as waste-to-energy projects (Shao, 2020), energy facilities such as nuclear power plants (Takahashi, 1998), and special transportation facilities such as viaducts (Li & Ma, 2015), where the main reasons for public resistance include concerns about property value, physical health, and environmental quality.

Preference Behavior to Public Service Facilities

With the increasing improvement of urban public service facilities (DeVerteuil, 2013) and land-use constraints, special public service facilities with almost no explicit forms of pollution (Andrews et al., 2007), including prisons, drug rehabilitation centers, mental hospitals, and aid stations (Takahashi, 1998) has also entered the NIMBY category. These facilities do not have apparent environmental conflicts like pollution or risk aggregation facilities, and it is difficult to measure the substantial adverse externality hazards from objective technical indicators. Due to the specificity of their servicing groups and the adverse effects of stigmatization, they cause potential risk perceptions and varying degrees of psychological resistance among nearby residents, and these facilities can be called stigmatized public service facilities.

- Some areas are also influenced by accumulated habits and traditional culture, resulting in undesirable NIMBY behavior because of cultural perception differences and cultural complexes. For example, in late 2010, the Province of British Columbia, Canada, planned to establish a hospice in a community near UBC, but was strongly petitioned and opposed by the community (mainly Chinese immigrants) (Li & Li, 2020). Likewise, events such as "Anti-funeral hall in Guangdong Huazhou" and "Opposing cemetery construction in Qingdao" reflect specific Chinese people's opposition and NIMBY behavior related to death, such as funeral facilities (Wu et al., 2017), hospice institutions (Yang et al., 2018), and eldercare institutions (see, e.g. Jing, 2019; Wang, & Han, 2020) et al. It can be seen that the Chinese's low acceptance of death-related facilities and strong resistance and the taboo against death-related matters are fundamental reasons triggering the NIMBY effect of eldercare institutions.

Methods

Research Sites

In this chapter, six of Guangzhou's eldercare institutions were selected as research objects, and the main selection reasons are listed as follows. Firstly, in terms of the degree of aging, the aging of the population is particularly significant after more than 20 years of development since Guangzhou entered an aging society in 1992. By the end of 2018, the number of registered elderly people aged 60 and above in Guangzhou had reached 1,693,000, accounting for 18.25% of the registered population; eight of the city's 11 districts have an elderly population of more than 100,000. Secondly, Guangzhou is at the forefront of the country in exploring diversified senior care services and has now implemented more comprehensive community-based eldercare and elderly canteen services than other cities. By 2020, there were more than 200 public and private senior care institutions of different types in Guangzhou, which means that the presence of eldercare institutions has become one of the most visible social phenomena in Guangzhou. The increased presence of senior care institutions in the community is also a nascent development with much research feasibility and academic value. Thirdly, Guangzhou is located in the Greater Bay Area with rapid economic development, and the city is at the forefront of urban development in China's local area with a high urban land price. As a result, many eldercare institutions face the risk of opposition and move into the community to save land and money.

Data Collection

The research team went to Guangzhou eldercare institutions for a ten-day initial research in August, 2018 to gain a preliminary understanding of the current situation of the phenomenon of NIMBY in eldercare institutions. It took half a year for the team to collect information and retrieve data on eldercare institutions in Guangzhou, including types of eldercare institutions, establishment time, size, community distance, and other relevant factors with the purpose of building a database of eldercare institutions in Guangzhou. Finally, six typical eldercare institutions were selected as case sites for follow-up research, on-site observation, and interviews, including Jiangnan Eldercare Home, Songhe Nursing Home, Tianlu Lake Senior Care Center, Ocean Express Tsubaki Xuanmao Senior Living Apartment, Beautiful Home & Nursing Home, Furexin Senior Residence.

A total of 16 relevant respondents were interviewed using semi-structured interviews, including two government and community-related personnel in charge, eight middle and senior managers of eldercare institutions, and six residents in the surrounding area. Interviews lasted an average of 56 minutes with the interviewees aged between 17 and 73 years old and with a gender ratio of seven males and nine females.

Findings

Influence of Culture on NIMBY Complex

It is believed that complexes are the embodiment of the individual's unconscious and their deeper roots lie in archetypal experiences deeply embedded in some historical or cultural patterns (Kirsch, 1991). These unconscious complexes of emotions, perceptions, feelings, and beliefs that are deeply embedded in the heart have a significant impact on human behavior. Although China has changed dramatically since the reform and opening-up period, common folk still retain the superstitious tradition of fengshui (风水). It is thought that natural energy space can invisibly influence and even change people's fortune in terms of wealth, emotions, and health. When individuals are exposed to or are near certain inauspicious people or things, their fortune will change in a bad direction, and this bad fortune will affect people's daily life (Wang et al., 2020).

Additionally, it is often considered inauspicious or bad luck to be close to or contact a dying person. As a result, the people's acceptance of funeral homes, cemeteries, and other facilities related to death is relatively low. The underlying reason why people have a strong resistance and taboo against eldercare institutions is that the concentration of older people reminds them of death. Under the influence of accumulated habits and traditional culture, such beliefs not only affect the site selection of individual houses but also has an important impact on the construction of public facilities. For example, Nanjing funeral parlors have been relocated several times with the city's expansion and eventually formed an interactive mechanism with the city (Wu et al., 2017).

> The taboo of 'death' is the root of our opposition. To the end of our communication with the community, we will always talk about the older people holding funerals in the community after death, which is unlucky and affects their luck!
>
> (R1)

> People hate funeral parlor cars. If they see them every month and witness the throwing of paper money too often, the community will complain.
>
> (R8)

From this point of view, the NIMBY effect of community eldercare institutions is because of the dissatisfaction and resistance of the surrounding residents to the people who use the facilities. This kind of psychological dislike of the residents toward the elderly facilities in a specific cultural context is also a distinct characteristic of the Chinese NIMBY effect that differs from Western-style NIMBY (He, 2009).

Stigmatization and Ageism

Stigma was first introduced into the humanities and social sciences by Goffman (1963). According to Link and Phelan (2001), the characteristics of a stigmatized group include mistrust and unpopularity, manifested as labeling, negative stereotyping, cognitive separation, status loss, and discrimination. Stigmatization of older adults usually comes from two major sources. First, it stems from perceptions, prejudices, and stereotypes (Perdue & Gurtman, 1990) and focuses on phenomena such as physical aging, psychological aging, and degradation of social functions and roles (Wu, 2008) within the framework of age discrimination. Older adults are often treated as a vulnerable group with weaknesses, illnesses, disabilities, lack of vitality, high dependency, and large health care expenditures (Wu, 2008). Iversen et al. (2009) pointed out that people usually form negative or positive stereotypes, prejudice, and/or discrimination against older people from a cognitive, affective, and behavioral perspective because of their actual or perceived age.

Meanwhile, it comes from the cognitive and emotional level of individual consciousness, which is influenced by cultural and other factors, and people's emotional orientation is one of the crucial sources of stigmatization (Palmore, 1971). For example, physical stigma such as perceptions of older people as having infectious diseases or body odor, wearing dirty clothes; social stigma such as walking around older people and not talking to them; and moral stigma such as blackmail that demeans the moral character of older people. In addition, according to Jiang and Zhou (2012), family, society, media, and library materials are the principal sources that reinforce negative attitudes toward aging. The "trust crisis" brought about by the intensified social transformation in China continues to spread and intensify under the catalyst of the Internet and social media influence, resulting in a gradually deepening of the social and behavioral stigma against older people. To some extent, stigma has become the primary impression and common perception of the elderly by other social groups (Xiong, 2019).

> After the Peng Yu case, there are yearly media reports on the elderly being blackmailed and so on. These will certainly affect our nursing home construction; there are complaints that he passed by daily out of the community from the front of our nursing home and are worried about the fear of loading the elderly and asking us to install cameras.
>
> (R9)

Considering all factors, stigmatization leads to unfair treatment of those who bear the stigma (whether individuals or groups) by those who inflict the stigma upon them based on prejudice, which has negative consequences (Wu, 2008). The cognitive bias and emotional rejection of the elderly group by individuals will undoubtedly further deteriorate the living environment of the elderly. Negative perceptions and attitudes of aging held by society can have important effects on older adults' behavior, self-concept, self-acceptance of aging, mental health, lifestyle, and occupation, and may even lead to less positive overall self-evaluation of older adults (Wu, 2008). From a cultural perspective, a cross-cultural comparison study by Laidlaw et al. (2010) found that older Chinese adults have more negative aging experiences. Therefore, the focus on aging in contemporary China is to support these individuals financially and in terms of life care and address discrimination, stigma, and even intergenerational disharmony in the overall social environment. By providing the elderly with spiritual comfort and security, it could contribute to improving the quality of life of the dependent elderly.

Subjective Distortion and Emotional Amplification

Compared to the potential health and safety risks associated with high pollution and high-risk NIMBY facilities, residents' perception of the NIMBY effect of community eldercare institutions is much more subjective and ambiguous, largely stemming from the fear and taboo of death in traditional Chinese cultural concepts. People often give different reasons to make up for their deficiency in the virtue of respecting and loving the elderly in order to disguise their true intention of psychological taboos such as elderly dying in the neighborhood brings more "bad luck" to people nearby (Jiang, 2017); the frequency of ambulances entering and leaving the neighborhood brings inconvenience to the community residents; and the fear of knocking down the elderly. All in all, the main reasons for the NIMBY attitudes toward community elderly care institutions are as follows. Firstly, the environmental impact of noise and living odors from the activities of the elderly; secondly, health concerns about potential disease transmission; thirdly, the occupation of public leisure space due to the transformation of public resources into elderly institutions; and fourthly, concerns about potential monetary loss, such as a drop in house prices as people try to avoid living in neighborhoods with eldercare institutions. However, these stated reasons are subjective assumptions and exaggerations of individuals. They are more likely to be compelled by rumors to amplify the negative effects of eldercare institutions, and this becomes a pain point for the governance of the NIMBY problem.

Under the influence of the NIMBY complex, the impact of the NIMBY effect is often subjectively misinterpreted and amplified by the group (Yang et al., 2018). This results in more confusion about its actual adverse results, which leads to similar results like other polluted and risky neighborhood facilities in the NIMBY process of elderly institutions, such as risk perception, psychological fear (Slovic, 1987), trust deficit, and rumor spreading (Ma & Li, 2015). Although not everyone develops opposing attitudes toward NIMBY facilities (Litvin et al., 2019), the higher the subordination of subjects, the faster the rate of crisis and risk alienation in general (Wang et al., 2017). Especially with the help of better interconnection conditions, some rights conflict including NIMBY movements usually gets much stronger subjective misinterpretation and emotionally fueled possibility.

However, it is noteworthy that not all participants in the NIMBY movement are entirely dominated by narrow territorial thinking and overreaching emotions (Kraft & Clary, 1991). The general public rationally seeks institutionalized solutions despite their unconscious inner impulses or deep-rooted cultural beliefs. Once their interests are not taken seriously or satisfied, the public's social psychology will be arbitrarily amplified, thus contributing to the risk of group polarization (Wang & Du, 2020). From this point of view, effective communication is still an important way to prevent misunderstandings and emotional amplifications.

From Psychological Distance to NIMBY

According to Lefebvre (1991), space is a product of various ideologies in which varying social relations pervade. Natural laws, geographic distance, human psychological perception, and other elements can combine to influence individuals' preferences and proximity to surrounding facilities (Wu et al., 2017). Recreational facilities such as libraries or parks are usually popular when choosing a place to live. In comparison, facilities related to health care, medical care, nursing care, or even death are necessities but also something that is not supposed to be placed in their backyard. Different types of facilities also have different NIMBY effects. Medical and health facilities have a mild NIMBY effect; eldercare institutions have a moderate NIMBY effect, while funeral facilities have the most substantial NIMBY effect.

Meanwhile, the distance between residential location and neighboring facilities is positively correlated with risk perception (Kraft & Clary, 1991). Residents under the influence of the NIMBY complex are psychologically repulsed by community eldercare institutions and the older people who live in it. Thus, under the force of "facility impact—public resistance," a specific impact space is formed in the city centered on the NIMBY facilities, so the closer the neighbor NIMBY facility is to the community, the stronger the opposition it receives (Yan & Li, 2018). In this NIMBY space, the objective reality space is the physical space occupied by people or facilities, while the subjective conceptual space is the psychological space for people's perception and measurement. It is shown that the size and scale of NIMBY space increase asymptotically with the increase of distance from the neighboring facilities, and after reaching the farthest critical distance, the NIMBY risk perception and psychological distance disappears, at which point the NIMBY space is maximized (Wu et al., 2017). It can be seen that the subjective conceptual space has an important influence on the objective reality space. Therefore, increasing the objective reality space is an effective form of generating the security of the subjective perception (Yang et al., 2017). Reducing the psychological distance between people and the elderly to reproduce relationships under spatial production is another effective solution.

Discussion

Special Features and Convertibility as NIMBY Facilities

Stigmatization of the elderly is the most important factor that triggers the NIMBY effect in eldercare institutions, which determines that the targeted object of the NIMBY effect is not the facilities, equipment, or service operators, but the elderly who live in it. This creates special features and convertibility of eldercare institutions as NIMBY facilities. In the traditional NIMBY phenomenon, the target of NIMBY is mainly the facilities or equipment itself that have a negative and actual impact on the community. While the difference between the NIMBY of eldercare institutions and others is that the community residents seldom oppose the facilities and equipment needed for the operation of eldercare institutions and even welcome the facilities and space that can be shared by the community residents. Instead, what the community residents oppose is not the eldercare institutions themselves but their service recipients.

This means that in the NIMBY effect of eldercare institutions, what we should reflect on is not the problem of eldercare institutions, but rather the NIMBY phenomenon targeting "people" rather than "objects" and how to bring it into people's acceptance range to avoid NIMBY resistance. The complexity lies precisely in the subjective nature of "people," i.e. the causes of NIMBY will be the actual economic loss, environmental impact or health damage, and emotional identification with people, which emotions and psychological factors will influence.

Such perspectives will provide us with a different solution to the traditional NIMBY effect and the possibility of converting resistance to acceptance. Local managers usually fall into a confrontational misconception when dealing with

NIMBY conflicts (Yang et al., 2017). The production of community eldercare institutions as a specific spatial form is behind reshaping social relations and redistribution of rights. According to Wang & Wang (2018), a reasonable and effective multi-faceted consultation mechanism can be constructed to solve the problem of NIMBY in order to ensure the healthy and effective development of related industries and, therefore, promote the overall welfare of the region. Based on the analysis of its particularity, we believe that promoting the common participation of residents, reducing their risk perception and appropriate multiple compensations are all feasible solutions.

Traditional Taboos on Death and Modern Fears of Aging

Influenced by traditional culture, death is often viewed as taboo (He & Heugten, 2020). It is widely believed that someone who encounters a funeral will be unlucky and their fortune will be affected. People will avoid death-related occasions, directly originating from the reality of "fear of aging and death" social psychology. Most Chinese prefer avoiding or shunning death-related topics such as children should not talk about death in front of their parents (Ikels, 2004), and in the face of serious illnesses such as cancer, the patient may be kept in the dark about their condition by their family (Shi et al., 2019). This leads to a cultural phenomenon where everyone is afraid of talking about death and individuals lack the ability to think and communicate about their own aging and death.

The NIMBY effect is a manifestation of social panic under the onset of a rapidly aging society and the escape of the social panic of the public toward aging as a whole. The gathering of the elderly in the eldercare institutions will produce a visual and psychological impact on the surrounding residents, so many of them choose to avoid this psychological impact without the corresponding psychological preparation. In order to ease the psychological fear, the opponents concentrate their fears of health conditions, aging, and death as an emotional expression of their opposition to community eldercare institutions. As long as the eldercare institutions are not built in my neighborhood, they can think less about the aging and death issues by means of "out of sight, out of mind."

However, beneath the conflict between traditional superstition and the moral pressure to respect the elderly, most people prefer to cover up their underlying reasons for avoiding aging and fear of death. It is found that the community's opposition to eldercare institutions is not based on the actual economic, environmental, or health losses, but more on emotional worries and concerns, which are gradually formed and accumulated. The deeper reasons for community-based NIMBY opposition should lie in cultural norms because the main concerns mentioned above are potential concerns rather than actual events. It can be seen that in the face of the rapidly aging society, neither the society nor the individual is psychologically prepared or culturally adjusted for the reality of a rapidly aging population.

Balance of Interests and Joint Participation

Although some scholars consider the NIMBY effect as an emotional manifestation of public selfishness (e.g. Vig & Kraft, 1990), it is also, to some extent, especially for the Chinese, a reflection of the awakening and a heightened sense of widespread self-awareness (Davies, 2005). Indeed, in the process of rapid urban development and land use progress, the production of space is of immediate relevance to every urban resident, which often results in space as a focus of social conflict (Wang & Wang, 2018). As a production process of urban space, the construction of the NIMBY facility has obvious spatial planning attributes (Yang et al., 2018), and the undeniable fact that it brings about implications to neighboring residents as the city develops.

NIMBY conflicts are bound to occur due to conflict of interests, including the economic benefits and the balance of rights vs. interests of adjacent residents (Davies, 2005). Therefore, it is also necessary to consider the reasonable rights and interests of the neighboring residents and protect their interests within a specific scope. Through constructing a pluralistic governance framework, it could alleviate the disputes between different subjects (Yang et al., 2018), and bring the protesters into a reasonable system means to recognize differentiated rights demands and individualized interest expressions in pursuing consensus.

Meanwhile, in order to avoid public emotions from fueling and fermenting, relevant governments and companies should be sensitive and attentive to the public's psychological perceptions. Previous studies have shown that the closed nature of the decision-making process of NIMBY facility projects leads to a general lack of public trust in the government and magnifies the public's negative perceptions of NIMBY facilities (Chen, 2018). The perception of unfairness and opacity in the decision-making process is the main reason for the public's involvement in various NIMBY movements (Liu et al., 2018). As a result, introducing civic participation, innovative governance, and constructing living communities are all conducive solutions toward solving the neighborhood avoidance problem (Sun et al., 2016), which not only facilitates the sharing of community benefits but also helps the public slowly accept the rationality of eldercare facilities in the community.

NIMBY Behavior and Filial Culture

The occurrence of the NIMBY phenomena in eldercare institutions reflects, to some extent, the actual contemporary views and behavior of Chinese people toward the elderly after they are free from the ethical and moral bondage of their families. In China's filial cultural value system, it includes not only filial piety for biological parents but also the construction of an ethical society that cares for the elderly. The stigmatization of the elderly and the NIMBY effect of eldercare institutions reflect the change in the social atmosphere of "respect for the elderly, filial piety." Under the traditional effect of moral pressure, people complain about community eldercare institutions based on noise, health, and other non-objective reasons, all of which are emotional expressions of the conflict between the traditional culture of respecting the elderly and the modern society's fear of the elderly. The taboo, concealment, and distancing also expose people's NIMBY behavior and fear of death, and the conscious act of reducing contact with the elderly and staying away from them, to some extent, also exposes the impact of today's society on the traditional concept of filial piety and the hidden danger of the eroding social value of filial piety and its influence on the younger generation.

It has to be admitted that the NIMBY effect caused by the construction of eldercare institutions not only reflects the public's defense of space rights and interests but also reveals the ethical deficiency under the threshold of social security, which goes against the traditional Chinese virtue of respecting and caring for the elderly. Thus, it is called for the respect for the elderly and increased eldercare services (Jiang & Zhao, 2009) to bridge the separation between social cognition and filial piety. It is believed that this problem could be solved by negotiating the interests of different stakeholders, strengthening mutual understanding and recognition, and establishing ties of common interests.

Conclusion

The psychological distance manifested through taboos and stigmatization that people feel toward the elderly contributes to the behavioral distance from community-based eldercare institutions. It has deep-rooted cultural origins, and although not everyone upholds this concept, it is easily driven and infected by emotions and has a significant impact on the construction of urban facilities and social harmony. It points out that the object of NIMBY is not the eldercare facilities, equipment, or service operators, but the older people themselves, which reflects the growing fear of old age and NIMBY behavior. Behind it lies the conflict between the traditional culture of avoiding death and the fear of getting old in modern life, in contrary to the traditional values of Chinese filial piety.

This chapter explores the crisis of Chinese filial piety culture from the opposite perspective and raises awareness of the aging problem and its relationship with the reconstructed traditional values in today's society. It advocates people to understand the elderly and the aging problems correctly and improve social perception and attitudes toward the elderly by strengthening death-related education, emotional communication, and physical interaction with the elderly to eliminate or reduce the NIMBY effect as much as possible in this interactive process. The formation of a diverse and positive attitude toward the concept of aging is helpful to maintain and improve the dignity and status of the elderly and promote the better integration of the elderly into society holistically to benefit society.

Funding

This research was partially funded by the Ministry of Education in China, Youth Project of Humanities and Social Sciences (Grant No. 20YJCZH127), and National Natural Science Funds of China (Grant No. 42001158). This funder has no role in the research design, the writing of the article, or the decision to submit the article.

References

Andrews, G. J., Cutchin, M., Mccracken, K., Phillips, D. R., & Wiles, J. (2007). Geographical gerontology: The constitution of a discipline. *Social Science & Medicine*, 65(1), 151–168. https://doi.org/10.1016/j.socscimed.2007.02.047

Cao, Z., Hu, X., Xiao, H., Liu, C., & Lai, G. (2009). 成都市老年人养老意愿和社会支持网研究 [A research on aged people's pension willing of Chengdu and the social support net]. *Journal of Sichuan Institute of Education*, 25(12), 20–24. https://kns.cnki.net/kcms/detail/detail.aspx?FileName=SJXB200912007&DbName=CJFQ2009

Chen, S. (2000). 中国养老模式研究综述 [Summarizing on China supporting model research]. *Population Journal*, 3, 30–36+51. https://doi.org/10.16405/j.cnki.1004-129x.2000.03.008

Chen, S. (2002). 四书五经 [*The Four Books and the Five Classics* (2nd edition)]. Yuelu Publishing House.

Chen, X. (2018). 不同类型邻避运动的成因及其治理 [The study on the causes and governance of different types NIMBY movement]. *Journal of Sichuan Vocational and Technical College*, 28(3), 26–31. https://doi.org/10.13974/j.cnki.51-1645/z.2018.03.005

Davies, A. R. (2005). Incineration politics and the geographies of waste governance: A burning issue for Ireland? *Environment and Planning C-Government and Policy*, 23(3), 375–397. https://doi.org/10.1068/c0413j

DeVerteuil, G. (2013). Where has NIMBY gone in urban social geography?. *Social & Cultural Geography*, 14(6), 599–603. https://doi.org/10.1080/14649365.2013.800224

Gao, X., Wu, D., Xu, Z., & Yan, B. (2015). 中国老龄化地理学综述和研究框架构建 [A review and frame-work setting of geographical research on aging in China]. *Progress in Geography*, 34(12), 1480–1494. https://kns.cnki.net/kcms/detail/detail.aspx?FileName=DLKJ201512002&DbName=CJFQ2015

Goffman, E. (1963). *Stigma: Notes on the Management of Spoiled Identity*. Prentice-Hall. https://www.researchgate.net/publication/37093346_Stigma_Notes_on_the_Management_of_Spoiled_Identity

He, L., & Heugten, K. V. (2020). Chinese migrant workers' care experiences: A model of the mediating roles of filial piety. *Qualitative Health Research*, 30(1), 1749–1761. https://doi.org/10.1177/1049732320925420

He, Y. (2009). "中国式"邻避冲突—基于事件的分析 ["Chinese" adjacent to avoid conflict, based on the analysis of events]. *Open Era*, 12, 102–114. https://kns.cnki.net/kcms/detail/detail.aspx?FileName=KFSD200912012&DbName=CJFQ2009

Ikels, C. (2004). *Filial Piety: Practice and Discourse in Contemporary East Asia*. Stanford University Press. https://www.researchgate.net/publication/40421866_Filial_Piety_Practice_and_Discourse_in_Contemporary_East_Asia?_sg=h6M3CzOJpks67FiUEhYr68kd4xHpakcfBrrSPazZUTuOmAxxd10SB1p8U8XVGYQO4u5jLkb9vLwZoaw

Iversen, T. N., Larsen, L, & Solem, P. E. (2009). A conceptual analysis of ageism. *Nordic Psychology*, 61(3), 4–22. https://doi.org/10.1027/1901-2276.61.3.4

Jiang, C., & Zhao, X. J. (2009). 中国老年照料的机会成本研究 [Study on the opportunity cost of eldercare in China]. *Management World*, (10), 80–87. https://doi.org/10.19744/j.cnki.11-1235/f.2009.10.010

Jiang, W. (2017). 社区养老如何走出"邻避困境"——基于海口社区养老风波的分析 [How to get out of the "Nimby Dilemma" of community Insititution -- Based on the Analysis of Haikou Community Insititution]. *Human resource development*, (3), 25–27. https://doi.org/10.19424/j.cnki.41-1372/d.2017.03.014

Jiang, Z., & Zhou, Z. (2012). 老年歧视的特点、机制与干预 [Characteristics, mechanism and intervention of ageism]. *Advances in Psychological Science*, (10), 1642–1650. https://kns.cnki.net/kcms/detail/detail.aspx?FileName=XLXD201210016&DbName=CJFQ2012

Jing, R. (2019). 社区养老设施邻避效应的治理—基于邻避效应研究综述的分析 [Management of NIMBY effect in community eldercare facilities—Based on analysis of NIMBY effect research review]. *Economic Research Guide*, 36, 23–24. https://kns.cnki.net/kcms/detail/detail.aspx?FileName=JJYD201936010&DbName=CJFQ2019

Kirsch, T. B. (1991). *Cultural Complexes in the History of Jung, Freud and Their Followers*. Inner City Books. https://www.researchgate.net/publication/345591774_Cultural_Complexes_in_the_History_of_Jung_Freud_and_their_Followers

Kraft, M., & Clary, B. (1991). Citizen participation and the NIMBY syndrome, public response to radioactive waste disposal. *Political Research Quarterly*, 44(2), 299–328. https://www.researchgate.net/publication/233870270_Citizen_Participation_and_the_NIMBY_Syndrome_Public_Response_to_Radioactive_Waste_Disposal?_sg=z58ufeXXtrHGA-MYXzJV1InGke6V9cu3QtR9L_PtDIhWlrC1Q8MtwAwbaQ5sKJe3vz3P4Vvzlh_kgbk

Laidlaw, K., Wang, D., Coelho, C., & Power, M. (2010). Attitudes to ageing and expectations for filial piety across Chinese and British cultures: A pilot exploratory evaluation. *Aging & Mental Health*, 14(3), 283–292. https://doi.org/10.1080/13607860903483060

Lefebvre, H. (1991). *The Production of Space*. Oxford: Blackwell.

Li, B., & Li, X. (2020). 国外邻避冲突治理路径的经验分析 [Empirical analysis on the governance path of NIMBY conflict in foreign countries]. *Inner Mongolia Science, Technology & Economy*, 21, 30–31. https://d.wanfangdata.com.cn/periodical/nmgkjyjj202021010

Li, J., & Ma, B. (2015). 公众为何反对?一起高架桥规划邻避冲突的案例研究 [Why is the public against it? A case study of NIMBY conflict in viaduct planning]. *Journal of Chinese Academy of Governance*, 5, 89–93. https://doi.org/10.14063/j.cnki.1008-9314.2015.05.017

Li, Z., & Lu, H. (2009). 中国的尊老敬老文化与养老 [On the relation between culture of respecting, revering the old and providing for the old in China]. *Population Journal*, 5, 27–31. https://kns.cnki.net/kcms/detail/detail.aspx?FileName=RKXK200905004&DbName=CJFQ2009

Link, B. G., & Phelan, J. C. (2001). Conceptualizing stigma. *Annual Review of Sociology*, 27(1), 363–385. https://www.researchgate.net/publication/234838557_Conceptualizing_Stigma?_sg=M50S9ClNG5gILJMTlW6gPnynXQ_AkSwOVesIQEHMWkBrtiuO1afBfmU8_wHl-FhDa4BfjVR6vRm-uP4

Litvin, S. W., Smith, W. W., & McEwen, W. R. (2020). Not in my backyard: Personal politics and resident attitudes toward tourism. *Journal of Travel Research*, 59(4), 674–685. https://doi.org/10.1177/0047287519853039

Liu, R., Ye, K., Liu, Q., Chen, Y., Liang, B., Bai, L., & Wang, P. (2017). 深圳市某区75岁及以上高龄老年人养老需求现况及其影响因素评估 [The current state of the pension requirements of the elderly people aged 75 years or older in a district of Shenzhen City and the influencing factors]. *Henan Medical Research*, 26(1), 5–7. https://kns.cnki.net/kcms/detail/detail.aspx?FileName=HNYX201701003&DbName=CJFQ2017

Liu, T., Yau, Y., & Yuan, D. (2018). Efficacy beliefs, sense of unfairness, and participation in LULU activism. *Cities*, 83, 24–33. https://doi.org/10.1016/j.cities.2018.06.005

Ma, B., & Li, J. (2015). 我国邻避效应的解读:基于定性比较分析法的研究 [Interpretation of NIMBY effect in China: Based on qualitative comparative analysis]. *The

Journal of Shanghai Administration Institute, *16*(5), 41–51. https://kns.cnki.net/kcms/detail/detail.aspx?dbcode=CJFD&dbname=CJFDLAST2015&filename=SHXY201505004&uniplatform=NZKPT&v=6-6vU6uxnakOde7AAiuU85SVGn84ehFsyjgTFWsZyc87WgHbMT2xeu1vzTmba082

Ma, Q. (2003). 孝文化与代际公正问题 [Filial piety culture and intergenerational justice]. *Morality and Civilization*, *4*, 8–13. https://kns.cnki.net/kcms/detail/detail.aspx?FileName=DDYW200304002&DbName=CJFQ2003

Ma, Z. (2003). 关于孝文化批判的再思考 [Re-thinking on the criticism of filial piety culture]. *Studies in Ethics*, *6*, 35–39. https://doi.org/10.13904/j.cnki.1007-1539.2003.04.002

O'Hare, M. (1977). Not on my block you don't: Facility siting and the strategic importance of compensation. *Public Policy*, *25*(4), 407–458. https://www.researchgate.net/publication/255515228_Not_on_my_block_you_don%27t_-_facilities_siting_and_the_strategic_importance_of_compensation

Palmore, E. (1971). Attitudes toward aging as shown through humor. *The Gerontologist*, *11*(3), 181–186. https://doi.org/10.1093/geront/11.3_Part_1.181

Perdue, C. W., & Gurtman, M. B. (1990). Evidence for the automaticity of ageism. *Journal of Experimental Social Psychology*, *26*(3), 199–216. https://doi.org/10.1016/0022-1031(90)90035-K

Rowles, G. D. (1986). The geography of ageing and the aged: Toward an integrated perspective. *Progress in Human Geography*, *10*(4), 511–539. https://doi.org/10.1177/030913258601000403

Shao, Q. (2020). 环境正义、风险感知与邻避冲突的协商治理路径分析——基于国内垃圾焚烧发电项目的案例思考 [On deliberative governance path of environmental justice, risk perception and NIMBY conflicts—A case study of domestic refuse incineration power plant projects]. *Journal of Tianjin Institute of Administration*, *22*(2), 22–32. https://doi.org/10.16326/j.cnki.1008-7168.2020.02.003

Shi, W., Yang, L., Liu, L., & Tan, W. (2019). 恶性肿瘤患者告知影响因素与告知模式的研究进展 [Research progress on influencing factors and informing models of malignant tumor patients]. *Cancer Development*, *17*(3), 271–276. https://kns.cnki.net/kcms/detail/detail.aspx?FileName=AZJZ201903007&DbName=CJFQ2019

Slovic, P. (1987). Perception of Risk. *Science*, *236* (4799), 280–285. https://doi.org/10.1126/science.3563507

Sun, L., Zhu, D., & Chan, H. W. (2016). Public participation impact on environment NIMBY conflict and environmental conflict management: Comparative analysis in Shanghai and Hong Kong. *Land Use Policy*, *58*(58), 208–217. https://doi.org/10.1016/j.landusepol.2016.07.025

Takahashi, L. M. (1998). Controversial facility siting in the urban environment resident and planner perceptions in the United States. *Environment and Behavior March*, *30*(2), 184–215. https://www.researchgate.net/publication/258132438_Controversial_Facility_Siting_in_the_Urban_Environment_Resident_and_Planner_Perceptions_in_the_United_States

Tornstam, L. (2006). The complexity of ageism: A proposed typology. *International Journal of Ageing and Later Life*, *1*(1), 43–68. https://doi.org/10.3384/ijal.1652-8670.061143

Vig, N. J., & Kraft, M. E. (1990). *Environmental Policy in the 1990s: Toward a New Agenda*. Congression Quarterly Press. https://www.researchgate.net/publication/274107848_Environmental_Policy_in_the_1980s_Reagan's_New_Agenda

Wang, D., & Wang, W. (2018). "空间生产"视角下邻避现象的包容性治理 [Inclusive governance of NIMBY from the perspective of "production of space"]. *Administrative Forum*, *25*(4), 85–91. https://doi.org/10.16637/j.cnki.23-1360/d.2018.04.013

Wang, G., & Du, Y. (2020). 社会燃烧理论视域下"中国式邻避"的生成与治理 [The generation and governance of "Chinese-style NIMBY" from the perspective of social combustion theory]. *Leadership Science*, 22, 34–38. https://doi.org/10.19572/j.cnki.ldkx.2020.22.010

Wang, G., Liu, Y., & Chi, Y. (2017). 舆论危机的异化极化效应研究 [Alienation mechanism and polarization effect of public opinion crisis]. *Journal of Management Science*, 20(3), 149–161. https://kns.cnki.net/kcms/detail/detail.aspx?FileName=JCYJ201703011&DbName=CJFQ2017

Wang, K. (2019). "价值冲击"与"现实困境"的双重叠加:嵌入式养老院的建设困局与路径选择 [The double superposition of value shock and realistic dilemma]. *Shanghai Urban Management Journal*, 28(1), 60–66. https://kns.cnki.net/kcms/detail/detail.aspx?FileName=CGZJ201901013&DbName=CJFQ2019

Wang, K., & Han, Z. (2020). "别闹大":中产阶层的策略选择—基于"养老院事件"的抗争逻辑分析 [Why "Not to Make It Big"?—A logical analysis of the middle class resistance on nursing home incident]. *Journal of Public Administration*, 17(2), 84–94+170. https://kns.cnki.net/kcms/detail/detail.aspx?FileName=GGGL202002007&DbName=DKFX2020

Wang, K., Xu, H., & Huang, L. (2020). Wellness tourism and spatial stigma: A case study of Bama, China. *Tourism Management*, 78, 1–12. https://doi.org/10.1016/j.tourman.2019.104039

Wu, F. (2008). 认知、态度和社会环境:老年歧视的多维解构 [Cognition, attitude and social environment: A multi-dimensional explanation of old age discrimination]. *Population Research*, 4, 57–65. https://kns.cnki.net/kcms/detail/detail.aspx?FileName=RKYZ200804006&DbName=CJFQ2008

Wu, Y., Zhai, G., & Zhan, L. (2017). 城市邻避空间及其演变轨迹—以南京市殡葬邻避空间为例 [NIMBY space and its evolution: A case study of Nanjing funeral NIMBY space]. *Human Geography*, 32(1), 68–72+122. https://doi.org/10.13959/j.issn.1003-2398.2017.01.010

Xiong, T. (2019). 我国老年群体媒介形象的污名化研究 [*A study on the stigmatization of media images of the elderly in China*]. [Master dissertation, Heilongjiang University]. CNKI. https://doi.org/10.27123/d.cnki.ghlju.2019.001171

Yan, D., & Li, J. (2018). 中国邻避冲突的设施类型、时空分布与动员结构—基于531起邻避个案的实证分析 [Facilities type, temporal and spatial distribution and mobilization structure of NIMBY conflicts in China: An empirical analysis based on 531 NIMBY cases]. *Urban Problems*, 9, 4–12. https://doi.org/10.13239/j.bjsshkxy.cswt.180901

Yang, F., He, Y., & Zhao, Z. (2017). 城市市政基础设施的邻避效应评价方法研究 [Study on Evaluation Method of NIMBY Effect of Urban Municipal Infrastructure]. *Journal of Beijing University of Technology (Natural Science Edition)*, 53(3), 518–524. https://doi.org/10.13209/j.0479-8023.2017.025

Yang, L., Chen, L., & Liu, H. (2018). 空间正义视角下的邻避冲突与邻避设施供给要件探析—以武汉某临终关怀医院抗争事件为例 [The supply component and optimization path of NIMBY facilities from the perspective of spatial justice: Study of a hospice protest event in Wuhan]. *Journal of Huazhong University of Science and Technology (Social Science Edition)*, 32(1), 125–133. https://doi.org/10.19648/j.cnki.jhustss1980.2018.01.018

Zhang, S., & Zhao, Y. (2017). 城市小型社区嵌入式养老设施设计研究 [A study on the design of small care facilities for the elderly embedded in urban communities]. *Acta Architecture Sinica*, 10, 18–22. https://kns.cnki.net/kcms/detail/detail.aspx?FileName=JZXB201710005&DbName=CJFQ2017

7 Dimensions of Eldercare and Quality of Life of Elderly People in an Old-Age Home in Kolkata

Saheli Guha Neogi Ghatak

Introduction

The demographic profile of India is experiencing a dramatic transition which has led to a paradoxical situation where the demographic cohort consists of a large working-age group of people on the one hand and a significant proportion of the 60 and above the age group of the elderly population on the other as this population of 60 and above is growing explosively. The assessment of the perception of quality of life (QOL) has become an imperative field of discussion nowadays. Vienna International Plan of Action on Aging (1983) strengthened that the concept of QOL of the Elderly is equally important with longevity.

The rise of the middle class and rapid disintegration of the family system in West Bengal are two important social changes in the post-independence era. Several interrelated factors connected to the complex reforms known as economic liberalization of the 1990s caused serve erosion of intergenerational reciprocity and eldercare tradition in Bengali families. Modern age in Bengal acted adversely to the family support for the elderly both in rural and urban settings (Chatterjee, 2009). With a diversely fragmented pattern of the traditional support base (the family), the nuclear family has been substituting the extended kinship structure leading to psychological isolation (Parsons, 1943). Correspondingly the structuralist-functionalist and modernization theorists view of the breakdown of the traditional norms and increased weakening of the ties between adult children and their parents (Chattopadhyay & Marsh, 1999; Goode, 1963; Parsons, 1943), age selective migration and global employment opportunities have distanced the cohorts who were earlier living together. Thus, coercive inter-generational interface, changing roles and expectations of women, urban space crunch and privacy, helped the flourishing of Old Age Homes (OAH).

Nowadays, elderly people claim that society should not only confirm their inclusion with dignity but also provide care. Inadequate understanding of various dimensions of their QOL is largely responsible for the elderly being denied a dignified existence. After all, the last stage of life course holds as much potential

DOI: 10.4324/9781003254256-10

for growth and development as earlier stages (Raju, 2006). The burgeoning elderly population is driving the prerequisite of eldercare. Serious attention to eldercare needs to be given for better QOL of elderly in OAH.

Quality of Life of Elderly

QOL is an individual's perception of his/her position in life, based on culture and value systems in which they live, concerning their goals, expectations, standards, and concerns. It is an inclusive concept influenced by the multifaceted ways of people's physical health, psychological state, level of independence, social relationships, and their relationship to appropriate features of their environment (WHO-QOL Group, 1995).

Bowling et al. (2013) stated that elderly people's views of the key dimensions of QOL might differ across the community and aged care settings, and there are differentials between the dimensions of QOL between community-dwelling elderly and elderly living in age care homes. The significant themes of QOL for community-dwelling elderly involve a positive outlook, psychological well-being, having good health and functioning, social relationships, leisure activities, neighborhood resources, adequate finance, and independence. Residents of age care homes give preference to physical comfort, functional capability, privacy, autonomy, dignity, meaningful activity, meaningful relationships, and safety. Besides these discrepancies, elderly people's perspective in explaining QOL may vary based on their socio-demographic background, health status, gender, and ethnicity.

Cummins (1997), ascribed QOL as both objective and subjective, each alliance being the cumulative of seven domains: material well-being, health, productivity, intimacy, safety, community, and emotional well-being. Objective domains include culturally relevant measures of objective well-being. Subjective domains include the satisfaction of the elderly weighted by their importance to the individual. Gabriel and Bowling (2004) conducted one study on 999 elderly of 65 years old and above in Britain suggested that QOL includes- good health and mobility, economic empowerment, good social relationships, help and support, living with family, good neighbors, access to local facilities and services (including transport), feel safe, positive psychological outlook and acceptance of surroundings, engagement in hobbies and leisure activities and maintaining social activities and retentive role in society, enjoy life with independence and control over life. QOL of elderly people is a multidimensional paradigm that is valuable in evaluating and adding life to years. It is important to use domains of QOL from elderly people's perspective and recognize that these domains will fluctuate based on a person's life circumstances, social network, and personality.

Care is no more limited to private concerns nowadays, family fragmentation, entry of women into paid workforce indicates the care of the elderly as one of the major public issues. Owing to urbanized, industrialized society, unitary family type, growing emphasis on individualization, and altering value system, the position of the elderly certainly deteriorates. Elderly people are no longer properly cared for by the family and social network in the post-neo-liberal era and they are not considered as an essential contributor in family and society by providing the assimilated knowledge thus, making institutional care more important. OAH is no longer an alien concept in India; likewise, in Kolkata also there is unforeseen growth of these eldercare homes. The significant reasons for deciding on living in OAH are—diminishing joint family system, expansion of dual-career families, insufficiency of care-taker in family, obligatory marginalization and exclusion, shortage of spaces in apartment, avoidance of family battle (specifically with children), wish for independent living with dignity and peace of mind as well as receive better care services in exchange of money. The perception of care of the elderly is not limited to a family obligation but, OAH has become a significant source of providing care to the elderly. Availability of formal care appears to influence the probability to move to institutional care (Larsson & Thorslund 2002; Tennstedt et al. 1990). The issue of eldercare indicates the involvement of numerous social issues. The perception of the QOL of the elderly can be understood based on the perception of receiving care. The issue of care is pertinent specifically for QOL of elderly people living in a family setting or an institution (Gerritsen et al., 2004). Assessing different dimensions of care received by the elderly in OAH, gender difference, and connection between care and QOL was the major consideration for this research. Perception of receiving care varies based on social adjustment capability and the form of intra-generational–interpersonal relationship that in turn, develop the perception of QOL of elderly (male and female) residing in OAH in Kolkata.

The most important apparatuses of good life quality among the elderly are generally similar to those of adult people, such as good subjective physical and emotional well-being, adequate financial resources, substantial social relationships, social activity, care, and a good living environment. (Lowenstein & Ogg 2003). Health, Activities of Daily Living (ADL), and functional ability are connected not only to survival but also to life satisfaction, dependency, or/and need of care (Iwarsson et al., 1998; Slivinske et al., 1998) are affective and social components of QOL. Jamuna and Reddy (1993) observed that the family is the primary care provider of the elderly and it is the quality and quantity of inter-generational interactions within a family that ultimately determines the quality of eldercare. Concerning social participation, older women are more likely than older men to visit family and friends, which reflects their social adjustment pattern (Linn, Hunter, & Perry, 1979).

The Rationale of the Study

The empirical observation was made to understand various dimensions of care in OAH in Kolkata and the gender differences in perception of receiving care and

QOL. In India, women are always designated as a caregiver but in their old age, women need care, so as care receivers, how they are different from their counterparts and how their perception of care of elderly determine their QOL was the area of research for the present study.

Objectives

The objectives of this chapter were (1) to ascertain the dimensions of receiving care in OAH and perceived QOL of the elderly and (2) to understand the Intra-generational–interpersonal relationship and social adjustment pattern of the elderly in OAH as an important factor of QOL of elderly.

Method

Variables

Care

Care means providing and receiving assistance in a supportive manner (Phillips, Ajrouch, & Hillcoat-Nallétamby, 2010). Care is a central part of life, binding together families, friends, and communities. It is embedded in social relations, therefore, embodies love, solidarity, exchange, altruism, and spirituality. Formal care is paid and formally organized; institutional care is formal care. Here OAH care is taken into consideration. Informal care is unpaid and associated with family, friends, neighbor care. Informal care is given to dependent persons, such as the sick and elderly, outside the framework of organized, paid, professional work. (Malcolm et al. 2005). With the changing structure, nature, and roles within the family, the traditional patterns of care are changing. Friends as caregivers are also gaining importance in providing care. (Vaarama et al., 2008).

Quality of Life

An elderly person's QOL is the degree of well-being felt by the individual. QOL is defined based on the multidimensional assessment, by both intrapersonal and social normative measures of the person-environment system of an individual in time-past, current and anticipated. (Lawton, 1991). World Health Organization conceptualized QOL in cross-cultural terms as an individual's perception of his/her position in life, in the framework of the culture and value systems in which they live, and in the context of their goals, expectations, standards, and concerns. It is a comprehensive ranging concept, affected in a composite way by the person's physical health, psychological status and level of independence, social relationship, as well as their relationship to salient features of their environment (WHO-QOL Group, 1995).

Intra-Generational–Interpersonal Relationship

An intra-generational–interpersonal relationship is the type of relationship within a particular group of people. Here the term indicates the relationship of the elderly with other elderly boarders in the OAH, their friendship, and companionship.

Social Adjustment

Adaptation of the person to the social environment is an adjustment that may take place by adapting the self to the environment or by changing the environment (Campbell, *Psychiatric Dictionary*, 1996). It is the types of relationships that involve the accommodation of the individual to circumstances in his/her social environment for the satisfaction of his/her needs or motives. Both the social and emotional aspects of adjustment were considered as measured variables.

Sample—100 elderly (50 males and 50 females) were taken chosen based on purposive sampling from 10 OAHs within the jurisdiction of Kolkata.

The sample selection criteria:

a Selection of OAHs
- OAH having at least 20 boarders
- OAH with health check-up system weekly/fortnightly
- OAH with other facilities (Yoga, meditation, physiotherapy, etc.) and recreational activities

b Selection of Respondents
- 60 years of age of elderly
- Elderly who are OAH boarders for at least five years
- Elderly who are capable of ADLs[1] in both subgroups

Tools used:

1 General information schedule consists of open-ended and close-ended questions on socio-demographic status, different dimensions of care, and intra-generational–interpersonal relationships).
2 The Social Adjustment Scale (Dr. Roma Pal, Agra University, 1989).
3 WHO-QOL BREF Questionnaire, 1996.
   Data collection—Telephonic interview was taken due to the pandemic situation.
   Statistical test—Mean, Standard Deviation, and Chi-square.

Results and Interpretation

Table 7.1 Socio-Demographic Profile of Elderly

Age (in year)	Male (N = 50) No. (%)	Female (N = 50) No. (%)	Total (N = 100) No. (%)
65–69	23 (46)	20 (40)	43
70–74	19 (38)	18 (36)	37
74 and above	8 (16)	12 (24)	20
Educational Status			
Illiterate	2 (4)	4 (8)	6
Primary	4 (8)	8 (16)	12
Secondary	8 (16)	18 (36)	26
Graduate	22 (44)	16 (32)	38
Post Graduate	6 (12)	4 (8)	10
Professional	8 (16)	0	8
Economic Status			
No income	01 (2)	05 (10)	06
Less than Rs. 10,000	00	05 (10)	05
10,001–20,000	18 (36)	17 (34)	35
20,001–30,000	23 (46)	18 (36)	41
30,001 and above	8 (16)	05 (10)	13
Marital Status			
Married	06 (12)	4 (8)	10
Unmarried	30 (60)	20 (40)	50
Widow/widower	14 (28)	25 (50)	39
Divorce/separated	0	1 (2)	02
Caste			
General	24 (48)	28 (56)	52
SC	16 (32)	14 (28)	30
ST	6 (12)	6 (12)	12
OBC	4 (8)	2 (4)	6
Family Type			
Nuclear	32 (64)	28 (56)	60
Joint	18 (36)	22 (44)	40

Demographic Profile of Sample

Most elderly people in this sample belonged to the 60–64 years of age group. The educational background of the elderly is a vital social indicator that has a direct and facilitating effect on their QOL through factors like living conditions and economic status. It is generally presumed that an individual's educational level improves her awareness for health promotion and adopting preventive care measures (Gupta, 2014). In this study, 38% of the elderly were graduates, most both males and females were having a monthly income of 20,001 to 30,000/month. Work, retirement, income, and savings give the identity of an individual within the family and society and also facilitate the improvement of QOL (Gupta, 2014). A majority of OAH residents were unmarried male elderly and female were widows which were also reflected by various studies at both national and international levels. The reasons for the increase in the number of widows can be understood based on the age difference between marriage partners, the difference in life expectancy between males and females, and the share of men and women remarrying (Mohanty and Gulati, 1993). All the respondents were from the Hindu community and most (64% males and 56% females) were from nuclear families (Table 7.1). Various studies have established the associations between socio-demography and the QOL (Gupta, 2014) of the elderly.

These results confirmed the feminization of the elderly. The need to provide appropriate services to the increasing oldest-old (74 and above age) population was also highlighted from the data. Such tendencies were recognized by CMIG in the UNFPA report, 2011/2014 on West Bengal, which specified that rising feminization of aging was prominent in West Bengal, analogous to the other seven state reports, with the sex ratio being 1135 females per 1000 males in the 60+ age group. Nearly two-thirds of the elderly (63%) were in the 60–69 age group confirming aging as a significant contemporary phenomenon requiring instant attention (UNFPA-BKPAI, 2011/2014).

Social Adjustment of Elderly Living in Old Age Home

Social adjustment of the elderly was analyzed based on The Social Adjustment Scale (SAI) scores (Pal, 1989). The social adjustment scale consists of two-part emotional and social adjustment. Mean (M) and standard deviation (S.D.) were calculated based on emotional adjustment, social adjustment, and total SAI scores (Table 7.2). The mean of total SAI of the male elderly in OAH was M-86.84 and the score for female boarders in OAHs was M-88.66 and S.D. was 8.03 and 7.65, respectively.

The social adjustment score highlighted the gender differences of adjustment of male and female elderly. The higher mean value showed higher social adjustment. Thus, the male elderly were less adjusted than the female elderly. Indian society with its patriarchal social arrangement has always given the male more supremacy and authority in the household in terms of decision-making rights and economic domain than the female, so in old age, male members face more difficulty to adjust with changing and diminishing status and role, which affect

Table 7.2 Social Adjustment Scale Score of Male and Female Elderly in OAH

SAI—Score	Male (N = 50) Mean	S.D.	Female (N = 50) Mean	S.D.
SAI—Emotional	39.37	4.57	41.24	5.21
SAI—Social	44.56	6.51	48.3	6.09
SAI—Total	86.84	8.03	88.66	7.65

their perception regarding QOL too. Moreover, women socialized to be adjusted through the culture of adjustment. Feminization of some services, especially the role of caregivers, is one way to perpetuate the culture of adjustment among women. Elderly females in OAH also adjusted more as they received the training of adjustment from their childhood as is reflected by the narratives:

> Male 67 years, retired professor, single, was unhappy with the food services in OAH and repeatedly complained to the authority yet no changes happened in the everyday menu.
>
> Female 69 years widow, mother of NRI son, had no objection to food and other services as she thought it was her destiny to stay in OAH alone. She did not complain about the food menu rather she thought the menu was appropriate for elderly people.

According to cognitive adaptation theory (Taylor, 1983), the adjustment process in old age centers around an attempt to regain mastery over the event in particular and one's life in general, as elderly in OAH do not have mastery over the everyday life event in particular and one's life in general, they have to live within the particular rules of OAH. The socialization process of female elderly consequently helped them to adjust to OAH more than their counterpart.

Intra-Generational–Interpersonal Relationship of Elderly in Old Age Home

One of the factors that make old people stay in OAHs is companionship as an elder in companionship points to intra-generational–interpersonal relationships. Data (Table 7.3) highlighted that there is a significant difference between male and female elderly based on their intra-generational–interpersonal relationship. Female elderly have a greater intra-generational–interpersonal relationship than males as their social adjustment is higher than male elderly boarders. Female boarders are friendlier and adjustment comes as a natural functional capacity outcome from them. Women elderly have a large number of friends and attend more religious activities in comparison to men (Linn, Hunter, & Perry, 1979). The following narratives elucidate the issues-

> Male 69 years old retired elderly, spent time with other co-boarders and felt happy as he did not feel insulted while talking to them which was quite common while he stayed with his son's family. In the present pandemic situation, the co-boarders sat in distance and passed time by discussing various social and political activities of the country.
>
> Another female 71 years old, widow, felt her communication with other co-boarder received approval and inclusion. Due to the pandemic, she could not go to different religious places with her friends in OAH but she spent time with them every day by chatting with each other and by seeing T.V. together by keeping distance from each other.

Table 7.3 Comparison of Male and Female Elderly Boarders in Terms of Intra-Generational–Interpersonal Relationship

Intra-generational–interpersonal relationship		Male	Female	X^2
1	Have contact with other boarders			10.44*
	a Frequently	14	30	
	b Sometimes	24	14	
	c Rare	12	06	
2	Co-boarders pass the time together—have tea, gossiping, chatting			
	a Frequently	12	28	11.28*
	b Sometimes	28	14	
	c Rare	10	8	
3	Do religious activities together			
	a Frequently	04	20	26.84*
	b Sometimes	14	22	
	c Rare	32	08	
4	Go for an outing together			
	a Frequently	12	06	10.27*
	b Sometimes	22	12	
	c Rare	16	32	
5	Exchange gifts			
	a Frequently	06	18	17.09*
	b Sometimes	18	20	
	c Rare	32	12	

The intra-generational–interpersonal relationship was conceptualized based on the rate of contact with others/boarders/neighbors, spending time together, religious activities, and going for outings together. In OAH, the elderly as a community passed the time together chatted, exchange gifts, etc., as the communication accommodation theory. (Gallois et al., 2016) substantiates. The theory suggested, communicators are expected to accommodate the person they are talking with by adopting their mode of communication. Accommodation is executed for seeking approval, inclusion, affiliation, or interpersonal goals. While communicating with other co-boarders' elderly receive more approval, inclusion, and affiliation than inter-generational communication. Thus, the intra-generational–interpersonal relationship has a positive influence on the QOL of the elderly.

According to Socioemotional selectivity theory (Carstensen, 1992), elderly people analytically enhance their social networks for satisfying their emotional needs through available social partners. Social networks become more selective as people age. The elderly accentuates the emotion-regulating function of interaction and emotionally fulfilling relationships. The intra-generational–interpersonal relationship builds on the basis of the available social partner in OAH that satisfy the emotional need of the elderly in OAH. The importance of intra-generational relationships for the QOL or well-being of the elderly was also supported by the Convoy Model of Social Relations. (Kahn and Antonucci, 1980).

Gabriel and Bowling's (2004) survey of QOL, in Britain, found that having good social resources was said to be part of having a good QOL. Neighborhood resources, or neighborhood social capital, also contribute to a good QOL, just as having good relationships with their neighbors contributed to good QOL.

Dimensions of Receiving Care in Old Age Home

Receiving care in own home is the best option for elderly people but when the children are away from home, the elderly have to live alone or in the case of unmarried, widow/widower elderly without children or elderly who seek personal space often prefers to stay at OAHs. Nowadays, OAHs are not an alien concept rather, the acceptance of OAHs as care homes are quite familiar and acceptable.

In this research, different dimensions of care of the elderly in OAH were identified following the care model of Nolan et al. (1995).

Data demonstrated (Table 7.4) various dimensions of receiving care in OAH. In the case of receiving *instrumental care* such as receiving food on time, cleaning and personal hygiene-related assistance, technological help, etc., both elderly males and females informed that they received instrumental care regularly and

Table 7.4 Dimensions of Receiving Care in OAH

Type of care	Response of elderly based on Receiving care	Male	Female	X^2
Instrumental care	Receive food on time			
	a Yes	46	48	0.70
	b No	04	02	
	Receive all assistance related to cleaning and personal hygiene			
	a Yes	46	47	0.15
	b No	04	03	
Preventive care and supervisory care	Medical care[a]			
	a Always	26	22	1.59
	b Sometimes	18	24	
	c Rare	06	04	
	Other health care facilities (yoga, physiotherapy, etc.)			
	a Always	32	28	0.8
	b Sometimes	14	16	
	c Rare	04	06	
	Arrange recreational facilities[b]			
	a Always	16	20	1.77
	b Sometimes	26	26	
	c Rare	08	04	

(*Continued*)

Table 7.4 Dimensions of Receiving Care in OAH (*Continued*)

Type of care	Response of elderly based on Receiving care	Male	Female	X^2
Anticipatory care	Technological help[c]			
	a Always	12	28	10.68*
	b Sometimes	30	17	
	c Rare	08	05	
	Receive help from OAH regarding marketing, medicine, food, etc.			
	a Always	16	30	8.43*
	b Sometimes	28	18	
	c Rare	06	02	
Preservative care	Measures taken during COVID-19 in OAH[d]			
	a Always	16	20	1.77
	b Sometimes	26	26	
	c Rare	08	04	
Reciprocal care	Care from OAH authorities and boarders[e]			
	a Always	14	28	8.14*
	b Sometimes	26	15	
	c Rare	10	07	
(Re)constructive care	Help for physical and mental healing[f]			
	a Yes	12	10	0.23
	b No	38	40	

* Significant at 0.05 level.

a. Regular health checkups, supervision about medicine intake and other medical issues.
b. Watching T.V., arrangement of religious and other tours, celebration of various festivals, cultural programs, etc.
c. Help related to the handling of android mobile phone, e-banking, registration for vaccination, WhatsApp communication with children and other relatives and friends.
d. During pandemic COVID-19, various measures were taken by OAH such as giving food in a personal room, maintaining distance in T.V. room, restriction of visitors, vaccination, etc.
e. Through regular interaction, gifts exchange, etc.
f. Help regularly with technical tasks, i.e. using a catheter, wound dressing, and medicine, help with improving physical functions (walking, training memory, etc.).

there is no significant difference of opinion among elderly males and females. Most of the elderly, both males and females informed about their frequently received preventive and supervisory care in the form of receiving regular health check-ups, supervision about medicine intake and other medical issues, and other health care facilities such as yoga, physiotherapy, other recreational facilities (watching T.V., arrangement of religious and other tours, the celebration of various festivals and cultural programs). *Preservative care* was received by both male and female elderly in OAH. During pandemic, various OAH have taken different measures to prevent the spread of COVID-19, such as giving food in a personal room, maintaining distance in T.V. room, restriction of visitors, vaccination, etc. The elderly in OAH also received *Reciprocal Care* from OAH authorities and boarders. The intra-generational–interpersonal relationship helped the elderly male and female to receive care from co-boarders through regular interaction, gifts exchange, etc. *(Re)constructive care* was also received by both male and female elderly in OAH in the form of receiving regular technical tasks, i.e. using a catheter, wound dressing and medicine, help with improving physical functions (walking, training memory), etc. Most of the elderly said "No" because they did not require that help as these narratives explain

> Female, 69 years old widow felt that her QOL would have deteriorated during the pandemic if she would not stay in OAH. She was provided food on time, cleaning and personal hygiene were maintained, received regular health check-ups, etc., all everyday life issues were taken care of by OAH authorities. Life was easier in OAH during the pandemic. She spent her time watching T.V in a common room sitting at a distance and could continue interaction with other boarders keeping distance and wearing the mask. She said all of her friends and relatives who stayed with their family had lots of problems related to a regular health check-up, medicines, etc., and felt lonely and anxious. During the lockdown, it was difficult for the elderly who lived alone to manage everyday life food, medicines, and the economy. But she felt blessed to stay in OAH as everything was taken care of by OAH authorities and she was safe and arrangements for vaccines were also made by OAH.
>
> Female 72 years old widow retired professor, mother of a married daughter, narrated that her experience in OAH was a quite happy one. She used to stay with her daughter's family initially after her husband's death, but later, she shifted to OAH as she wanted her own space and freedom. She was happy in OAH as she never felt any problem in OAH rather felt dignified life and all of her necessities were fulfilled by the OAH staff. All kinds of assistance regarding buying medicines, fruits, and other goods were taken care of by staff members of OAH.
>
> Female, 67 years old, spinster retired govt. employee, was happy in OAH because she could nurture her hobbies like singing and painting in OAH and also had many friends with whom she used to gossip, went to various religious places, and performed in various cultural programs organized by OAH before the pandemic. She was hopeful that she will again perform on stage after the pandemic and thanked the OAH authority for taking care of all food, medicine, vaccine, and arrangement of psychological counseling during the crisis period. She also informed that during the pandemic she lost her only brother and her co-boarders and OAH staff helped her to cope with that grief.
>
> Male 67-year-old widower, father of NRI daughter and narrated that: He had to face a lot of problems while handling the smartphone. His daughter taught him many things before going abroad, but he forgot most. But in OAH, the young staff trained him enthusiastically about all the technical issues of smartphones such as what's an app video call, e-commerce, e-banking, online medical assistance, online Yoga class, etc. He explained this kind

of support as a boon in OAH while his friends in the family set up did not receive any such support from his family members rather humiliated by family members for asking technical help.

The above narratives elucidated different types of care received by elderly boarders in OAH in Kolkata. It was found that OAHs in Kolkata provided all the seven categories of care, i.e. instrumental caregiving; preventive caregiving; supervisory caregiving; anticipatory caregiving, preservative caregiving; reciprocal caregiving, and (re)constructive care.

Data revealed a significant difference between male and female boarders in terms of their responses based on receiving anticipatory care and reciprocal care. In the case of other care dimensions, there was no significant difference between male and female elderly as other types of care OAH facilities were understood in terms of objective indicators. In the case of receiving anticipatory and reciprocal care, the perception of care differs because of the socialization pattern of women, which trained them as a caregiver.

Quality of Life of Elderly in Old Age Home

Data highlighted (Table 7.5) the WHO-QOL-BREF scores of 10 elderly (5 males and 5 females) living in OAH. Mean and SD of physical QOL of elderly males were 62.72 and ± 9.87 and female 59.08 and ± 8.48; psychological QOL were 55.87 and ±8.63 and 58.86 ± 7.43, respectively for male and female elderly; social QOL were 57.59 and ± 9.3 and 59.47 and ± 7.6; environmental QOL were 58.36 and ± 8.7 and 60.12 and ± 98.56 and the overall QOL of elderly were 58.65 and ± 9.12 for male and 59.38 and ± 8.11 for female elderly living in OAH. Data revealed that physical QOL of the elderly male was better than female elderly but psychological, social, and environmental QOL were better for female elderly in OAH. The following narratives clarify such issues:

> Female, a 69-years-old widow, mother of NRI son, narrated that she felt safe and having better QOL within OAH and her son was also relatively less tensed for her than her nephew whose mother lived in a flat alone. She stated that she had seen her nephew struggling to send medicines and daily necessary goods to her mother. She concluded that when any elderly would

Table 7.5 Quality of Life of Elderly in OAH (WHO-QOL-BREF Scale Score)

Gender	Physical QOL Mean (S.D.)	Psychological QOL Mean (S.D.)	Social QOL Mean (S.D.)	Environmental QOL Mean (S.D.)	Overall QOL Mean (S.D.)
Male	62.72 (9.87)	55.87 (8.63)	57.59 (9.3)	58.36 (8.07)	58.65 (9.12)
Female	59.08 (8.48)	58.86 (7.43)	59.47 (7.6)	60.12 (8.56)	59.38 (8.11)

Quality of life of elderly in OAH (N = 10)

not have the option to stay with their children, then it's better to stay in OAH than staying alone at home.

Male, 72 years old, widower, felt quite anxious and lonely in OAH after the sudden death of her wife. He did not talk to all boarders but he had selective friends in OAH. Pandemic made him more depressed as he was not allowed to go outside OAH.

The above narratives highlighted a lack of adjustment capacity among male elderly, which relates to a lesser score on the QOL scale. In the pandemic and lockdown scenario, elderly women justified their living in OAH as a safe and better place to stay by comparing it with their friends and relatives living in a family setting. Female elderly mentioned that they had to follow various rules of OAH such as isolation and physical distancing, etc.; still, they were connected with fellow boarders and they were less worried about their health check-ups and medicines, unlike their known person in family settings.

Conclusion

This study attempted to understand various dimensions of receiving care in OAH and the QOL of the elderly along with intra-generational–interpersonal relationships and social adjustment of elderly in OAH as a significant factor of QOL of elderly. The result of the analysis showed that the female boarders of OAH had better social and emotional adjustment than the male boarders. Intra-generational–interpersonal relationships of female elderly were better than their counterparts and perception of anticipatory care and reciprocal care was also better among elderly females than male counterparts, which brings the difference in their perception regarding QOL. The male boarders revealed more rigidity in their social and emotional aspects of adjustment than the female boarders.

In this research, seven dimensions of receiving the care were reflected on following Nolan. Those are

1. *Instrumental care*: hands-on caregiving mostly recognized as caregiving (Food on time, medicine, cleaning, personal hygiene, and other everyday life required things)
2. *Preventive care*: the purpose of preventing both physical and mental illness (regular health check-ups, physical and mental deterioration, arrangement of recreational facilities—watching T.V. together, celebration of Rabindra Jayanti, pooja, etc.)
3. *Supervisory care*: the supervision on daily routine (medicine intake in proper time, regular medical check-up, arrangement of things for the elderly along with protection of self-esteem and dignity).
4. *Anticipatory care*: decisions and behavior based on the possible future needs of the elderly (marketing, medicine, food, etc., especially help related to the handling of android mobile phone, e-banking, registration for vaccination, WhatsApp communication with children, and other relatives and friends).

5. *Preservative care*: the preventive measures taken by OAH authorities (giving food in a personal room, maintaining distance in T.V. room, restriction of visitors, vaccination, etc.).
6. *Reciprocal care*: perceived care by the OAH authority and caregiver and from the co-boarders, and
7. *(Re)constructive care*: Rebuilding an identity on the foundation of a person's history.

The perceived feeling of QOL of female elderly related to receiving the care was better than their male counterparts.

As the social adjustment and intra-generational–interpersonal relationships of female elderly were better, their perception of care and QOL was also better. Women are always labeled as better caregivers but this study revealed women as better care receivers also than males. They endure and are satisfied with a diminutive amount of care so, their perception of QOL is better. Various theoretical writings and empirical research explored the assumption that women provide extensive unpaid care for children, the elderly, and disabled family members (Land 1978). Care research was initially linked to feminism during the early 1980s, revealing and exposing to the public gaze what was hitherto assumed to be a natural female activity. Similarly, in the Indian scenario, care was related to functional, societal norms assumed that females should be more caring rather than their male counterparts. Females are constantly portrayed as caregivers rather than care receivers. Hence, in old age, when marginalization and diminishing power and the need for assistance arises from physical or cognitive incapacities necessitate the care, the male elderly is not pleased with the care they receive in comparison to the earlier attentive care they used to receive, whereas their female counterparts being habituated as caregivers rather than receivers, are satisfied with the expanse of care received. So, their perception concerning care is positive and it enables good QOL. The forgiving nature of females helps them toward a positive perception of care. Thus, the social adjustment and intra-generational–interpersonal relationships of female elderly are also better than the male boarders (Table 7.3). The women also demonstrated personal qualities of flexibility, tolerance, strong cultural and religious values, self-care activities, and care for others.

Following social constructionist theories of aging QOL of the elderly is associated with the social reality of received care which shifts over time and social roles that come with maturation (Dannefer and Perlmutter, 1990; Kuypers and Bengtson, 1973). QOL of the elderly is understood based on social meaning, social realities, social relations, attitudes toward aging and the aged, life events, and timing. The improved perceptual QOL can be achieved through adjustment and forgiveness and through involvement in productive activity (voluntary/paid social work—teaching, accounting, supervisor, etc.) or unproductive work (nurturing hobbies—listening to music, playing musical instruments, painting, drama, playing an indoor game with co-mates, etc.) The activity theory of aging states that aging in activities benefit the elderly to overcome loneliness, depression, improve their mental health, and enhance self-esteem, and thus, they become forgiver, which will support them to make better perception regarding their QOL.

Across the world, countries are experiencing population aging. The growth rate of the elderly population is more rapid in developing countries like India and the demographic transitions, socio-economic and political changes together with increased individualism have altered the living conditions of the elderly. The diversity among the elderly and varied inter-related influencing aspects from their environment needs significant consideration of researchers and policy planners. Care as an important factor of QOL of elderly in OAH and gender difference of receiving care which creates difference perception about their QOL need to be considered by policymakers. Policies related to OAH care need to be strengthened. Proper regulation and surveillance of OAH facilities and care services are required failing which licensing of OAH should be canceled.

Note

1. In Gerontological literature, ADL are operationalized as personal-care activities such as ambulating (walking), transferring (getting up from a chair), dressing, eating, drinking, personal hygiene (bathing, using the toilet), and taking medication, etc. (Dunlop, et al. 1997; Everard et al., 2000; Raju, 2002).

References

Bowling, A., Hankins, M., Windle, G., Bilotta, C., & Grant, R. (2013). A short measure of quality of life in older age: The performance of the brief older people's quality of life questionnaire (OPQOL-brief). *Archives of Gerontology and Geriatrics*, 56(1), 181–187. Retrieved from http://www.journals.elsevier.com/archives-of-gerontology-and-geriatrics

Campbell, A. (1996).Psychiatric Dictionary. Definitions of social adjustment, Retrieved from http://www.definitions.net/definition/social+adjustment.

Campbell, A., Converse, P. E., & Rodgers, W. L. (1976). *The Quality of American Life*. New York: Russell Sage. https://www.russellsage.org/publications/quality-american-life

Carstensen, L. (1992). Motivation for social contact across the life span: A theory of socioemotional selectivity. *Nebraska Symposium on Motivation*, 40: 209–54. https://europepmc.org/article/MED/1340521

Chakraborty, I. (2016). Alleviating the Angst of Aged Women: Initiative of the Calcutta Metropolitan Institute of Gerontology (CMIG), Kolkata; Stree Shakti-The Parallel Force UNDP funded project report on Innovative practices for care of elderly women in India. Retrieved from https://www.researchgate.net/publication/303975703_An_initiative_of_Stree_Shakti-_The_Parallel_Force_supported_by_UNFPA_i

Chatterjee, P. (2009). The Coming Crisis in West Bengal, *Economic & Political Weekly*, Vol. XLIV No. 09, pp 42–45. In UNFPA-BKPAI Survey for West Bengal (2014). Building a Knowledge Base on Population Ageing in India Report, *The Status of Elderly in West Bengal, 2011*.

Chattopadhyay, A., & Marsh, R. (1999). Changes in living arrangement and familial support for the elderly in Taiwan 1963–1991. *Journal of Comparative Family Studies*, 30, 3, 523–37. https://utpjournals.press/doi/10.3138/jcfs.30.3.523

Cummins, R. A. (1997). A comprehensive quality of life scale (ConQol). Fifth Edition, School of Psychology, Deakin University, Melbourne; https://sid.usal.es/idocs/F5/EVA66/ComQol_I5.pdf

Dannefer, D., & Uhlenburg, P. (1999). Paths of the life course. In V.L. Bengston, D. Gans, and N.M. Putney (Eds.), *Handbook of Theories of Ageing*, Second Edition. New York: Springer.ing Company.https://books.google.co.in/books?id=7qpHuXKsaC0C

Dannefer, D., & Perlmutter, M. (1990). Development as a multidimensional process: Individual and social constituents. *Human Development*, 55, 108–113. https://doi.org/10.1159/000276506

Dunlop, D. D., Hughes, S. L., & Manheim, L. M. (1997). Disability in activities of daily living: Patterns of change and a hierarchy of disability. *American journal of public health*, 87(3), 378–383. https://doi.org/10.2105/AJPH.87.3.378

Everard, K. M., Lach, H. W., Fisher, E. B., & Baum, M.C. (2000). Relationship of activity and social support to the functional health of older adults. *The Journal of Gerontology, Series B, Psychological Science and Social Science*. Jul;55(4), S208–12. doi: 10.1093/geronb/55.4.s208. PMID: 11584883.

Gabriel. Z., & Bowling, A. (2004). Quality of life from the perspectives of older people. *Ageing & Society*, 24, 675–691. http://discovery.ucl.ac.uk/1648/1/quality-oflife.pdf

Gallois, C., Gasiorek, J., Giles, H., & Soliz, J. (2016). Communication accommodation theory: Integrations and new framework developments. In H. Giles (Ed.), *Communication Accommodation Theory: Negotiating Personal Relationships and Social Identities across Contexts* (pp. 192–210). Cambridge University Press, UK.

Gerritsen, D., Steverink, N., & Ribbe, M. (2004). Finding a useful conceptual basis for enhancing the quality of life of nursing home residents. Retrieved from https://link.springer.com/article/10.1023/B:QURE.0000021314.17605.40

Goode, William, J. (1963). *World Revolution and Family Patterns*. Glencoe: Free Press.

Gupta, N. (2014). *Quality of life of older women in urban India*. Doctoral Dissertation, Dept. of Social Science, TISS. http://hdl.handle.net/10603/19504

Iwarsson, S., Isacsson, A., & Lanke, J. (1998). ADL Independence in the elderly population living in the community: The influence of functional limitations and physical environment demands, *Occupational Therapy International*, 3, 52–61. https://doi.org/10.1002/oti.74

Jamuna, D., & Reddy, L. K. (1993). Impact of age and length of widowhood on the self concept of elderly widow. *Indian Journal of Gerontology*, 7, 91–95. http://gerontologyindia.com/articles.htm

Kahn, R. L., & Antonucci, T. C. (1980). Convoys over the life course: Attachment, roles, and social support. In Baltes P. B. Brim O. (Eds.), *Life-span development and behaviour* (Vol. 3, pp. 254–283). New York: Academic Press.

Kuypers, J. A., & Bengtson, V. L. (1973). Competence and social breakdown: A social psychological view of Aging. *Human Development*, 16(2), 37–49.

Land, H. (1978). Who cares for the family? *Journal of Social Policy*, 3, 7, 357–384. https://doi.org/10.1017/S0047279400007893

Larsson, K., & Thorslund, M. (2002). Does Gender Matter?: Differences in Patterns of Informal Support and Formal Services in a Swedish Urban Elderly Population. *Research on Aging*, 24(3), 308–336. doi:10.1177/0164027502243002

Lawton, M. P. (1991). A multidimensional view of quality of life in frail elders. In J. E. Birren, J. E. Lubben, J. C. Rowe, & D. D. Deutchman (Eds), *The Concept and Measurement of Quality of Life in the Frail Elderly* (pp. 3–27). Academic Press.

Linn, M., Hunter, K., & Perry, P. (1979). Differences by sex and ethnicity in the psycho-social adjustment of the elderly. *Journal of Health and Social Behavior*, 20(3), 273–281. https://doi.org/10.2307/2136451

Lowenstein, A., & Ogg, J. (2003). Oasis—Old age and autonomy: The role of service systems and intergenerational family solidarity. Final Report. Haifa, Israel: University of Haifa, Center for Research and Study of Aging.

Malcolm J. Johnson, Vern L. Bengtson, Peter G. Coleman and Tom L. Kirkwood (Eds.) (2005). *The Cambridge handbook of age and aging* (pp. 670–681). Cambridge: Cambridge University Press.

Mohanty B. Leela Gulati. (1994). In the Absence of their Men: The Impact of Male Migration on Women. New Delhi: Sage Publications, 1993. 174 pages. Tables, Appendices. *Indian Journal of Gender Studies*, 1(2):269–271. doi:10.1177/097152159400100211

Neerja, Vasudeva, P., & Verma, (2000). A study of need for formal source of support for the aged. *Indian Journal of Psychological Issues*, 8(2), 26–32.

Nolan, M., Keady, J., & Grant, G. (1995). Developing a typology of family care: implications for nurses and other service providers. *Journal of Advanced Nursing*, 21, 256–65.

Pal, R. (1989). Social Adjustment Inventory Scale, In Das, P.R. and Shah, A.F. (2014) Attitude towards self and others as predictor of social adjustment. *Indian Journal of Positive Psychology*, 5(2), 206–208. https://doi.org/10.15614/ijpp%2F2014%2Fv5i2%2F53007

Parsons, T. (1943). The kinship system of the contemporary United States. *American Anthropologist*, 45, 22–38. https://doi.org/10.1525/aa.1943.45.1.02a00030

Phillips, J., Ajrouch, K., & Hillcoat-Nallétamby, S. (2010). Care. In *Key concepts in social gerontology* (pp. 43–45). SAGE Publications Ltd, https://www.doi.org/10.4135/9781446251058.n11

Raju, S. (2002). *Health Status of Urban Elderly: A Medico-social Study*. Delhi: B R Publishing Corporation.

Raju, S. (2006). Aging in India in the 21st Century: A Research Agenda; a country-specific report, United Nations Office on Ageing and the International Association of Gerontology in 2002.

Slivinske, L.R., Fitch, V.L., Wingerson, N.W. (1998). The Effect of Functional Disability on Service Utilization: *Implications for Long-Term Care, Health & Social Work*, 23(3), 175–185, https://doi.org/10.1093/hsw/23.3.175

Taylor. S. E. (1983). Adjustment to threatening events: A theory of cognitive Adaptation. *American Psychology* 4, pp. 237–239. https://psycnet.apa.org/doi/10.1037/0003-066X.38.11.1161

Tennstedt, S. L., Sullivan, L. M., McKinley, J. B., & D'Agostino, R. B. (1990). How important is functional status as a predictor of service use by older people? *Journal of Aging and Health*, 2, 439–441. https://doi.org/10.1177/089826439000200402

UNFPA-BKPAI Survey for West Bengal (2014). Building a Knowledge Base on Population Ageing in India Report, *The Status of Elderly in West Bengal, 2011*.

Vaarama, M., Pieper, R., & Sixsmith, A. (Eds.) (2008). *Care-related Quality of Life in Old Age. Concepts, Models and Empirical Findings.* New York: Springer. https://www.springer.com/gp/book/9780387721682

Vienna International Plan of Action on Aging (1983). United Nations, New York, 1983.

WHO-QOL Group (1995). *Field Trial WHOQOL-100, Fact, Definitions and Questions.* Geneva. https://www.who.int/mental_health/who_qol_field_trial_1995.pdf

Section IV

Care Issues of Marginalized Elder Groups in China and India

8 Successfully Aging Alone

Long-Term Singlehood and Care during COVID-19 in India

Ketaki Chowkhani

Introduction

"Who will look after you when you are old and sick" is a question that is often asked to aging single people, sometimes out of genuine concern and more often to chide them about how they missed the bus of marriage and coupledom. This question becomes more poignant during the COVID-19 pandemic, especially for long-term older single people living alone. Under the Maintenance and Welfare of Parents and Senior Citizens Act 2007, children are required to look after their parents.[1] While this act is undergoing some changes in recent times, it still does not include the role of non-kin in later life caregiving.[2] The law, hence, does not recognize single people's existence in old age, especially those who are never married and without children. Even legal heirs are not bound by the law to look after their guardians.

Unlike elsewhere, the age of retirement in India is 60 years. Hence, those who are single and do not have children to look after them need to start planning for their old age sooner than those who have children, often from the ages of 40 and 50 onward. This demographic needs to already plan successfully aging alone, especially because they don't have children to look after them, which renders them non-existent in the face of the law. Legally, they do not have "anyone" to look after them since they do not have children, but as I shall demonstrate, they socially have mobilized a network of support to counter the gaps in the law.

In this chapter, I examine self-care strategies long-term single people, specifically between the ages of 40 and 50, used during the COVID-19 pandemic lockdown to manage chronic illness and maintain health and well-being. The chapter uncovers how studying older single people's lives contributes to understanding diverse strategies of self-care and reconfigures caregiving issues outside the traditional family, especially in the case where the law does not recognize their existence. The study provides us with a two-pronged insight, one into caregiving practices among older single people living alone, and two, into successfully aging alone. The chapter is divided into three sections. The first section examines the self-care practices employed by long-term single people living alone; the second section examines their social support system with regard to care and illness; and the third section theorizes care and aging from a singlehood standpoint.

DOI: 10.4324/9781003254256-12

Self-Care, Singlehood, Aging, and the Pandemic in 2020

My working definition for self-care is borrowed from WHO, which defines self-care as:

> The ability of individuals, families and communities to promote health, prevent disease, maintain health, and cope with illness and disability with or without the support of a healthcare provider. The scope of self-care as described in this definition includes health promotion; disease prevention and control; self-medication...
>
> (WHO, 2019, x).

Telemedicine, healing from a distance, is also an important part of self-care especially during a pandemic (Leite, Hodgkinson, & Gruber 2020). Arima Mishra (2010) notes that "self-care marks the shift of medical care and treatment from hospital/clinic to the home or community" and that it "also changes the relationship between patient and doctor—it shifts from a paternalistic model of care to one of equal sharing" (Mishra, 2010, 75). With self-care, Mishra notes that "patients are seen as partners in the healing process" (Mishra, 2010, 84). She notes that "recognition must be given to the diverse ways people seek to construct ways to understand well-being and empowerment. Self-care in biomedical discourse does not allow such diversity and alterity" (Mishra, 2010, 95). In this chapter, I seek to understand this very diversity of self-care practices by examining older long-term singles.

Audre Lorde (1988) famously wrote about self-care not as self-indulgence, but as an act of self-preservation and political warfare. Today, self-care is popularly tied to lifestyle improvement and the neo-liberal market, thus losing its radical edge.[3] In the chapter, I will examine how self-care for older single people is an intrinsic part of their singlehood, and as the title of the chapter suggests, it contributes to successful aging alone.

Gangopadhyay (2021) examines how the market is stepping in to provide medical care, especially in the form of self-care in the context of older married people in urban India. She notes that older adults, all of whom are or were married, and have children, and especially those who live alone, are relying on the market rather than the family for self-care and successfully aging alone. Their attachments and reliance are shifting from family to the market, which creates a new form of aging. In my chapter, I notice that these networks are expanded. Long-term single people, unlike married or divorced/widowed people in Gangopadhyay's study, use friendship networks and solitude as a form of self-care.

Research has shown that never married people who live alone are better equipped to quarantine and are more comfortable with self-isolation and solitude (DelFattore, 2020; DePaulo, 2020a, 2021). Pioneering singles studies scholar Bella DePaulo (2020a), in a number of articles, writes about stories of single people who are navigating a pandemic, living alone, and thriving; and that size of the household matters more than social class in contracting the disease.

She maintains that those who live alone are safer since they are less exposed to infections and are also less likely to put other people at risk (DePaulo, 2020b). Research has also pointed out that the lockdown made married women more vulnerable to domestic violence and increased instances of violence have been reported (Ghoshal, 2020). The lockdown also increased women's labor at home (Dixit & Chavan, 2020). While many single people might have lost jobs or suffered otherwise, this clearly points out that single people who live alone are at an advantage during the pandemic.

DePaulo (2009, 2011a, 2020c), drawing from data from the West, has noted that lifelong older single people who are living alone, are doing just fine. Elyakim Kislev (2019), again drawing from data from the West, maintains that never married long-term single individuals do better as they grow older since they are used to managing on their own and they have developed support networks. He notes that for older singles, growing old alone is something they have always been doing. Investing in social support makes older people single people happier and increases their well-being. Singles are more likely to have a wider social support than currently or previously marrieds. They are also more likely to have cross-sex friendships.

Furthermore, scholarship in India (Agrawal, 2012; Bhatia et al., 2007; Samanta et al., 2015) has pointed out that older people who live alone are more lonely and prone to illness. Most of this scholarship does not take into account long-term single people who chose to remain single and live alone. This chapter intends to address this gap in research. While the data that I examine is limited, it nevertheless opens up an important area of inquiry on the under-studied older long-term single living alone.

Methodology

My working definition for singlehood for this chapter is those who are not in a romantic relationship, have never been married or had children and who live alone. The term long-term singlehood, borrowed from Lahad (2017), is used to refer to those who have been single for a considerable period of time ranging from a few years to over 25 years. The chapter draws on in-depth interviews conducted in 2020 in the months of May and June with five single, middle-class women and men between the ages of 40 and 50 who live in metropolitan Mumbai, as well as smaller urban centers like Pondicherry, and Khargone in Madhya Pradesh. All of them live alone without family or roommates. These women and men belong to different linguistic communities. Their backgrounds are similar: educated, English speaking, middle class, and urban. They are all in so-called "respectable professions." Because of the pandemic and restrictions on travel, the interviews were conducted through phone calls and video calls, and some interviews were audio or video recorded with the consent of the participant. Consent forms were obtained from the participants and the names have been changed to protect their identity. The group of interviewees is purposefully small because the attempt is to open up the question of aging, singlehood, and self-care during a pandemic lockdown to closer examination. The chapter's scope is also limited because it specifically examines a homogenous group of women and men who are middle class and English educated.

In designing the questionnaire, I did not follow the self-care inventory to assess self-care levels, but borrowed from the self-care questionnaires to ask questions about physical and emotional/psychological well-being. The open-ended questionnaire that I designed sought to include personal strategies of self-care.

Self-Care Practices of Long-Term Older Singles Who Live Alone

On 25 March 2020,[4] India went into lockdown to control the rise of COVID-19 cases. The lockdown lasted from six to eight weeks, and more in certain parts of the country. People could not step out of their homes unless they wanted to buy essential goods like groceries, milk, or medicine. Private medical clinics were shut and people were wary of visiting hospitals. During such a situation, self-care, where possible, removes the burden from hospitals, and occupies an important form of medical intervention and risk prevention. In this section, I examine the self-care strategies of long-term older singles and what that tells us about living in a single-headed household, aging, and self-care. Some of these singletons have chronic illnesses while others are non-patients who might have experienced short-term illness during the lockdown.

Most non-patients used similar strategies to maintain health. Anita, GPS, and Dwaipayan laid great emphasis on eating right, focusing on their diet, keeping immunity up, and cooking healthy food. Because none of them were able to or needed to step out to eat, and had the time to cook all their meals, they learned new recipes, followed a strict diet, all of which contributed to maintaining both physical and emotional well-being. Exercising at home and having a routine and structure to the day also helped Anita, GPS, and Dwaipayan maintain their health. Reading, listening to music, watching Netflix, listening to podcasts were some of the strategies Anita, GPS, and Dwaipayan used to promote emotional well-being. One person mentioned sexually pleasuring himself as a form of self-care and release of tension. Regularly talking to friends and natal family also helped them stay in touch with others as well as provide emotional support. Anita, GPS, and Dwaipayan mentioned that maintaining hygiene and sanitizing was a new form of self-care that they adopted during the pandemic.

Some of the non-patients also experienced minor illnesses and they used home remedies prescribed by friends and family to recover. Forty-year-old GPS felt he was sinking into depression and was aware of it. He overcame it by doing physical exercises and breathing exercises, sleeping on time and going out just to see people's faces. He also experienced dry cough due to dust allergy and cotton fibers from cotton factories in the area. He resorted to hot water and clove—home remedies suggested by family—as well homeopathy to overcome the cough. Dwaipayan in Mumbai was the only one who visited a doctor to recover from a fever. Many of the non-patients received help from a distance from family and friends when they experienced minor illnesses. They were able to maintain social and family ties, while leading independent lives and looking after themselves. Research has shown that single people are more likely to be in touch with family and friends than married people are (DePaulo, 2006; Kislev, 2019; Klinenberg, 2012).

Some other non-patients engaged in creative and spiritual pursuits to maintain emotional well-being. Dwaipayan got back to playing on his harmonica. Forty-seven-year-old Anita notes that living alone during the lockdown was "like a retreat. We all need to retreat." She noted how she felt very comfortable in her own company and valued her solitude. More importantly, Anita said "[you] can't go out, so go within." It is this introspective connection with the self in solitude which I argue later, helps one to theorize self-care from a singlehood standpoint. Anita, who speaks about going within, is not an introvert. Her idea of going within is not an introversion, but rather a form of introspection[5]. While eating healthy and exercising, keeping in touch with loved ones are standard measures of self-care, it is the use of creativity and solitude as effective strategies of self-care which are novel and lie outside biomedical discourses, as well as certain complementary and alternative therapies. These also point to the different strategies that older long-term single people use to cope during times of distress.

Some of the strategies of self-care that patients with chronic illnesses employ are similar to non-patients. Sima and Ratna have been reaching out to friends, taking help from social support and their chosen family, focusing on eating healthy, exercising, sleeping longer hours, and maintaining a daily routine. Some also use creativity as a form of emotional well-being. Forty-nine-year-old Ratna trained her memory with numbers, chain linking, anchoring, pegging and so on. Others used telemedicine before and during the pandemic. Ratna reached out during the pandemic to a homeopath friend who gave her recommendations for her frozen shoulder. All the forms of telemedicine that the chronic patients use seem effective and have been developed over a period of time, starting well before the pandemic. These patients have also been living in single-headed households for a while, and they have successfully been able to develop networks of care outside the family space.

Ratna has also used complementary and alternative therapies, which often include home remedies as a strategy of self-care. Ratna took homeopathy during the lockdown. She also talks extensively about turning within as a form of self-care. She took a philosophic as well as spiritual approach to life, which was aided by solitude. She ruminated:

> acceptance of life as it is, things you cannot change you make the best of it, no matter what the circumstances, there has to be a shift in your consciousness so that you are able to accept and do the best, have a positive mind set and going within…now there is no option but to go within and deeper, which is a very enjoyable experience.

Like Anita, Ratna spelt out the importance and inevitability of going within during the pandemic and its joyful effects. Like Anita, she is also not an introvert, and her solitude and going within is a result of introspection and not introversion. Her introspection has helped her accept her chronic illness and the circumstances of the pandemic. Solitude is key here, where despite having a strong support network, she thrives in her own space and company.

Solitude and introversion apart, some chronic patients were also able to exercise their agency to evolve their own self-care strategies. Ratna who has vertigo, hypertension, diabetes, cervical spondylitis, and a painful frozen shoulder evolved strategies of self-care based of their own through research. This is often referred to as the de-professionalization of medicine (Bhardwaj, 2010, 42). Ratna rejects the dominant biomedical discourse. She even practices an eclectic mix of therapies, and her mode of self-care cannot be contained within complementary or alternative therapies. Ratna experimented and tested herself to see what works for her body, guided by her own extensive research, allowing her to go entirely off insulin. She paid close attention to her diet and nutrition, understood the importance of gut and cellular health, of natural foods, and "willed herself to stay healthy." As an editor, she is able to discern between research by established authorities and quacks. She notes that this "knowledge acquisition does not happen overnight you build up on knowledge over a period of time." She speaks about an intimate knowledge of her own body, which she says even a doctor will not know. "If you listen to your body, your body will tell you," she says.

Michel Foucault characterizes self-care as a turning toward oneself that takes moral precedence over care for others as well as an ethical act that combines complex relations with others and knowledge of the self (Fornet-Betancourt et al., 1984, 116 and 118). Many of the participants care for themselves as an ethical project as well as share a complex relationship with their family, peers, and friends. They place self-care and solitude above anything else, without forgetting their ties with family and friends. Their families play an important role in their lives, acting as people who offer advice and support as well as friends who often act as families of choice in the absence of a natal family. Yet, there are differences between the ways patients and non-patients perceive and practice self-care. While many of the self-care strategies are similar between non-patients and patients, some of the patients have a deeper self-knowledge of their own bodies and their investment in their health is an integral part of their self-care.

Social Support among Older Long-Term Single People

Even though single people in my study seem to be good at self-care, they still have formed a support system of their own. Gangopadhyay (2020) points out that increasingly older people prefer living on their own rather than with her children, or in institutional arrangements. Her findings suggest a change in filial ties, with elders relying more on domestic help, shopkeepers, and drivers rather than on their families. Unlike the older people in Gangopadhyay's study, life-long single people in my study have developed a different network which comprises of friends, chosen family, siblings, doctors, and work colleagues. This difference can be attributed to the fact that long-term singles are more likely to form support networks outside the family (DePaulo, 2006; Klinenberg, 2012).

Dwaipayan regularly kept in touch with his friends, and would call his parents and sister every day. But when he fell sick, he immediately contacted a hospital and went alone to the doctor to get himself treated. He recovered quickly. Similarly, throughout the lockdown, Sima was in regular touch with her younger brother who lived close by, and would often visit him to help him with the household chores and have lunch with him. As a patient on regular anxiety medications, she was advised by her brother to call her doctor to regulate her dosage; but she refused. As her interview with me progressed, she slowly came around to using telemedicine. "I am thinking of calling him [the doctor] one of these days, the thought has just struck me," she confided. She elaborated that her doctor had asked her to feel free to call her anytime. The anxiety medicine led her to put on weight, and as the country shut down, Sima's gym trainer took the initiative to send her a workout plan on WhatsApp. She also relied on some trusted friends to talk to when she panicked. Like Dwaipayan, she didn't use the services of a domestic worker, and managed on her own, describing herself as being independent.

Anita also elaborates on her independence. "I like solitude, I enjoyed the lockdown. [I had] queries from married friends. How are you managing? [It was] pity, condescension. [I thought to myself] my goodness you are stuck with a man. I am cool, used to it. My goodness! [I like] being in my own cocoon. Less you interact with these people… I avoid such friends" Anita's quote shows that support is of various kinds, and as DePaulo (2020d) notes, many older people value positive solitude, which becomes their support and form of care. Similarly, Gangopadhyay et al. (2018) apply the Successful Aging Model to understand how older adults in New Delhi are increasingly focusing on the "self" in terms of self-reliance and self-development. This shift in understanding aging also contributes to how we understand older long-term singles and the changing forms of caregiving practices.

Ratna, on the other hand, valued both her solitude, as well as had a strong support network. She was very close to some family friends who cared for her like family after her father passed away. She strangely referred to them as her "local guardian," a term often used by young women who live alone away from their families. One of her family friends would call her every day and get medicines and other supplies for her. She would catch up with another friend over the phone in the evenings every day. She also received ample support from all quarters. She noted, "people help us in different ways. This person I know sent me a video that helped a lot. Another friend sent me a few videos, there was support from all around… I have a very good circle of friends so that aspect is also taken care of."

GPS, on the other hand, was the one helping other people. The organization he worked in was located in a small town, and since it involved social work, he practically knew everyone in town, from the egg and chicken vendors to the school teachers. This relationship with the town's people was not at a superficial level. He, and the team of 47 people working under him, would be regularly invited to functions such as weddings, tonsuring of a child's head, death ceremonies, as well as into their homes for a chat or a meal. He had built a strong relationship with the people in town, something which was an integral part of his work. These thousands of people were like his extended family. At the same time, he was directly responsible for his large team of young people, and he often helped them in medical emergencies during the lockdown. GPS's support came from colleagues that he worked with, and the large community that was built as a result of his work.

In all these narratives, one notices that long-term single people draw their social support from various sources, which include friends, doctors, institutional settings like the workplace, siblings, and chosen family. While most are still in touch with their natal families, their main forms of physical and emotional support lie outside the traditional support systems. The other unique feature of single people's support during the lockdown is solitude. Single people often rely first on themselves before turning to others (DePaulo, 2011b). Their form of self-care while aging is a two-pronged approach to solitude and social networking. The following section will examine this approach from a singlehood standpoint.

Theorizing Self-Care and Aging from a Singlehood Standpoint

The participants' responses have suggested that older single people are going within, and using solitude and self-knowledge as a strategy of self-care. DePaulo (2011b) has written about Carol Kahn's research on how long-term single people's attachment person, or "secure base" is often primarily themselves rather than others. Kahn notes that long-term single people have the "interdependence of turning inward for self-care and connection to self with turning outward for connection to others" (DePaulo, 2011b). Elsewhere I have argued that a singlehood standpoint is a return to the self.[6] Singlehood offers us productive solitude, returns to the self within as well as a connection to communities. In their strategies of self-care, older single people who are living alone are using both strategies of turning inward and outward to deal with chronic illness and maintain health and well-being. They are turning within to heal themselves from negative emotions, bad health and to experience joy, and they are turning outward for advice and help and socialization. Most of their self-care as they grow older comes not from mandates of the law, but from practices of singlehood that they are already equipped with, and which they have been using for a few decades.

Long-term single people living alone, unlike earlier research, are also not lonely or more prone to illness or suffering. While some might have a chronic illness like Ratna, they are coping well with a vast network comprised of friends, chosen family, colleagues, doctors, and siblings. Despite the law not recognizing their existence, they are thriving. As scholarship has already pointed out, long-term single people are more likely to build a community of friends and caregivers outside the nuclear or joint family. Examining aging and care from a singlehood standpoint, especially during a pandemic, leads us to different results and shows us that it is possible to age alone successfully—despite legal non-recognition—if one has built both a robust social support as well as learned to enjoy positive solitude.

Notes

1. I would like to thank Jagriti Gangopadhay for pointing out the role of the law.
2. https://www.firstpost.com/india/how-indias-new-bill-on-welfare-of-parents-senior-citizens-will-motivate-younger-generation-to-care-for-elderlies-9827571.html
3. https://www.theguardian.com/commentisfree/2019/aug/21/self-care-radical-feminist-idea-mass-marketv. Accessed on 13-02-2021.
4. https://www.thehindu.com/news/national/pm-announces-21-day-lockdown-as-covid-19-toll-touches-10/article31156691.ece. Accessed on 13-02-2020.
5. I thank Dr. Saumitra Basu for this observation.
6. https://www.youtube.com/watch?v=8sdJAXIQ9T4. Accessed on 06-05-2021.

References

Agrawal, S. (2012). Effect of living arrangement on the health status of elderly in India: Findings from a national cross sectional survey. *Asian Population Studies*, 8(1), 87–101.

Bhardwaj, R. (2010). Medical pluralism in India: The interface of complementary and alternative therapies with allopathy." In Arima Mishra (Ed.), *Health, Illness and Medicine: Ethnographic Readings* (pp. 75–101). Hyderabad, Orient Blackswan.

Bhatia, S. P. S., Swami, H. M., Thakur, J. S., & Bhatia, V. (2007). A study of health problems and loneliness among the elderly in Chandigarh. *Indian Journal of Community Medicine*, 32(4), 255–258.

DelFattore, J. (2020, April 11). Singles say they're better prepared to self-quarantine, but many fear getting short changed in medical treatment. *The Washington Post*. https://www.washingtonpost.com/health/singles-say-theyre-better-prepared-to-self-quarantine-but-many-fear-getting-shortchanged-in-medical-treatment/2020/04/10/0f0b972c-7368-11ea-87da-77a8136c1a6d_story.html

DePaulo, B. (2006). *Singled Out: How Singles Are Stereotyped, Stigmatized, and Ignored, and Still Live Happily Ever After*. New York, St Martin's Griffin.

DePaulo, B. (2009, December 7). Men and Women who have always been single are doing fine. *Psychology Today*. https://www.psychologytoday.com/us/blog/living-single/200912/men-and-women-who-have-always-been-single-are-doing-fine

DePaulo, B. (2011a, January 19). If you are single, will you grow old alone? 6 nation study. *Psychology Today*. https://www.psychologytoday.com/us/blog/living-single/201101/if-you-are-single-will-you-grow-old-alone-6-nation-study

DePaulo, B. (2011b, May 16). Can you be your own source of comfort and security? A bold question about attachment. *Psychology Today*. https://www.psychologytoday.com/ca/blog/living-single/201105/can-you-be-your-own-source-comfort-and-security-bold-question-about

DePaulo, B. (2020a, May 22). Single in a pandemic: Not the same old stories. *Medium*. https://belladepaulo.medium.com/single-in-a-pandemic-not-the-same-old-stories-8bbf0bafcc02

DePaulo, B. (2020b, April 21). Who's safe? Living alone may be better than youth or wealth. *Psychology Today*. https://www.psychologytoday.com/us/blog/living-single/202004/who-s-safe-living-alone-may-be-better-youth-or-wealth

DePaulo, B. (2020c, October 1). Women who stayed single, no kids, in their 70s: How are they doing? *Medium*. https://belladepaulo.medium.com/women-who-stayed-single-no-kids-in-their-70s-how-are-they-doing-3d8052bd502a

DePaulo, B. (2020d). Old and alone: Even professionals do not understand this. *Psychology Today*. https://www.psychologytoday.com/us/blog/living-single/202011/old-and-alone-even-professionals-do-not-understand?fbclid=IwAR39wHEameR6gIvyqlJm8Fzj_SRp6XX8IlmV5cpTyricck21XF3JwcrkYC4

DePaulo, B. (2021, March 13). Covid singles are supposedly lonely and miserable. But some of us are thriving instead. *NBC News*. https://www.nbcnews.com/think/opinion/covid-singles-are-supposedly-lonely-miserable-some-us-are-thriving-ncna1261021

Dixit, M., & Chavan, D. (2020). Gendering the Covid-19 pandemic: Women locked and down. *Economic and Political Weekly*, LV(17), 13–17.

Fornet-Betancourt, R., Helmut, B., Alfredo, G. M., Gauthier j. d. (1984). The ethic of care for the self as a practice of freedom: An interview with Michel Foucault. *Philosophy & Social Criticism*, 12(2–3), 112–131. https://doi.org/10.1177/019145378701200202

Gangopadhyay, J. (2020). Examining the lived experiences of ageing among older adults living alone in India. In M. K. Shankardass (Ed). *Ageing Issues and Responses* (pp. 207–219). Singapore, Springer.

Gangopadhyay, J. (2021). Ageing and self-care in India: Examining the role of the market in determining a new course of growing old among middle class older adults in urban India. *Ageing International*. Published online on August 11, 2021. https://doi.org/10.1007/s12126-021-09461-7.

Gangopadhyay, J., Bapna, N., Jain, A. et al. (2018). Understanding the everyday processes of aging in urban Delhi. *Ageing International*, 45, 255–27. https://doi.org/10.1007/s12126-018-9329-7

Ghoshal, R. (2020). Twin public health emergencies: Covid-19 and domestic violence. *Indian Journal of Medical Ethics*. Published online on May 7, 2020. https://doi.org/10.20529/IJME.2020.056.

Kislev, E. (2019). *Happy Singlehood: The Rising Acceptance and Celebration of Solo Living*. California, University of California Press.

Klinenberg, E. (2012). *Going Solo: The Extraordinary Rise and Surprising Appeal of Living Alone*. New York, Penguin Press.

Lahad, K. (2017). *A Table for One: A Critical Reading of Singlehood, Gender and Time*. Manchester, Manchester University Press.

Leite, H., Hodgkinson, I., & Gruber T. (2020). New development: "Healing at a distance"—telemedicine and COVID-19. *Public Money & Management*. https://doi.org/10.1080/09540962.2020.1748855.

Lorde, A. (1988, 2017). *A Burst of Light and Other Essays*. New York, Ixiga Press.

Mishra, Arima. (2010). Deconstructing "self-care" in biomedical and public health discourses. In Arima Mishra (Ed), *Health, Illness and Medicine: Ethnographic Readings* (pp 75–109). Hyderabad, Orient Blackswan.

Samanta, T., Feinian, C., & Vanneman, R. (2015). Living arrangements and health of older adults in India. *The Journals of Gerontology Series B: Psychological Sciences and Social Sciences*, 70(6), 937–947.

WHO. (2019). *Consolidated Guideline on Self-care Interventions for Health: Sexual and Reproductive Health and Rights*. Geneva, World Health Organization.

9 Loss of the Only Child and Caregiving for Grandchildren among Older Adults—A Qualitative Case Study in China

Ji Wu and Xue Qiu

Introduction

Loss-of-only-child families are families that have lost their only child for various reasons, such as an illness or accidental injury. In the context of the lives of Chinese people, centered on children, the heavy trauma of losing the only child has plunged millions of people into grief and despair, having to face challenges in accepting the loss. Their world gradually goes out of control, making it difficult to free themselves from depression, frustration, decadence, fear, and other psychological disabilities (Mu, 2016). China's traditional social culture, represented well in statements such as "raise children to provide in old age" and "no offspring is the gravest offence against filial piety," along with the social security lag, often make the older adults who have lost their only child choose self-isolation. They cut themselves off from social ties and the community, making it difficult to reintegrate into society and eventually affecting the rebuilding of their social life (Fang 2018). Due to China's one-child reproductive culture, the problems of one-child families and those that have lost their only child will persist for a long time (Xu & Zhang, 2020). Single children might leave behind children after their demise, and for financial reasons, spouses may choose to entrust them to the bereaving older adults to raise in their old age. In such cases, the grandchildren may provide the older adults with emotional and spiritual support (Zhao, 2020). To provide better care to the grandchildren, the adults need to readjust their lives in old age. They enter a complex, multistage process of adapting to the loss of their only child and being a caregiver. This study therefore attempts to describe the life and multistage adaptation process of the older adults who simultaneously grieve and become a caretaker of grandchildren from an insider's perspective using grounded theory.

Literature Review

The perspectives of domestic and international studies on the loss of an only child include both issue-based and person-based perspectives, while the research paradigm includes grand and personal narratives. In these two dimensions, valuable results have been obtained on the dilemmas (Xiao & Yang, 2014), needs (Dai & Li, 2020), and countermeasures (Chen et al., 2020) for older adults who have lost their only child; social assistance and security (Wang & Fang, 2019); social support reconstruction (Wang et al., 2021a); and mental health (Wang et al., 2021b). Research based on personal narratives makes it easy to break away from the label of "older adults who have lost their only child" constructed by the mainstream discourse and explore their life and inner experiences. The academic community explores the narratives of personal experiences, which can be divided into two stages: causal research that explores the internal logic from the perspective of subjects or relationships and processual research that explores the interpretation of paths from the perspective of individuals or communities.

In 2012, scholars who focused on the causality of internal logic tended to focus on "loss-of-only-child families" from a strategic perspective of social construction and help them reconstruct their families (Yang & Wang, 2012). From the perspective of public policy, Cheng explored the scope of the problem in the eyes of the public in 2013 (Cheng, 2013). By constructing a spatio-temporal analysis of the family, Guo examined the complex impact of the "absent presence" of the deceased child on the temporal arrangement and spatial production strategies in the lives of the remaining family in 2014 (Guo & Jiang, 2014). In the same year, in the context of social governance, Zhang analyzed the dilemma of organizational participation by parents who had lost their only child, its internal logic, and ways to solve it (Zhang & Liu, 2014).

Scholars who have focused on processual research have conducted qualitative and comparative studies of four self-organizations for older adults who have lost their only child. In 2018, Fang proposed that the "spiritual community" function of self-organizations for such older adults should be strengthened through government leadership, joint participation by various social actors, and self-improvement of self-organizations to promote their smooth resocialization (Fang, 2018). Based on the conceptual tools of "structural edge" and "psychological edge," in 2020, Xu constructed a model of social marginalization of individuals based on the strong self-awareness of Chinese older adults who have lost their only child and have gradually closed their psychological edges due to drastic changes in their life. A dual-path model of individual social marginalization is thus constructed (Xu & Zhang, 2020).

Both causal and processual studies have interpreted the life situations of such older adults in an experiential way. Although they have not addressed the topic of raising the third generation, the research perspective and paradigm are of referential significance to this study. Based on the existing studies, two questions need to be considered: What are the stages of life adaptation that older adults who have lost their only child go through from the moment of loss to the moment they are interviewed? What positive actions do the older adults take in the process of life adaptation?

Research Process

Data Sources and Collection

Twelve older adults from four cities in H Province, China, were selected as the respondents for the study (Table 9.1). All these individuals had lost their only child more than seven years ago and were raising their grandchildren with their

Table 9.1 Basic Information of the Interviewed Older Adults

Number	Age	Sex	Years since the loss	Community type	Grandchildren/age	Marital status	Health status	Source of income
D1	65	Female	10	Urban	Granddaughter/13	Widowed	Thyroid, uterine tumor	Labor insurance, special grant, granddaughter's subsistence allowance
D2	58	Female	7	Rural	Granddaughter/12	Married	Prolapsed disk	Special grant, old partner working
D3	55	Female	9	Rural	Grandson/10	Married	Allergenic	Social security, special grant, partner working, grandson's subsistence allowance
D4	66	Female	8	Urban	Grandson/10	Widowed	Unable to move freely	Pensions, special grant
D5	68	Female	12	Urban	Granddaughter/17	Married	Gastritis, femoral necrosis	Special grant, partner working
D6	72	Male	10	Urban	Grandson/15	Married	Unable to move freely	Special grant, odd jobs
D7	58	Female	9	Rural	Granddaughter/9	Married	Stomach trouble	Special grant, odd jobs
D8	64	Male	10	Urban	Granddaughter/13	Married	Physically weak	Special grant, odd jobs
D9	65	Female	9	Rural	Grandson/16	Widowed	Psychasthenia	Special grant
D10	55	Female	10	Urban	Granddaughter/12	Married		Special grant, social security, partner working
D11	62	Female	10	Rural	Grandson/10	Married		Special grant, partner working
D12	56	Female	8	Urban	Granddaughter/9	Widowed		Special grant, pensions, odd jobs

spouse or alone. Each older adult was interviewed for about 60 minutes and was asked about life in old age after the loss and the changes that were needed to care for the grandchildren. All interviews were transcribed verbatim at the end of the interview, totaling over 200,000 words.

Three rounds of interviews were conducted. The first was with seven older adults, which resulted in a preliminary theoretical framework. In the second round, three older adults were interviewed, and the subcategories of "couples forming caregiving alliances," "beginning to focus on oneself," "loss-of-only-child identity in the cultural dimension," and "new ways of living as a caregiver" were added to complete the framework. In the third round, two older adults were interviewed, and no new categories emerged.

Data Analysis

This study adopted a grounded theory approach to analyze the interview transcript data of the older adults and conducted an exploratory study on the process of resilience in the adults with the inter-constructed identities of losing their only child and being a caregiver through open, spindle, and selective coding. Grounded theory provides a clear set of research methods and procedures, and through the collection and analysis of data from interviews and data in the local context, one can use the original theoretical framework for localized innovation and construct a discourse system based on the national context (Niu, 2010).

The open coding process was used to label and define phenomena in the information on the older adults and extract concepts and categories. This yielded 168 concepts and 98 initial categories, with 12 deeper subcategories derived by generalizing the initial categories. Spindle coding is a cluster analysis of the categories formed by open coding that establishes associations between the different categories to form a larger class of genera (Radford, 2008). This process thus clustered the 12 subcategories formed by open coding into three main categories (Table 9.2).

Table 9.2 Spindle Code Scoping

Main category	Subcategory
The self-healing stage of the child's recent death	The medicalization and somatization of grief
	Action strategies for coping with the pain of loss
	Blood relationship support and intimacy indifference
	Entrusting their future to their grandchildren
Stages of raising grandchildren after the death of an only child	Constructing a grandchild raiser identity
	Emotional identity as older adults who have lost their only child
	Discourse strategies centered on raising grandchildren
	Separating their future from that of the grandchildren
Stages of constructing the identity of the caregiver of the elderly	Constructing caregiver identity
	The cultural dimension of the identity of losing one's only child
	The discourse strategy for caregiver construction
	New ways of living as a caregiver

Figure 9.1 Resilience: Three-stage caregiver identity construction among the older adults.

By analyzing the eight main categories of dilemmas, social support, the self-healing stage of the child's recent death, the stage of raising the oldest grandchild, the stage of new role construction, the intimate relationship caregiving alliance, social involution, and the identities of the older adults who had newly become a caregiver, as summarized in the spindle coding, a model of the social adaptation of these adults was constructed, as shown in Figure 9.1. Resilience is finding the facts, truth, and true meaning of oneself and the world (Guo, 2019). The process of social adaptation among these older adults to the loss-of-only-child identity and caregiver identity construction, that is, their dual identities, is neither a complete resurrection nor a transformative metamorphosis. However, it can be a different kind of epiphany and change or an unconscious and gradual growth.

Explanation of the Multistage Process of Social Adaptation

The Self-Healing Stage after the Child's Recent Death

The older adults who had just lost their child faced the grief, suffered mental trauma and physical health problems, and saw their cognition and behavior change dramatically. Amid this extreme grief, they had begun helping themselves in various ways; raising their grandchildren was both stressful and healing at this stage.

Medicalization and Somatization of Grief

D7: "At that time, I did not even know that I was depressed for a long time. In fact, I was very optimistic and courageous before I visited the doctor twice in H city on my own and was informed by the professor that this disease is not a mental illness and that I'm just excessively sad."

After their child's death, older adults may diagnose themselves with depression or believe that their spouse is mentally unbalanced. They consider their state of extreme sadness to be a state of illness.

D5: "I was not well. I was allergic to everything I ate. It was too hard. I had to cook separately for the grandchild. I don't even know how tired I was."

D9: "Earlier, we were both in good health. But after our child died, our health was not good. We had to go to the hospital for injections every now and then."

Somatization of grief occurred in the vast majority of the older adults who were interviewed, and their health deteriorated rapidly in the short term, with various physical illnesses or immune deficiencies.

Action Strategies for Coping with the Loss

In the face of such extreme grief, the older adults adopted various ways to cope with their pain.

D4: "At that time I just didn't know what to do. I used to go outside to walk around, regardless of the wind and rain. Her grandfather has been bedridden for years and had to be turned over every 2 hours. I sent my oldest grandson off to a nursery and went out for a walk, knowing that I'd be back in 2 hours to turn him over, feed him, and still walk after the whole thing. Anyway, I have to come back every 2 hours, no matter where I go."

Some interviewees thus chose to go out, escape their home environment, and take walks to relieve their emotions without forgetting their family responsibilities.

D10: "When I think about my son, I go to his grave and look at it. I can't stand it, and I cry at his grave to feel better. I cry every time I visit his grave, and the people who look after the graveyard know me well and look after me every time I go there, just in case I pass out."

Other seniors thus found a specific way to let out their emotions before returning to their lives and responsibilities.

Blood Relationship Support and Intimacy Indifference

Since the death of their child, the siblings of the older adult interviewees had been caring for their health and day-to-day lives, assisting them in dealing with the aftermath of their child's death and providing support in several ways. This companionship and care made the older adults feel supported and gave them the strength to keep going.

D10: "With the lawsuit to be filed over there, there was a family. He had an uncle and brother or someone who helped us with the lawsuit. We were already late by 10 days or so when we went back to the old house, back to the relatives, and they still helped us with the lawsuit."

D2: "While going downstairs, I sprained my foot at night. So I called my sister and her husband. There was no way out. I had to have the surgery. Her husband was at the hospital taking care of me, and my sister was at home taking care of my grandchild. How embarrassing it was. My brother-in-law took care of me for 10 days. Without them, I wouldn't have made it this far."

In contrast to this, the vast majority of the interviewees felt that there a lack of intimacy and too much indifference immediately after their child's death.

D5: "When my child had just died, my husband was drinking and smoking all the time, and I didn't want to talk, and we didn't have much to say. At that time, it felt like the sky was falling, all understandable. What is there to say?"

The couples coped with their own grief, each partner suffering in their own way, and neither had the energy to support the other.

Entrusting Their Future to Their Grandchildren

After the loss of their child, quite a few of the elderly felt like following their children; however, the grandchildren left in their care gave them a sense of responsibility. For some of the interviewees, their grandchildren reminded them of their children.

D10: "My grandson looks like my son, and when I see him, I feel that my son is still alive and that there is still hope in life."

The concept of "raising children to provide in old age" is deeply rooted in China, as children are the center of the family, subject to the lifelong efforts and hopes of their parents. The sudden pain of losing a child can plunge parents into endless grief for a long time, with some even feeling suicidal (Xie, 2016). Before the death of their only child, they entrusted the older adults to raise their children, and raising grandchildren became the motivation for the older adults to live.

D12: "I tried to sell the house to cure my son. He knew it wouldn't work and told me not to sell it. He asked me to keep the house to take good care of the grandchild."

D8: "My son left me my grandchild. I have to raise him/her and fulfil the my son's responsibility."

With respect to the future, the older adults expected their grandchild to grow up quickly and achieve something in return. They transferred their expectations from their deceased child to their grandchild, as if to give them hope in life again.

D1: "My life is so hard. I thought before that when my child got married and had my grandchild, my difficult times would cease, and I would be able to enjoy my blessings, but then my child passed away. I keep telling my grandchild now, 'you have to study hard, get in to a good university, and earn a high income in the future so that grandma can enjoy her blessings.'"

The interviewees thus entrusted their future to their grandchildren, believing that they could repay them when they grow up and achieve something and hoping to be happy along with them.

Raising Grandchildren after the Death of an Only Child

Constructing a Grandchild Raiser Identity

New experience of entering the loss-of-only-child group for the first time. Several interviewees reported that, in the immediate aftermath of their child's death, they muddled through their days taking care of their grandchildren and kept thinking about their child, trying to seek support from the lost-child group.

Older people who had just entered the lost-child group had new people to interact with and had many new positive experiences but gradually lost their initial enthusiasm when they got to know the group and realized that it was not a healing space.

D4: "When I first entered the group, I knew that I was not the only one who had lost my child, and I felt good when I read the messages posted in the group. After a while, I realized that it was nothing special, and I couldn't be happy anymore."

As their grandchildren started to look for their father and mother, the grandparents realized that they were growing up and needed better companionship and education. They felt that they were not doing enough. Gradually, they took a break from their grief and used more energy to raise their grandchildren.

D7: "Later, I understood it all at once. It was my grandson looking out for his father all day long. I told him that his dad was on a business trip, but the child was not happy and went to school. I told myself that I need to change for the child, and I gradually got better as the child started schooling."

Determining that raising grandchildren is one's own business. From this stage onward, all the interviewees saw raising their grandchildren as their responsibility. Some realized this the moment their child died, while others realized this only sometime after.

D3: "She [my daughter-in-law] gave me a year of reprieve [to adjust to the pain of loss] before I had to raise the grandchild."

Interviewer: "Doesn't she raise the child?"

D3: "In today's society, how many young children can think about the older adults? It is certainly me who has to raise the child. If the son dies, the daughter-in-law almost never comes back to see the child. She will pretend that she never gave birth, never raised the child; [there are] too many similar cases. We also come across this kind of belief that the old woman has to raise grandchild."

While taking their responsibilities to the next level, the older adults provided extensive care and began to pay attention to every aspect of their grandchildren's growth.

D1: "[Before picking up my grandchild] we packed up my grandchild's room in advance and prepared the items he needs to use."

D9: "He's only 1.6 m tall, and everyone his age has grown taller than him. When we go shopping with him, he does ask for anything. He's timid (sigh)."

Some of the older adults made adequate material preparations within their ability before picking up their grandchildren. Others expressed their concerns about their grandchildren's growth, from their health to their personalities; these concerns stemmed from their attention to the details of their grandchildren's growth.

Emotional Identity as Older Adults Who Have Lost Their Only Child

After accepting their responsibility of raising their grandchildren, the interviewees had tried to immediately cope with the death of their child and took the lead in breaking through emotionally to accept their loss-of-only-child identity. The first step in the gradual emotional acceptance was to go out and participate in activities for such people, confronting loss with a new mood in the lost-child community.

D3: "Going to the activities, I realized that I am not the only person who has lost their only child, and I felt better with these people around me." The second step was to slowly accept being part of the lost-child community and cope with people looking at them differently.

D4: "When I am with a lot of older people who have lost children, I don't mind what others say about me. But if I am on my own, I still care about what people think."

The third step was talking about other people's losses without talking about their own.

D7: "When people are together to talk about the loss of their only child, I can talk about some of my own opinions, but I still can't stand to talk about my loss."

Older people who have lost their only child are unable to accept the new identity immediately but gradually push themselves emotionally to face it.

Discourse Strategies Centered on Raising Grandchildren

At some point, the grandchildren discover that everyone else has parents except them and might start to look for them. The grandparents themselves might not have fully accepted their child's death and may not know how to respond to their grandchildren's needs, so they have to resort to deceptive discourse to appease their grandchildren and themselves.

D7: "When my grandson saw that other children were playing with their fathers, he came home and kept asking, 'Grandma, where is my father, and why doesn't he play with me?' and I said, 'Your father has gone to work.' My grandson said, 'Grandma, you're lying to me. Other fathers also work. Do I have no father?' Then he sat on the floor and cried (choking). He (grandson) just doesn't understand. I can't help it, and I can only continue to fool him. I said: 'Dad has gone to work abroad and went to the United States.' My grandson said: 'Is my father a superman and saving the world?' (Sobbing) 'Yes, Dad is saving the world, he can't come back.' I just can't tell him that his father is gone, he is too young, and I can't tell him that."

Reconstruction of intimate relationships. In response to their grandchildren's need for care and love, the elderly have to communicate and be strong as a couple to better care for their grandchildren.

D11: "My partner and I are not happy to talk about anything other than what groceries we buy in our daily lives as such, and the remaining communication is only about the grandchild."

The women in the interviewed families were usually responsible for taking care of their grandchildren, while the men were responsible for earning money.

D3: "It's so hard for us. We have no income and still have to raise my grandchild, so my partner has to go out and do renovations, and I'm at home to take my grandchild to and from school."

Such rebuilding of couples' relationships starts with the newfound focus on caring for the grandchildren. They gradually start communicating and dividing the care tasks to provide better care for their grandchildren and fulfill their responsibility.

Separating Their Future from That of the Grandchildren

Compared to the first stage, the older adults who have lost their only child have separated their own future from that of their grandchildren and do not give themselves too many expectations while expecting less from their grandchildren. They no longer expect their grandchildren to do well on exams or to repay them but simply feel that their grandchildren are capable of supporting themselves.

D6: "I don't expect him to get good grades now but just [go to] an average college. I don't have many years left to live, so I hope he can take care of himself when we're gone."

At this stage, the interviewees began to focus on the relatives and friends around them, and some of them reassumed the responsibility of caring for their parents as well.

D12: "At that time [referring to sometime after the death of the child], my mother in my old home was sick and could not stand up, so even though I felt bad, I had to go and take care of my mother."

D2: "At that time [when the child died], we really couldn't take care of my husband's father, so we sent him to a nursing home, and now we go to see him every other month. No matter what happens to ourselves, we still have to take care of our parents."

Although they were older adults themselves and had the responsibility of caring for their grandchildren, as time progressed, there was a growing concern for their lives beyond the loss of their only child.

Constructing the Identity of the Caregiver of the Elderly

Constructing Caregiver Identity

Expectations for the future—"Taking care of the grandchild even for one day counts."

At this stage, the expectation of the older adults is that their grandchildren will be healthy in the future, and they have no expectations with respect to their grandchildren's future achievements. Taking care of the grandchild for a single one also matters.

D10: "I don't know when I'll be gone. I'm trying to live one more day to raise my grandchild. I won't know when I'm gone, and he will suffer."

Missing children and caring for grandchildren co-exist. The older adults no longer dwell on whether they miss their child; they have come to accept that the feeling of loss will always be there, and they are convinced that this will not interfere with their ability to care for their grandchildren. They understand that they can simultaneously miss their children and raise their grandchildren.

D7: "It's impossible for this pain to go away, it only slows down. Why? It is like swiping TikTok videos and seeing the scene in question and remembering it. It is impossible to say you do not miss them, and after all these years, you can slowly understand on your own. The children also miss their parents, and the grandchildren have to be taken care of."

The older adults made their grandchildren the center of their lives. They spend their days working around their grandchildren, with the vast majority of the family's expenses being spent on them. They choose to rely on their families when they are sick, afraid of spending money and not having time to go to the doctor.

D3: "I'm busy every day, but I did not do anything other than picking up the grandchild to and from school, cleaning up the house, completing the tasks set by the teacher. When I'm sick, I have no time to see a doctor, other than [when it's serious I am] forced to go to the hospital. The grandchild is too busy studying, busier on the weekend than the usual days."

In addition to overcoming difficulties on their own, they also take formal and informal social support. The lack of guardianship is a difficult legal dilemma for the older adults to overcome, and gaining guardianship is subject to cumbersome legal procedures (Liu, 2017).

D4: "His (grandson) household registration is not on my side of the family, and he can't enjoy many benefits here. I went to the community secretary and said: 'You see, there are only two people in my family. I'm not well and have to take care of my grandson, so I can't go anywhere. Please help me to solve the custody matter.' The secretary knew all of us who had lost our only child, so he/she helped us when we were in a really difficult situation. I have filed papers with the court to file a lawsuit on his side of the family. No matter how difficult it is, I have to take custody."

Some of the interviewed elderly people who had lost their only child took the initiative to seek support from the community to overcome their hardships using their special identity, making sure they got the custody of their grandchildren.

The Cultural Dimension of the Identity of Losing One's Only Child

At the caregiver stage, the elderly reach a deeper loss-of-only-child identity in the cultural dimension. Some of the interviewees had already accepted the fact that their families had no offspring, that their "bloodline" was broken, and that there would be no one to take care of them or visit their graves.

D3: "After my son died, I was trying to make a living. I ran out of tricks, and I knew that there was someone in the neighboring province that could not pay social security, but I paid for my old partner."

D1: "After my son died, I scattered his ashes in the river. My aged partner's ashes were also scattered in the river after she died, so I go to the riverside when I miss them."

By accepting the traditional cultural loss, they have fully recognized their identity as older adults who have lost their only child.

D5: "He has no father, no mother, no uncle, no aunt. If I don't take care of him, how can he live? He will not survive. Everyone says that I took good care of him, and he would not have grown up so well without me. Sometimes I think it is good to have this grandson as my company, and I'm getting back the feeling of being a mother little by little."

In this stage, the older people who had lost their only child saw themselves as the sole caregivers of their grandchildren, and the affirmation of their caregiving behaviors by people outside the family allowed them to further recognize their status as caregivers.

The Discourse Strategy for Caregiver Construction

The discursive strategy of deception. The grandchildren grow up, go to school, and increasingly pester their grandparents about their parents. The grandparents know that their grandchildren already have some knowledge of the truth and that they cannot continue to deceive them by concealing the truth. At this stage, the older adults fully accept the loss-of-only child identity. They open up to their grandchildren and discuss the death of their parents.

D4: "I said that 'Your dad actually just left the world.' The kid had ideas and said to me, 'Why did he die? Can't you bring Dad back to life? How come you can't bring him back to life?' (crying)."

Action strategies to focus on the personal growth of grandchildren. First, the older adults focus on their grandchildren's learning and try to improve their grades, including paying for remedial classes, teaching themselves, seeking the care of teachers, and using smartphones.

D9: "Everyone studied ahead over the holidays, and my grandchild was sick and didn't finish. The teacher started the class too fast, and he did not keep up. I approached the teacher to explain this situation of being sick and asked the teacher to help tutor after class as well. I ask their classmates to use WeChat to teach me, and I learned and then taught him, and just kept up little by little."

D10: "Now all tasks have to be completed on the phone. I just learned to use WeChat to complete the check-in study in the circle of friends so that it can motivate him to study."

In addition to their achievements, the older adults were also concerned about the growth of their grandchildren, especially the changes during adolescence. At this stage, they are particularly concerned about the children's relationship with their peers and whether they have friends of the same age. However, if their grandchildren are unwilling to communicate with them, they actively seek help from loss-of-a-child organizations to find ways to respond to their grandchildren's rebellious behavior in adolescence.

D5: "I don't even dare to communicate with him with an attitude. I'm afraid that he is sensitive and will think more. When he reached puberty, he was rebellious, and I did not know how to deal with it, so I asked HD Public Welfare [a social welfare organization for the loss of an only child] to help. They found us a counseling psychologist, and the child was not as rebellious as before. I feel that it may be related to the age; he'll behave well after growing up."

Intimate relationship care alliance. As the period of caring for their grandchildren grew longer, the couple became comfortable with the division of labor in caring for their grandchildren.

D3: "He doesn't just sit around waiting for dinner when he comes home now. He also helps me with the housework."

D11: "My husband and I, one coaxes, the other coerces in front of my grandchild, who has also become obedient."

Couples developed a tacit understanding and increased intimacy when caring for their grandchildren.

D1: "Before I didn't eat or drink or sleep by myself, but later on, my grandchild had to eat, and so I had to eat and sleep on time."

D6: "The house is small, and I am afraid that smoking and drinking will affect my grandchild, so I have reduced the frequency."

The couples reconstruct their relationship to care for their grandchildren, forming an intimate care alliance. This alliance manifests itself in the changes in the couple's lifestyle revolving around caring for their grandchildren. Older people who have lost their only child adjust their emotions and behaviors and even change their bad habits, forcing themselves to return to a normal life in order to be able to make their grandchildren's lives more regular.

New Ways of Living as a Caregiver

Beginning to focus on their own life. The older people who had lost their only child realized that sadness could not help them, and they began to focus on themselves while thinking about their children. Some of the interviewees said that they would find their own ways to have fun and enrich their lives in their free time.

D3: "I don't remember the age of my son when he died. I even forget what zodiac sign he was because I can't have emotions. I have them for nothing. I have to figure out how to get over them on my own."

D9: "I sometimes get into trouble with my grandchild, so I go out by myself and have some fun, talk to other parents, or else I just swipe TikTok videos and watch live streams."

Breaking through social involution. In the second stage, the elderly focus on caring for their grandchildren and are less willing to communicate externally.

The interviewees had stopped maintaining relationships outside the family, and their willingness to communicate had declined. Apart from spouses, parents, and siblings, their willingness to communicate with people outside the family decreased, and some of the older adults were no longer active within the loss-of-only-child group.

D3: "It's like I disconnected from the outside world on my own. The world outside [the home] seems to be irrelevant to me."

D4: "When I talk to people, I often don't make a sound. I often forget what I'm talking, and I don't talk in the loss-of-only-child group."

However, in the third stage, some of the elderly people interviewed said that they were afraid that there would be no one to take care of their grandchildren after their death. Therefore, to gain more social support and for the growth of their grandchildren, they took the initiative to break through their social circle of only siblings, former classmates, colleagues, and the lost-child group and actively started building interpersonal relationships.

D3: "I'm almost 70, with only a few more years to live. For all the activities I can attend, no matter how far, I take my granddaughter to attend. I add everyone I know on WeChat, and I give them all likes in the circle of friends. I really have no moves. I have to pave the way for my granddaughter. Otherwise, what should she do when I'm gone?"

They also focus on the support they can get from their grandchildren's school and foster the relationship between the teachers and their grandchildren. Further, they use the activities of the loss-of-only-child community to push their grandchildren in front of the media and increase media publicity for their grandchildren.

D1: "When the teacher gave free tutoring, I went to the school to put up a banner, in front of the principal and the teachers, I asked the teacher to recognize my grandchild as his/her goddaughter."

D1: "I would take my granddaughter to events for the lost, and people didn't know my name. They just knew I was my granddaughter's grandmother."

When asked they minded about the media publicity for their grandchild,

D1: "No, I don't mind; the publicity and coverage through the media are to expose her to society."

After these older adults recognize that they are the sole caregiver of their grandchild, they are no longer painfully disciplined but adapt to the current life and change their lifestyles.

Conclusion and Discussion

In the self-healing stage after the recent death of an only child, the eldercare deep in pain, the couple is indifferent, and each adopts their own action strategies to cope with the grieving process. However, they realize that they have to take responsibility for raising their grandchildren, sacrifice their future for them, and thus heal. While raising the grandchildren, sometime after the demise of the child, the elderly interviewed in this study decided that raising their grandchildren was their own responsibility. They only identified with the status of the loss of an only child at an emotional level, convincing their grandchildren that their parents are still alive to appease them and themselves. To adapt to the new reality, the couple rebuilt their intimate relationship and also cut off their own future from that of their grandchildren. In the stage of the elderly constructing the caregiver identity of the lost, taking care of their grandchildren even for one day counted. They discovered how to miss their child and yet care for their grandchild. They also accepted the loss-of-only-child identity at the cultural level. They told their grandchildren the truth about the death of their parents, couples formed a caregiving alliance, and they began to focus on their own lives, breaking through their original social circle and actively constructing interpersonal relationships.

After three stages of adaptation, the elderly generally accept the loss-of-only-child identity in the cultural dimension, construct a complex multiple identity as a caregiver for their grandchildren, rediscover their position in the world, and change their way of life. Simply put, these elderly have a deep and recurring awareness of the essential nature and functional role of their lives—that is, they are caregivers as well as elderly who have lost their child. They miss their children, take care of their grandchildren and family, and care for themselves at the same time. They rediscover the dignity and value of their lives; are willing to contribute to the improvement and enhancement of their grandchildren, spouses, families, and the world they live in; and find the extraordinary in the ordinary tasks of their daily lives.

Thus far, scholarly research on the care of grandchildren by the elderly who have lost their only child has focused more on the identity of the elderly as the caregiver (Rong et al., 2020), considering them as placing their spirituality and future on their grandchildren and self-imposing the legal responsibility to care for their grandchildren (Chen, 2019). This study found that caregiving is the intermediate stage of the social adaptation process of the elderly, and they still do not identify with the loss of their only child in the cultural dimension. Many of them begin to focus on themselves and start a new life in the third stage. Based on the idea of restoration, the elderly grow and develop in the process of accepting their loss and reach a consensus with identifying with their loss, taking care of their grandchildren, caring for their spouse and family, and focusing on themselves. They are gradually aware of their own independent existence and discover that they have a variety of functions and potentials, such as communication, care, and concern. They attempt to utilize their personal strengths and allow themselves to enjoy a less painful and somewhat better life. The three-stage process of interaction with the environment is a gradual return to the self and finding oneself, as the elderly find their proper place in the world, focus on themselves and their relationships with others around them, and care for themselves again.

References

Chen, L., Song, Y., & You, Y. (2020). Life restoration and future care preparation among older parents in Shanghai who have lost their only adult child. *Journal of Applied Gerontology, 39*(10), 1097–1105.

Chen, M. (2019). Research on the Problems and Countermeasures of Intergenerational Education in Urban Families Who Lost Their Alone. *Beijing Architecture University.*

Cheng, Z. (2013). The problems of only-child lose in public policy: An analysis based upon public cognition and subjective perception (in Chinese). *Population & Development, 19*(4), 65–72.

Dai, W., & Li, Q. (2020). The demands for old-age support of the "only-child-died" rural families based on different living arrangements (in Chinese). *Population & Development, 26*(1), 85–96.

Fang, S. (2018). Communities of mind and double involution: Research on the construction of self-organization of the old people who lost their alone (in Chinese). *Population and Society*, 34(3), 90–100.

Fang, S. (2018). Communities of mind and double involution: Research on the construction of self-organization of the old people who lost their alone (in Chinese). *Theory Monthly*, 5, 174–181.

Guo, J. (2019). Dominant point of view-social work theory and practice (in Chinese). *Social Science Literature Press*, 1, 1–44+211.

Guo, M., & Jiang, N. (2014). Absent presence: Family spatial and temporal analysis on the living conditions of the bereaved parents who lost their only child and the relationship transformation (in Chinese). *Northwest Population*, 35(6), 71–76+82.

Liu, X. M. (2017). Construction and policy choice of the spiritual consolation and care system for families who lost only one in cities (in Chinese). *Gansu Social Sciences*, 101–105.

Mu, G. (2016). On the national responsibilities and civil rights of the people who lost alone (in Chinese). *Dongyue Essays*, 37(8), 5–9.

Niu, J. (2010). Grounded theory and its application in journalism and communication. *Southeast Communication*, 4, 14–16.

Radford, M. L. (2008). Constructing grounded theory: A practical guide through qualitative analysis. By Kathy Charmaz. London: Sage Publications. *Library & Information Science Research*, 30(2), 158–159.

Rong, C., Caiming, X., Xiaolan, W., Duo, W., Weiwei, S., Yan, M., & Jinmin, L. (2020). The status quo and optimization strategies of the social support system for parents who have lost only one. *Population and Development*, 26(2), 108–115.

Wang, J., & Fang, W. (2019). A study on the social assistance to only-child-lost families (in Chinese). *Journal of Peking University (Philosophy and Social Sciences Edition)*, 56(5), 77–86.

Wang, C., Lin, S., Ma, Y., & Wang, Y. (2021a). The mediating effect of social support on the relationship between perceived stress and quality of life among shidu parents in China. *Health and Quality of Life Outcomes*, 19(1), 1–10.

Wang, Q., Zhang, S., Wang, Y., Jing, Z., Zhou, Y., Qi, K., ... Zhou, C. (2021b). Prevalence and risk factors of posttraumatic stress disorder among Chinese shidu parents: A systemic review and meta-analysis. *Journal of Affective Disorders*, 282, 1180–1186.

Xiao, Y., & Yang, G. (2014). The endowment dilemma analysis and the corresponding measures of elderly people who lost their only child under the strengths perspective (in Chinese). *Population & Development*, 20(1), 107–112.

Xie, Y. C. (2016). Special guardian system: The fundamental way out to solve the difficulty of signing for parents who lost their only one (in Chinese). *Shandong Social Sciences*, 6, 163–169.

Xu, X., & Zhang, N. (2020). "Psychological-structural" pathway of social marginalization—An empirical study on people who lost the only child in contemporary China (in Chinese). *Sociological Research*, 35(3), 145–168+245.

Yang, H., & Wang, W. (2012). The loss of only-children families and their reconstruction (in Chinese). *Research on Hot Issues*, 11, 21–26.

Zhang, C., & Liu, H. (2014). On organizational participation of only-child-died parents: Dilemma, inner logic and countermeasures-thinking based on social governance (in Chinese). *Journal of Central China Normal University (Humanities and Social Sciences Edition)*, 53(6), 31–39.

Zhao, X. (2020). Integrate the system to deal with the plight of the rural families bereft of their only child (in Chinese). *Zhongzhou Academic Journal*, 8, 73–79.

Section V
Eldercare Research in China and India

10 Does India Have Sufficient Data to Understand the Need for Eldercare?

Dona Ghosh

Introduction

Rapid gain in life expectancy and falling fertility rate have accelerated the share of the elderly (aged 60 years or above) to the total population of the world (WHO, 2015). However, such demographic transition has distinctive spread and divergent pathways across the globe. The problem of population aging was first manifested in the developed regions, for instance, the European and North American countries. It is expected to grow further by 75% in these areas in the coming 15 years. Although the phenomenon appeared later in the developing world, the Asian countries will soon be the most abundant resident of the world's total elderly population (He, Goodkind, & Kowal, 2016). Projection suggests that by 2050, Asia alone will have two-thirds (975.3 million) of the world's total elderly population, whereas it was only 341.4 million (or 55.3%) in 2015.

The average life expectancy in India has increased from 48.5 years (Rajan, Mishra, & Sarma, 1999) in 1971 to 67.9 years in 2010–2014 (NITI Ayog[1]). The additional years during old age have multiple influences on the individual and society, especially from the perspective of health. Old age is characterized by declining functional capacities that increase the risk of morbidities among elderly individuals. In India, elderly citizens suffer from the dual burden of diseases—communicable and non-communicable chronic ailments (Reddy, 1996).

Multiple illnesses and loss their functionality are common among seniors due to irregularity in treatment. The health situation becomes worse owing to inadequate support (Agrawal, 2012) and consecutively causes long-term disabilities in the late-life, if not controlled with appropriate treatment. It has been noticed that disability among the elderly is more common among the individuals, who, are positioned at a lower socioeconomic status (Kabir, 1992; Kabir et al., 2003), poorly educated (Beydoun & Popkin, 2005), economically dependent (Soneja et al., 1996), widow (Goldman, Korenman, & Weinstein, 1995), and females (Strawbridge et al., 1993; Verbrugge & Patrick, 1995).

Co-morbidity has a close association with functional disability (Soneja et al., 1996; Sengupta & Agree, 2002)—incidences of morbidity spur the risk of impairment (Strawbridge et al., 1993; Verbrugge & Patrick, 1995). In the developed countries, healthcare facilities are rooted in government policies

DOI: 10.4324/9781003254256-15

and extensive enough to cover almost all elderly individuals to provide medical facilities. This kind of health policy, undoubtedly, imposes an enormous economic burden on society (Haines, 1995), but has a direct impact on the mass's health-seeking behavior. It enables all elderly individuals to require medications and lessens the severity of chronic illnesses during old age. Therefore, the elders enjoy greater independence in maintaining daily living and need long-term care only for a short period.

In India, the government health care facilities are inadequate (Goel et al., 2003; Alam, 2007) and disproportionately distributed (Prakash, 1999; Srinivasan, Vaz, & Thomas, 2010), especially for meeting the changing demographics demand (Ingle & Nath, 2008). People often avoid government health institutes due to the extended waiting period, insufficient specialized personnel or scarcity of resources (Patil, Somasundaram, & Goyal, 2002). Therefore, a large share of the population relies on the private practices that snatch not only huge expenditure from their pocket (Pal, 2012) but also impose heavy strength on their meager earning/saving of old age, in the circumstances where, the individual-resource is, sometimes, insufficient even to meet the basic requirements (UNDP, 2000; Alam, 2007). It is noticed that the out of pocket health expenditure is continuously growing in India (Patil, Somasundaram, & Goyal, 2002), and elderly individuals are the worst victim of it—they frequently stop treatment to curtail the household costs. The majority of the elderly population live in poverty (Sen, 1994) and deprivations (Chambers, 1995). They most often cannot cope up with the continuously growing health care cost that intensifies their impoverishment (Brinda et al., 2012; Mohanty et al., 2014), and often deprive them of taking proper nutrition (Vedantam et al., 2010), and/or appropriate living condition (Prakash, 1999). Such deprivations further deteriorate the health conditions of the elderly in terms of both morbidity and disability (WHO, 2001).

From the above discussion, it is clear that population aging puts an enormous challenge on India's healthcare system. In the coming few decades, the increased size of the aged population will increase the demand for geriatric healthcare, and most of them will be immersed in financial distress. Therefore, we should urgently need a healthcare policy for older adults to avoid future deterioration of health conditions and the consecutive burden of long-term disability. However, we require an accurate estimation of healthcare demand and related data for any such healthcare policy. Detailed data from a wide, heterogeneous, and large population can give a clear impression about the desired objective.

Studies in geriatric health primarily engage small-scale primary survey for unit-level analysis or aggregate data with no detail of individual health characteristics of the elderly people. Till today, only a handful of organizations collect data on health and healthcare-seeking for India's aged. However, to understand the actual magnitude of the present and future healthcare need of the elderly population, we need a comprehensive database. This chapter aims to provide a systematic review of micro-level data sources that are available in the context of health problems of the aged in India. The contribution of this chapter is twofold.

It might be helpful for the researchers: a) to understand the strengths and weaknesses of the available micro-level data, particularly in the context of measuring health problems of the aged; and b) to address the gap areas in designing the future surveys.

Sources of Micro-Level Dataset on Health in India

Overview on Coverage

Study on Global Aging and Adult Health

Study on global aging and adult health (SAGE) is a part of the multi-country Longitudinal Study Programme, conducted by the World Health Organization (WHO). It has a special focus on the process of aging and the distribution of health problems and disabilities. In six countries, including India, SAGE has collected data through longitudinal study with a nationally representative sample of aging and older adults' health. The study's principal objective was to understand the health and well-being of the elderly (50 years and above) people of a nationally representative cohort in comparison with a smaller group of young individuals (18 to 49 years). The data were collected through face-to-face interviews in two rounds: Wave 0 (2002–2003); and Wave 1 (2007–2010). Wave 1 includes both follow-up and new respondents.

SAGE uses a probability sampling design and a multistage cluster sampling that involves five stages. Selected samples are representative both at the state level in the selected states and the sub-national level. It has captured the information on household (household characteristics, housing, household and family support, assets and household income, household expenditure) and individual (socio-demographic characteristics, work history, health state, anthropometrics, performance tests and biomarkers, risk factors, chronic conditions and health service coverage, health care utilization, social cohesion, subjective well-being and quality of life, caregiving) levels, on both aged and population.

SAGE has demarcated the population based on 2001 Census and adopted a stratified multistage cluster sample design for India. Instead of 28, it included 19 states in the sampling frame. Following "geographic location" and "level of development," only six states (Assam, Karnataka, Maharashtra, Rajasthan, Uttar Pradesh, and West Bengal) were selected. Each state was further divided into two residential divides: rural and urban. At the first stage, villages (for rural areas) and blocks (for urban areas) were selected from the states, using the probability proportional to the size of the population (following 2001 Census). The households were selected using systematic sampling. In total, the survey has constructed 12 strata (i.e. locality), where it interviewed 12198 individuals of 10424 households. To collect data, SAGE has used standardized instruments for five domains: (1) household questionnaire; (3) proxy questionnaire; (4) verbal autopsy questionnaire; and (5) appendices including showcards.

National Sample Survey

It is conducted by the National Sample Survey Office (NSSO), Government of India. To construct a national-level morbidity profile, NSSO has initiated a health survey in the seventh round (1953–1954). It later introduced a full-scale study in 1973–1974 (28th round) to find alternate health measures of morbidity. The health surveys later were extended to improvise social consumption (from 42nd round); and public distribution system, health services, educational services, and the aged's problems (from 52nd round). NSS conducts a nationwide health survey, which includes a separate section for the aged population from 52nd round (1995–1996). This section covers information on old age-related issues like morbidity; treatment-seeking behavior; health-related problems, perceived health status; financial independence, and health-related expenditure. NSS has measured mainly three types of the health status of the elderly population: observed health, perceived health, and physical mobility.

NSSO has adopted multistage stratified sampling. First Stage Units (FSU) of the surveys consist of census villages in rural areas (except Kerala[2]) and urban blocks in Urban Frame Survey (UFS). For large-sized FSUs, two hamlet-groups (hgs)/sub-blocks (sbs) were drawn from each sector. From each FSU, ten households were surveyed in both rural and urban areas. Households are identified as Ultimate Stage Units (USU).

At first, the investigator demarcates the exact boundaries of the sample FSU. After demarcation of boundaries, necessary hamlet-groups/sub-blocks are created. Each district is considered as a stratum. The district of a state/UT is divided into two strata: rural and urban stratum. If any town of the urban area of a district has more than one lakh population, it creates an additional stratum along with the residual urban area. Villages in the difficult areas of Nagaland and Andaman & Nicobar Islands also consist of the separate special stratum. From each stratum/sub-stratum, an optimum number of sample villages are selected by Probability Proportional to Size with Replacement (PPSWR). Finally, the village population in rural areas and the number of UFS Blocks households in urban sectors determine the sample size.

A list of selected FSUs is prepared. During list preparation, greater importance is given to the hamlet-groups/sub-blocks with the maximum percentage share of population and termed as hg/sb1. The remaining hamlet-groups/sub-blocks (hg/sb2) are selected using Simple Random Sampling (SRS). Once the list of FSUs/hamlet-groups/sub-blocks is prepared, it is stratified into three independent samples of households or Second Stage Strata (SSS): Survey on Health Care; Participation in Education; and Consumer Expenditure.

For the health survey, a list of households is prepared, where households from hg/sb1 are listed first, followed by the houses in hg/sb2. In an attempt to get a sufficient number, households are further divided into the following second stage strata: Stratum1 (households with at least one member hospitalized during last 365 days); Stratum2 (households having at least one child less than five years); Stratum3 (households with at least one member of age 60 years and above excluding those in Stratum1 and 2); Stratum4 (all remaining households). Ten households from each FSUs are selected to construct USUs.

Recent (60th and 71st) rounds of survey on health have used the population census of 2001 and 2011, respectively. 60th (71st) round has covered a total of 3,83,338 and 3,33,104 individuals from 73,868 and 65,932 households were surveyed in the 60th and 71st rounds, respectively. Among the total individuals, the elderly population consists of only 34,831 (in the 60th round) and 27,245 (in the 71st round) individuals.

Census[3]

A full-scale birth and death registration scheme, titled as Sample Registration System (SRS), was started by the Office of Registrar General of India in 1969–1970. SRS adopts a uni-stage stratified simple random sample without replacement except for the large villages. A baseline survey is conducted to map the essential sample areas and location of houses in the very beginning. After the selection of locations, sample units are identified. Information on sample households and women in the reproductive span and their pregnancy status is collected from the sample houses. Continuous enumeration involves both birth and death records, collected by the resident part-time enumerators and the full-time supervisors. At last, the two datasets are matched to eliminate the errors of duplication.

Census reveals data at ten years interval on the following aspects of individual and households: residential status, name, sex, date of birth, age, caste/class, educational/marital status, and relation to the head of household. Since the 1991 schedule of the census, additional questions on migration have been added. Considering the health related data, a separate section on the survival of children was added since the 2001 census schedule. However, the census does not capture any information on health, other than the age, of the senior citizens.

Indian Human Development Survey

Indian Human Development Survey (IHDS) has conducted two-panel national-level surveys in the year 2004–2005 and 2011–2012. In the first round, 215,754 individuals from 41,554 households across 1503 villages and 971 urban neighborhoods were surveyed. 2011–2012 survey has covered 204,565 individuals from 42,152 households, which includes 1,503 villages and 971 urban households. If we compare the total number of households or the individuals in both the surveys, it is observed that the number has reduced in the consecutive round. The reason is sample attrition re-interview of households of the previous survey to maintain the panel structure. For example, no information is available on 15,176 adult individuals 15 years and above and 8,423 dead persons (Barik, Desai, & Vanneman, 2018).

IHDS collects data on household characteristics and multiple individual-level information including medical issues, daily life activities, health, education, non-resident status, birth history, village characteristics, and crops. Two sections—"Education and Health Questionnaire" and "Medical Facility

Questionnaire" include extensive information on the individuals' health and the healthcare facilities in a locality. Medical Facility Questionnaire includes the organization level information like basic characteristics of the facility center, provision of services, employees' details and medical observation facilities. Although certain sections in the Education and Health Questionnaire targets children and fertile women, few sections include health information of all age groups. These sections cover the information on anthropometry, short-term and long-term morbidity and related costs of treatment, activities of daily living, and quality of care for out-patient services.

National Family Health Survey

The National Family Health Survey (NFHS) in India was initiated in the early 1990s under the stewardship of the Ministry of Health and Family Welfare (MOHFW), Government of India; and since then, it has conducted a series of surveys—1992–1993 (NFHS-1); 1998–1999 (NFHS-2); 2005–2006 (NFHS-3); 2014–2015 (NFHS-4) and 2019–2020 (NFHS-5). Intending to provide essential data on health and family welfare and emerging issues in the country, every consecutive round of NFHS keeps adjusting its components. NFHS-5 was supposed to be completed in 2019–2020. However, till today the data is available up to NFHS-4.

NFHS has adopted a uniform sample design representing nation, state/union territory, and district. It uses a two-stage stratified sampling technique, where each district is stratified into urban and rural areas. According to the village population and the percentage share of scheduled castes and scheduled tribes (SC/ST) population, the rural stratum is further sub-stratified into six almost equal substrata. For NFHS-4, 2011 census was used to select sampling frame for the Primary sampling Units (PSUs). PSUs consist of villages in rural areas and Census Enumeration Blocks (CEBs) in urban areas. PSUs with less than 40 households were assigned to the nearest PSU. In the second stage, a fixed number of 22 households are selected from each cluster using equal probability systematic selection.

NFHS rounds have covered almost all states and maintained a common set of health attributes (related to fertility, mortality, family planning, nutrition, health, and health care) across the rounds, aiming at making the dataset compatible for trend analysis. It uses various types of questionnaires like Household Questionnaire, Woman's Questionnaire (age 15–49), Man's Questionnaire (age 15–54) and Biomarker Questionnaire to target different population segments. The health of women was focused in the first two rounds of NFHS, where 89,777 and 89,199 ever-married women of age between 13 and 49 were surveyed in NFHS-1 and NFHS-2, respectively. From NFHS-2, information on children, men; and from NFHS-3 information on unmarried women was added to the database.

Longitudinal Aging Study in India

Employing computer-assisted personal interview (CAPI), Longitudinal Aging Study in India (LASI) covers around 1,500 individuals aged 45 and older from four states of India: Karnataka, Kerala, Punjab, and Rajasthan. The study's objectives were to understand scientific insights of population aging and required policy design, which is comparable at the international level. Therefore, the study followed a harmonized design, parallel to other international studies. It has three instruments: a household survey (includes household roster, housing and environment, consumption, household assets and debts, income, and health insurance); individual survey (includes demographics, family and social network; health, health care access and utilization, work and retirement, and individual assets); and community survey (local leaders, community demographics, infrastructure, and resources and health policy).

Discussion

Table 10.1 gives a brief description of the coverage of the datasets on health of the elderly population in the context of India. In this table, all the sources of datasets claim to have a nationally representative sample.

It is observed that the SAGE and LASI dataset are excellent datasets that provide comprehensive information about the health problems of the aged and the

Table 10.1 Description of Available Data Source on Health of the Elderly

Sources	Coverage of area	Coverage of time	Remarks
SAGE	Assam, Karnataka, Maharashtra, Rajasthan, Uttar Pradesh, and West Bengal	2002–2003 and 2007–2008	It had a special focus on the aged population but confined only to a few states of India
NSS Small surveys on Health and Morbidity	All India	1986–1987, 1995–1996, 2004, and 2014	It includes a separate column for the aged population from 52nd round
Census	All India	1981, 1991, 2001, and 2011	It includes individuals of all ages but does not cover important aspects of old age-related problems
IHDS	All states of India but not union territories (UTs). UTs are included only in the last round	2004–2005 and 2011–2012	The sample size is comparatively small to provide any national-level general conclusion especially, because of high attrition rates
NFHS	All India	1992–1993, 1998–1999, 2005–2006, and 2014–2015	Focuses on the health of women, children, and men of age below 49 years
LASSI	Karnataka, Kerala, Punjab, and Rajasthan	2010–2011	The data is not a national representative

Note: # Considered only full-scale surveys.

determinants of health. These data are also helpful for cross-national analysis. However, the surveys are confined to restricted sample sizes. Only a few states are selected, assuming they will represent the region of the country. However, it has ignored the heterogeneity in demographic characteristics and socioeconomic status of the elderly people across the states, even though they belong to the same region. For example, in both SAGE and LASI, Karnataka is taken as the representative of its neighboring states. However, as we consider the percentage share of elderly (60 years and above) population, Karnataka has only 9.2% compared to 12.3% in Tamil Nadu (Bharati & Singh, 2013). The percentage of education among 45 years or older respondents varies widely across the datasets. For example, the percentage share of the population who have more than ten years of education are 21.7 in LASI (2010–2011); 13.4% in NSS (2004–2005); 15.1% in IHDS (2004–2005); and 19.4% in SAGE (2007–2008) (Arokiasamy et al., 2012). It shows that only the LASI dataset has a close resemblance with SAGE data because the selected states in both the surveys have a higher literacy rate than the rest of the states and the overall literacy rate of the nation. Moreover, datasets like NSS, NFHS, Census, and IHDS include all states. Therefore, these studies have greater consistency with the national-level attributes. Except for IHDS, NSS, NFHS, and Census do not contain longitudinal aspects and cannot be compared across the rounds. Due to panel design, IHDS has advantages over NSS, NFHS and Census like "Application of better statistical models for controlling unobserved heterogeneity and better analysis of the role of exogenous shocks that occur between" the rounds.[4]

LASSI has conducted only one round, and that too is a pilot survey. The total number of respondents (45 years or older) is 1451, among which only 35.2% are 60 years or above. IHDS includes a wide range and comprehensive variables on health, but the focus is on 15–49 years of individuals (Li, Liu & BeLue, 2018). In IHDS-I, the percentage share of the elderly population (60 years and above) was only 8.28% (Desai et al., 2009). From the perspective of the inclusion of elderly individuals, the IHDS includes a tiny sample that might not be representative, even at the state level.

Table 10.2 compares the health-related variables of different rounds. Various domains and related variables are compared. It is observed that LASI has the most comprehensive measurement of health of the elderly in India. A part of the health variables mentioned in Table 10.2, LASI also includes details on angina, injury or fall, acute endemic diseases, immunizations for adults, such as the influenza vaccine, pneumococcal vaccine, hepatitis B vaccine, or typhoid vaccine, childhood health, family history, caregiving, food security, physical activities.

Conclusion

NFHS covers health variables of different domains, including bio-markers but neglects the elderly cohort. Although includes demographic characteristics of the entire population of the country, census data does not insight the details of health characteristics of the elderly population. IHDS, on the contrary, involves all social, demographic, economic, and health characteristics but suffers from

Table 10.2 Inclusion of Variables on Health of the Elderly

Domains	Health/healthcare information	SAGE	NSSO	IHDS	LASI
Health state descriptions	Overall health	In general, how would you rate your health today? Overall in the last 30 days, how much difficulty did you have with work or household activities?			Do you have any impairment or health problem that limits the kind or amount of paid work you can do? Do you have any form of physical or mental impairment? Which form of impairment do you have?
	Mobility	Overall in the last 30 days, how much difficulty did you have with moving around? Overall in the last 30 days, how much difficulty did you have in vigorous activities?	Status of physical mobility	(c) Does anyone in the household have any difficulty in walking 1 km?	
	Self-care	Overall in the last 30 days, how much difficulty did you have with self-care, such as bathing/washing or dressing yourself? In the last 30 days, how much difficulty did you have in taking care of and maintaining your general appearance (for example, grooming, looking neat and tidy)? In the last 30 days, how much difficulty did you have in staying by yourself for a few days (3 to 7 days)?			

(Continued)

Table 10.2 Inclusion of Variables on Health of the Elderly (*Continued*)

Domains	Health/ healthcare information	Variables/survey questions			
		SAGE	NSSO	IHDS	LASI
	Pain and discomfort	Overall in the last 30 days, how much of bodily aches or pains did you have? In the last 30 days, how much bodily discomfort did you have? In the last 30 days, how much difficulty did you have in your daily life because of your aches, pain, or discomfort?			Are you often troubled with pain? How frequently do you experience pain? Do you take any medication or therapy to get relief from the pain? Does the pain make it difficult for you to do your usual activities such as household chores or work? Have you had any of the following persistent or troublesome problems in the past two years? (pain or stiffness in joints; persistent swelling in feet or ankles; shortness of breath while awake; persistent dizziness or lightheadedness; back pain or problem; persistent headaches; severe fatigue or exhaustion; wheezing or whistling sound from the chest; cough with or without phlegm)

(*Continued*)

Table 10.2 Inclusion of Variables on Health of the Elderly (Continued)

Domains	Health/ healthcare information	Variables/survey questions			
		SAGE	NSSO	IHDS	LASI
	Cognition	Overall in the last 30 days, how much difficulty did you have with concentrating or remembering things?			Object naming
		In the last 30 days, how much difficulty did you have in learning a new task (for example, learning how to get to a new place, … etc.)?			Numeric ability
					Computation
					Literacy and executive function
					Drawing
	Interpersonal activities	Overall in the last 30 days, how much difficulty did you have with personal relationships or participation in the community?			
		In the last 30 days, how much difficulty did you have in dealing with conflicts and tensions with others?			
		In the last 30 days, how much difficulty did you have with making new friendships or maintaining current friendships?			

(Continued)

Table 10.2 Inclusion of Variables on Health of the Elderly (*Continued*)

Domains	Health/ healthcare information	Variables/survey questions			
		SAGE	NSSO	IHDS	LASI
Sleep and energy		Overall in the last 30 days, how much of a problem did you have with sleeping?			During the past one month, how often do you have trouble falling asleep? During the past one month, how often did you wake up during the night and had trouble getting back to sleep? During the past one month, how often did you wake up too early in the morning and were not being able to fall asleep again? During the past one month, how often did you feel unrested during the day, no matter how many hours of sleep you had? During the past 1month, how often did you take a nap during the day? In the past one month, have you taken any medications or used other treatments to help you sleep? Were these medications or other treatments recommended to you by a doctor?

(*Continued*)

Table 10.2 Inclusion of Variables on Health of the Elderly (*Continued*)

Domains	Health/ healthcare information	Variables/survey questions			
		SAGE	NSSO	IHDS	LASI
	Affect	Overall in the last 30 days, how much of a problem did you have with feeling sad, low, or depressed? In the last 30 days, how much of a problem did you have with worry or anxiety?			
	Vision	When was the last time you had your eyes examined by a medical professional?		Has a doctor ever diagnosed any member in the household as having cataract?	Have you ever been diagnosed with any eye or vision problem or condition, including ordinary nearsightedness or farsightedness?
		Do you wear eyeglasses or contact lenses to see far away (for example, across the street)?			Were you diagnosed with an eye or vision problem or condition in one or both eyes?
		Do you wear eyeglasses or contact lenses to see up close (for example, at arm's length, when you are reading)?			With which problem or condition were you diagnosed?
		In the last 30 days, how much difficulty did you have in seeing and recognizing an object or person you know across the road (about 20 meters)?			Have you ever undergone any treatment or corrective surgery for an eye problem or condition?

(*Continued*)

Table 10.2 Inclusion of Variables on Health of the Elderly (*Continued*)

Domains	Health/healthcare information	SAGE	NSSO	IHDS	LASI
		In the last 30 days, how much difficulty did you have in seeing and recognizing an object at arm's length (for example, reading)?			How good is your eyesight for seeing things at a distance, like recognizing a person across the street (or 20 meters away) whether or not you wear glasses, contacts, or corrective lenses? How good is your eyesight for seeing things up close, like reading ordinary newspaper print whether or not you wear glasses, contacts, or corrective lenses?
Oral health					In the last 12 months, have you ever been diagnosed with or suffered from any of the following oral problem(s)? Have you lost some or all of your natural teeth? How well can you chew solid foods such as chapati, apple, guava, or nuts?
Functioning assessment		Long periods of sitting could be 2 hours or longer		In the last 12 months, how many days was he/she not able to do normal activities due to this illness?	(g) Do you have difficulty with Walking 100 yards?

(*Continued*)

Table 10.2 Inclusion of Variables on Health of the Elderly (Continued)

Domains	Health/ healthcare information	SAGE	NSSO	IHDS	LASI
		Long periods of standing could be 30 minutes or longer		In the last 12 months, how many days was he/she received any treatment or advice?	Because of a health or memory problem, do you have any difficulty with maintaining daily activities?
		Performance of day to day work may be getting the work done, planning, organizing, doing tasks efficiently, performing in a way that is expected Difficulties in carrying food, water or children, or lifting and carrying things			
	Condition of Ailment			In the 30 days, for how many days was [NAME] ill? Did [NAME] have a fever in the last 30 days? Did [NAME] have a cough in the last 30 days? Did he/she breathe fast with short rapid breaths? Did [NAME] have diarrhea in the last 30 days? If had diarrhea, was there any blood in the stool with diarrhea?	

(Continued)

188   Dona Ghosh

Table 10.2 Inclusion of Variables on Health of the Elderly (Continued)

Domains	Health/healthcare information	SAGE	NSSO	IHDS	LASI
				If had diarrhea, when he/she had diarrhea, was there any change in the amount of liquid he/she took? If had diarrhea, was [NAME] given ORS [local name] solution? How long [NAME] been unable to do usual activities (incl. work, school, domestic work) in the last 30 days?	(b) Who first diagnosed you with high blood pressure or hypertension? (b) When were you first diagnosed with high blood pressure or hypertension? (Year or Age was recorded) (b) In order to control your blood pressure or hypertension, are you currently taking any medication?
Treatment of ailment			No. of days ill during the last 15 days (including hospitalization) No. of days with restricted activity during the last 15 days (including hospitalization) No. of days confined to bed during the last 15 days (including hospitalization) Nature of ailment during the last 15 days (including hospitalization)	In the last month, has [NAME] received any treatment or advice? (f) If received treatment or advice, from whom did [NAME] get advice or treatment? (f) If received treatment or advice, where did [NAME] get advice or treatment? # If received treatment or advice, What type of main treatment did she/he receive?	In order to control your blood pressure, are you under salt or other dietary restrictions? (diabetes and high blood sugar)

(Continued)

Table 10.2 Inclusion of Variables on Health of the Elderly (Continued)

Domains	Health/ healthcare information	\multicolumn{4}{c}{Variables/survey questions}
		SAGE	NSSO	IHDS	LASI
			Whether chronic ailment during the last 15 days (including hospitalization)	The last time you [THE RESPONDENT] had to visit a clinic, a hospital, a healer for a minor illness such as fever, cough/cold, or diarrhea for yourself or your children, who did you consult?	In which organs or parts of your body have you been diagnosed with cancer? Please identify all organs or parts of your body, starting with the first diagnosis
			Status of ailment during the last 15 days (including hospitalization)	The last time you [THE RESPONDENT] had to visit a clinic, a hospital, a healer for a minor illness such as fever, cough/cold, or diarrhea for yourself or your children, where was it located?	During the last two years, what type of treatments have you received for cancer?
			Total duration of ailment during the last 15 days (including hospitalization)	The last time you [THE RESPONDENT] had to visit a clinic, a hospital, a healer for a minor illness such as fever, cough/cold, or diarrhea for yourself or your children, why did you go then?	For which cancer(s) have you received the treatment?

(Continued)

190 Dona Ghosh

Table 10.2 Inclusion of Variables on Health of the Elderly (Continued)

Domains	Health/ healthcare information	Variables/survey questions			
		SAGE	NSSO	IHDS	LASI
			Nature of treatment during the last 15 days (including hospitalization)	The last time you [THE RESPONDENT] had to visit a clinic, a hospital, a healer for a minor illness such as fever, cough/cold, or diarrhea for yourself or your children, when did you go?	Are you receiving physical or respiratory therapy, or any other treatment for your lung disease?
			Whether hospitalized for treatment during the last 15 days?	The last time you [THE RESPONDENT] had to visit a clinic, a hospital, a healer for a minor illness such as fever, cough/cold, or diarrhea for yourself or your children, did you see a female or male health provider?	Which type of chronic lung disease do you have?
			Whether treatment taken on medical advice during the last 15 days (including hospitalization)	The last time you [THE RESPONDENT] had to visit a clinic, a hospital, a healer for a minor illness such as fever, cough/cold, or diarrhea for yourself or your children, do doctors and other health workers treat you Nicely/Somewhat nicely/Not nicely?	Have you ever had a heart attack?

(Continued)

Table 10.2 Inclusion of Variables on Health of the Elderly (Continued)

Domains	Health/healthcare information	Variables/survey questions			
		SAGE	NSSO	IHDS	LASI
			Level of care for treatment during the last 15 days (including hospitalization)	Usually, when you go to this facility, how many minutes do you have to wait?	When did you first have a heart attack?
			Reason for not availing govt. sources during the last 15 days (including hospitalization)	Did you go alone (with sick child) or were you accompanied by someone?	Was this the time when you were first diagnosed with heart disease?
			Reason for not seeking medical advice during the last 15 days (including hospitalization)		In the last two years, have you had a heart attack?
					Are you currently taking any medications because of your stroke or its complications?
					Are you receiving physical or occupational therapy because of your stroke or its complications?
					Have you had any subsequent stroke after the first diagnosed stroke you just told me about?
					In the last two years, have you consulted a doctor in connection with this most recent stroke?

(Continued)

192 Dona Ghosh

Table 10.2 Inclusion of Variables on Health of the Elderly (Continued)

Domains	Health/ healthcare information	Variables/survey questions			
		SAGE	NSSO	IHDS	LASI
					Do you still have any remaining problems because of your stroke(s), such as difficulty in moving or speaking?
					(d) Because of this stroke, do you have weakness in your arms and legs or decreased ability to move or use them?
					Have you ever been diagnosed with the following bone/joint diseases/problems?
					Which type of neurological or psychiatric problem(s) have you been diagnosed with?
					Are you currently taking tranquilizers, antidepressants, or other types of medication for neurological or psychiatric problem (s)?
					In the past two years, have you had a blood test for cholesterol?

(*Continued*)

Table 10.2 Inclusion of Variables on Health of the Elderly (*Continued*)

Domains	Health/healthcare information	Variables/survey questions			
		SAGE	NSSO	IHDS	LASI
			Whom consulted during the last 15 days (including hospitalization)		Have you ever been diagnosed with any of the chronic conditions or diseases like thyroid disorder, gastrointestinal problems (GERD, constipation, indigestion, piles, peptic ulcer, skin diseases, urogenital conditions or diseases, others In the last two years, have you been on dialysis? Do you ever pass urine while sneezing, coughing, laughing, or lifting heavy objects? In the past 12 months, have you visited any health care facility or any health professional has visited you? In the past 12 months, have you consulted any health care provider? What were the reasons for your last visit to the healthcare facility? What was your main reason for not seeking a visit?

(*Continued*)

Table 10.2 Inclusion of Variables on Health of the Elderly (*Continued*)

Domains	Health/ healthcare information	Variables/survey questions			
		SAGE	NSSO	IHDS	LASI
Anthropo-metrics, performance tests, and biomarkers	Blood pressure and pulse rates				
	Height and weight measurements				
	Waist and hip circumference measurements				
	Timed walk	Did the respondent complete the walk at the usual pace? Recorded (normal walk) time at 4 meters Did the respondent complete the walk at a rapid pace? Recorded (rapid walk) time at 4 meters			
	Relate to a vision test	Both distance and near vision are tested			
	Grip strength	Assess strength in the hands			
	Verbal recall tests	Interviewer read a list of 10 words and asked the respondent to repeat			Word recall
					In the past 12 months, did a health care provider ever recommend you to go to the hospital?

(*Continued*)

Table 10.2 Inclusion of Variables on Health of the Elderly (Continued)

Domains	Health/ healthcare information	SAGE	NSSO	IHDS	LASI
	Digit span test	Respondents have been provided with a series of numbers, starting with three digits, up to nine digits for forward span and starting with two digits up to eight for backward span			
	Verbal fluency	Interviewer asked to name animals (not insects) as much as possible in one minute			Verbal fluency
	Lung function	Pulmonary Function Test (PFT) values recorded by the spirometer			
	Delayed verbal recall/Test of long-term memory	Interviewer read a list of 10 words. Without reading the list again, respondents are asked to recall the words and repeat as many as they can remember after 10 minutes.			Long-term memory
	Blood tests	A finger prick technique is used to draw a blood sample from respondents			
Risk factors and preventive health behaviors	Tobacco use	Have you ever smoked tobacco or used smokeless tobacco?		(i) Does anyone in this household smoke cigarettes?	

(Continued)

Table 10.2 Inclusion of Variables on Health of the Elderly (*Continued*)

Domains	Health/ healthcare information	Variables/survey questions			
		SAGE	NSSO	IHDS	LASI
		Do you currently use (smoke, sniff or chew) any tobacco products such as cigarettes, cigars, pipes, chewing tobacco, or snuff?		(i) Does anyone in this household smoke bidis?	
		For how long have you been smoking or using tobacco daily?			
		On average, how many of the following products do you smoke or use each day?		(i) Does anyone in this household smoke chew tobacco or gutkha?	
		In the past, did you ever smoke tobacco or use smokeless tobacco daily?			
		How old were you when you stopped smoking or using tobacco daily?			
		How long ago did you stop smoking or using tobacco daily?			
	Drinking alcohol	Have you ever consumed a drink that contains alcohol (such as beer, wine, etc.)?		(i) Does anyone in this household smoke drink alcohol?	
		Have you consumed alcohol in the last 30 days?			
		During the past seven days, how many standard drinks of any alcoholic beverage did you have each day?			

(*Continued*)

Table 10.2 Inclusion of Variables on Health of the Elderly (Continued)

Domains	Health/ healthcare information	Variables/survey questions				
		SAGE	NSSO	IHDS	LASI
	Physical activities at work	In the last 12 months, how frequently [on how many days] on average have you had at least one alcoholic drink? In the last 12 months, on the days you drank alcoholic beverages, how many drinks did you have on average? Does your work involve vigorous-intensity activity, that causes large increases in breathing or heart rate (like heavy lifting, digging, or chopping wood) for at least 10 minutes continuously? In a typical week, on how many days do you do vigorous-intensity activities as part of your work? How much time do you spend doing vigorous-intensity activities at work on a typical day? Does your work involve moderate-intensity activity, that causes small increases in breathing or heart rate, for at least 10 minutes continuously? In a typical week, on how many days do you do moderate-intensity activities as part of your work?			

(Continued)

Does India Have Sufficient Data for Eldercare? 197

Table 10.2 Inclusion of Variables on Health of the Elderly (*Continued*)

Domains	Health/healthcare information	Variables/survey questions			
		SAGE	NSSO	IHDS	LASI
	Sports, fitness, and recreational activities	How much time do you spend doing moderate-intensity activities at work on a typical day? Do you walk or use a bicycle (pedal cycle) for at least 10 minutes continuously to get to and from places? In a typical week, on how many days do you walk or bicycle for at least 10 minutes continuously to get to and from places? How much time would you spend walking or bicycling for travel on a typical day? Do you do any vigorous-intensity sports, fitness, or recreational (leisure) activities that cause large increases in breathing or heart rate In a typical week, on how many days do you do vigorous-intensity sports, fitness, or recreational (leisure) activities? How much time do you spend doing vigorous-intensity sports, fitness, or recreational activities on a typical day?			

(*Continued*)

Table 10.2 Inclusion of Variables on Health of the Elderly (Continued)

Domains	Health/ healthcare information	Variables/survey questions				
		SAGE	NSSO	IHDS	LASI
		Do you do any moderate-intensity sports, fitness, or recreational (leisure) activities that cause a small increase in breathing or heart rate? In a typical week, on how many days do you do moderate-intensity sports, fitness, or recreational (leisure) activities? How much time do you spend doing moderate-intensity sports, fitness, or recreational (leisure) activities on a typical day?			
	Chronic conditions and health services coverage	Have you ever been diagnosed with/told you have arthritis (or by other names, rheumatism or osteoarthritis)? Have you been taking any medications or other treatment for it during the last two weeks? Have you been taking any medications or other treatment for it during the last 12 months? During the last 12 months, have you experienced pain, aching, stiffness, swelling in or around the joints...?		(a) Has a doctor ever diagnosed any member in the household as having tuberculosis?	(b) Has any health professional ever diagnosed you with hypertension or high blood pressure?

(Continued)

Table 10.2 Inclusion of Variables on Health of the Elderly (*Continued*)

Domains	Health/ healthcare information	Variables/survey questions			
		SAGE	NSSO	IHDS	LASI
		During the last 12 months, have you experienced stiffness in the joint in the morning after getting up from bed or after a long rest of the joint without movement? How long did this stiffness last? Did this stiffness go away after exercise or movement in the joint? These symptoms that you have said you experienced in the last 12 months, have you experienced them in the last 2 weeks? Have you experienced back pain during the last 30 days? On how many days did you have this back pain during the last 30 days?			
Health care utilization	Needing health care	When was the last time that you needed health care? The last time you needed health care, did you get health care? What was the main reason you needed care, even if you did not get care? Which reason(s) best explains why you did not get the needed health care?			

(*Continued*)

Table 10.2 Inclusion of Variables on Health of the Elderly (Continued)

Domains	Health/ healthcare information	Variables/survey questions			
		SAGE	NSSO	IHDS	LASI
	In-patient hospital care	Thinking about the health care you needed in the last three years, where did you go most often when you felt sick or needed to consult someone about your health?			
		Have you ever stayed overnight in a hospital or long-term care facility?	Nature of ailment for the medical treatment received as in-patient of a medical institution during the last 365 days	# Was she/he hospitalized in the last 30 days?	Over the last 12 months, how many times you were admitted as patient to a hospital/long-term care facility for at least one night?
		When was the last overnight stay in a hospital or long-term care facility?	Level of care for the medical treatment received as in-patient of a medical institution during the last 365 days	# If hospitalized, for how many days?	How many nights have you spent in the hospital during the past 12 months?
		Over the last 12 months, how many different times were you a patient in a hospital/long-term care facility for at least one night?	Type of ward for the medical treatment received as in-patient of a medical institution during the last 365 days		For the last hospitalization, how many months ago were you admitted to the hospital?
		What type of hospital or facility was it?	Time of admission for the medical treatment received as in-patient of a medical institution during the last 365 days		Which type of facility did you visit during your last hospitalization?

(Continued)

Table 10.2 Inclusion of Variables on Health of the Elderly (Continued)

Domains	Health/ healthcare information	Variables/survey questions			
		SAGE	NSSO	IHDS	LASI
		What was the name of this hospital or facility?	Time of discharge for the medical treatment received as in-patient of a medical institution during the last 365 days		How many nights did you spend in the hospital during your last hospitalization?
		Which reason best describes why you were last hospitalized?	Duration of stay for the medical treatment received as in-patient of a medical institution during the last 365 days		Why were you hospitalized? What is the main reason for your last hospitalization?
		How did you get there?	Any medical services like surgery received during in-patient of a medical institution during the last 365 days		During your last hospitalization, what kind of treatment/services did you receive?
		About how long did it take you to get there?	Any medical services like medicine received during in-patient of a medical institution during the last 365 days		(h) In your recent visit, how much did you or your household pay for health care provider's fees (consultation charges)? (h) In your recent visit, how much did you or your household pay for medicines from hospital? (h) In your recent visit, how much did you or your household pay for medicines from outside?

(Continued)

Table 10.2 Inclusion of Variables on Health of the Elderly (Continued)

Domains	Health/ healthcare information	Variables/survey questions			
		SAGE	NSSO	IHDS	LASI
					(h) In your recent visit, how much did you or your household pay for tests/investigation?
					(h) In your recent visit, how much did you or your household pay for hospital and nursing home charges including bed charges, food?
					(h) In your recent visit, how much did you or your household pay for operation theater charges, surgery charges, and related expenses?
					(h) In your recent visit, how much did you or your household pay for blood, oxygen cylinder?
					(h) In your recent visit, how much did you or your household pay for transportation?
					In your recent visit, how much did you or your household pay for expenses of the accompanying person(s) (food/accommodation)?

(Continued)

Table 10.2 Inclusion of Variables on Health of the Elderly (*Continued*)

Domains	Health/ healthcare information	Variables/survey questions			
		SAGE	NSSO	IHDS	LASI
		Who paid for this hospitalization? Anyone else?	Any medical services like X-ray/ECG/EEG/scan received during in-patient of a medical institution during the last 365 days		In your recent visit, how much did you or your household pay for expenditure not elsewhere reported (others)?
		Thinking about your last overnight stay, how much did you or your family/household members pay out of pocket for:	Any medical services like other diagnostic tests received during in-patient of a medical institution during the last 365 days		
		About how much in total did you or a family/household member pay out of pocket for this hospitalization? Overall, how satisfied were you with the care you received during your last (hospital) stay? What was the outcome or result of your visit to the hospital? Was this the outcome or result you had expected?			

(*Continued*)

Table 10.2 Inclusion of Variables on Health of the Elderly (*Continued*)

Domains	Health/healthcare information	Variables/survey questions			
		SAGE	NSSO	IHDS	LASI
	Pre-hospitalization medical treatment	For your last (overnight) visit to a hospital or long-term care facility, how would you rate your stay?	Nature of ailment for the medical treatment received before in-patient of a medical institution during the last 365 days Level of care for the medical treatment received before in-patient of a medical institution during the last 365 days Type of ward for the medical treatment received before in-patient of a medical institution during the last 365 days		
	After discharge medical treatment		Nature of ailment for the medical treatment received after in-patient of a medical institution during the last 365 days		What was your health status when you left the hospital? If left before recovery, why did you want to leave the hospital before you were recovered?

(*Continued*)

Table 10.2 Inclusion of Variables on Health of the Elderly (Continued)

Domains	Health/ healthcare information	SAGE	NSSO	IHDS	LASI
					Do you still suffer from the ailment you originally sought treatment for? Did your treatment continue after discharge? How long was the duration of treatment after discharge? How many kilometers from your residence is the health care facility in which you were most recently admitted? What is your travel time (one-way) to that facility? What was the main transportation mode you used last time when you visited that facility? After hospitalization, what was the change in your health condition? Rate your experiences about the last hospitalization or stay at a long-term care facility
	Out-patient care	Over the last 12 months, did you receive any health care NOT including an overnight stay in hospital or long-term care facility?	Any medical services like surgery received during the last 15 days for treatment (not as in-patient of medical institution)		In the past 12 months, how many times did you receive healthcare or consultation from a healthcare provider (including home visits)?

(Continued)

Table 10.2 Inclusion of Variables on Health of the Elderly (*Continued*)

Domains	Health/ healthcare information	Variables/survey questions			
		SAGE	NSSO	IHDS	LASI
		In total, how many times did you receive health care or consultation in the last 12 months?	Any medical services like medicine received during the last 15 days for treatment (not as in-patient of medical institution)		In which month and year was your most recent visit?
		What was the last (most recent) health care facility you visited in the last 12 months?	Any medical services like X-ray/ECG/EEG/scan received during last 15 days for treatment (not as in-patient of medical institution)		Which type of health care provider did you visit, or came to visit you, most recently in the past 12 months?
		What was the name of this health care facility or provider?	Any medical services like other diagnostic tests received during the last 15 days for treatment (not as in-patient of medical institution)		Which type of facility did you last visit to see that healthcare provider?
		Which was the last (most recent) health care provider you visited? Was this visit for a chronic condition, new condition, or for both reasons?			What was the main purpose of your visit? What is the main reason for your recent out-patient visit?
		Which reason best describes why you needed this visit?			What kind of treatment and/or diagnostics did you receive?
		For your last out-patient health visit/visit to health care provider, how would you rate?			Who accompanied you during your most recent out-patient visit?

(*Continued*)

Table 10.2 Inclusion of Variables on Health of the Elderly (Continued)

Domains	Health/ healthcare information	Variables/survey questions			
		SAGE	NSSO	IHDS	LASI
					Do you still suffer from the ailment you originally sought treatment for?
					How many kilometers is the health care facility from your residence?
					What was your travel time (one-way) to that facility?
					What was the main transportation mode you used last time you visited that facility?
					What was the outcome of your most recent visit to the health care provider?
					Overall, how satisfied were you with the health care you received at this visit?
					For your last visit to a hospital or health care facility, how would you rate your experience about the length of time you waited before being attended to
					For your last visit to a hospital or health care facility, how would you rate your experience of being treated respectfully

(*Continued*)

Table 10.2 Inclusion of Variables on Health of the Elderly (Continued)

Domains	Health/ healthcare information	Variables/survey questions			
		SAGE	NSSO	IHDS	LASI
					For your last visit to a hospital or health care facility, how would you rate your experience how clearly health care providers explained things to you
					For your last visit to a hospital or health care facility, how would you rate your experience of the way the health care staff is ensured that you could talk privately to providers
					For your last visit to a hospital or health care facility, how would you rate your experience of getting a health care provider of your choice
					For your last visit to a hospital or health care facility, how would you rate your experience about the cleanliness in the health facility
					In general, would you say your health is excellent, very good, good, fair, or poor?
Subjective well-being and quality of life	Feeling about life	Do you have enough energy for everyday life?	Own perception about the current state of health		

(Continued)

210 Dona Ghosh

Table 10.2 Inclusion of Variables on Health of the Elderly (*Continued*)

Domains	Health/healthcare information	SAGE	NSSO	IHDS	LASI
		Do you have enough money to meet your needs?	Own perception about change in the state of health		During the last 12 months, was there ever a time when you felt sad, blue, or depressed for two weeks or more in a row? (detail about depression)
		How satisfied are you with…your health?			
		How satisfied are you with … yourself?			
		How satisfied are you with…your ability to perform your daily living activities?			
		How satisfied are you with … your personal relationships?			
		How satisfied are you with … the conditions of your living place?			
		Taking all things together, how satisfied are you with your life as a whole these days?			
		How often have you felt that you were unable to control the important things in your life?			
		How often have you found that you could not cope with all the things that you had to do?			
		How would you rate your overall quality of life?			

(*Continued*)

Table 10.2 Inclusion of Variables on Health of the Elderly (*Continued*)

Domains	Health/ healthcare information	SAGE	NSSO	IHDS	LASI
	Healthcare expenditure	Taking all things together, how would you say you are these days? In the last four weeks, how much did your household spend on health care costs, excluding any insurance reimbursements?	(e) Whether any medical service provided free for medical treatment received as in-patient of a medical institution during the last 365 days		
		In the last four weeks, how much did your household spend on care that required staying overnight in a hospital or health facility?	(e) Cost of package for medical treatment received as in-patient of a medical institution during the last 365 days	(f) What was the total cost of doctor, hospital, and surgery for treatment of ailment	(h) What was the total amount that you or your household spent on this visit?
		In the last four weeks, how much did your household spend on care by doctors, nurses, or trained midwives that did not require an overnight stay?	(e) Cost of non-package for medical treatment (like doctor's/surgeon's fee (hospital staff/other specialists) received as in-patient of a medical institution during the last 365 days	(f) Were tests or medicines included in the fees of doctor, hospital, and surgery for treatment of ailment for out-patient as well as in-patient services in last 30 days?	How much in total did you spend on all your out-patient visits to health care facilities/providers (including your most recent visit) during the last 12 months?
		In the last four weeks, how much did your household spend on care by traditional or alternative healers?	(e) Cost of non-package for medical treatment (like medicines) received as in-patient of a medical institution during the last 365 days	(f) What was the total cost of medicine and tests and expenses not included in the doctors' and hospital fees for treatment of ailment for out-patient as well as in-patient services in the last 30 days?	During the past 12 months, have you used any of the following medications or health supplements without consulting a healthcare provider?

(*Continued*)

212   *Dona Ghosh*

Table 10.2 Inclusion of Variables on Health of the Elderly (*Continued*)

| Domains | Health/ healthcare information | \multicolumn{4}{c}{Variables/survey questions} ||||
		SAGE	NSSO	IHDS	LASI
		In the last four weeks, how much did your household spend on dentists?	(e) Cost of non-package for medical treatment (like diagnostic tests) received as in-patient of a medical institution during the last 365 days	(f) What was the total cost of tips, bus/train/taxi fare, or lodging while getting treatment for the treatment of ailment for out-patient as well as in-patient services in the last 30 days?	How much did you pay for these medications or health supplements during the last 12 months?
		In the last four weeks, how much did your household spend on medication or drugs?	(e) Cost of non-package for medical treatment (like bed charges) received as in-patient of a medical institution during the last 365 days		How much of this amount was reimbursed?
		In the last four weeks, how much did your household spend on health care products such as prescription glasses, hearing aids, prosthetic devices, etc.?	(e) Cost of non-package for medical treatment (like attendant charges, physiotherapy, personal medical appliances, blood, oxygen, etc.) received as in-patient of a medical institution during the last 365 days		
		In the last four weeks, how much did your household spend on diagnostic and laboratory tests such as X-rays or blood tests?	(e) Cost of transport for patient		

(*Continued*)

Table 10.2 Inclusion of Variables on Health of the Elderly (Continued)

Domains	Health/ healthcare information	Variables/survey questions			
		SAGE	NSSO	IHDS	LASI
		In the last four weeks, how much did your household spend on any other health care products or services that were not included above?	(e) Cost of other non-medical expenses incurred by the household (Rs.) (food, transport for others, expenditure on escort, lodging charges if any, etc.)		
		In the last 12 months, how many times did members of your household go to a hospital and stay overnight?			
		In the last 12 months, how much did the household pay for all costs associated with overnight stays in a hospital? Please exclude any expenses in the last four weeks that you have already told me about, and exclude any reimbursement from insurance			
		In the last 12 months, which of the following financial sources did your household use to pay for any health expenditures?			

(Continued)

Table 10.2 Inclusion of Variables on Health of the Elderly (Continued)

Domains	Health/healthcare information	SAGE	NSSO	IHDS	LASI
Financing healthcare expenditure (household members/persons are assigned codes at the beginning of the survey)		Is this person covered by any kind of health insurance plan? Is this person covered by any mandatory health insurance plans? Is this person covered by any voluntary health insurance plans? How much does your household pay for this person's voluntary health insurance each year? Is this person covered by insurance only because of his/her relationship with someone else who has health insurance?	Total amount of in-patient cost reimbursed by medical insurance company or employer Major source of finance for expenses of in-patient cost	(f) Were any of the expenditures for out-patient as well as in-patient services in the last 30 days covered by the insurance/ such as mediclaim or RSBY?	Are you covered by health insurance? What types of health insurance are you covered by? What does this health insurance cover? In which month and year did you first purchase/enroll in the health insurance policy provides? When did this health insurance benefit begin?

(Continued)

Table 10.2 Inclusion of Variables on Health of the Elderly (Continued)

Domains	Health/ healthcare information	Variables/survey questions		
	SAGE	NSSO	IHDS	LASI
	Who is enrolled in the insurance plan that gives this person health insurance?	Second most important source of finance source of finance for expenses of in-patient cost		What is the maximum amount of insurance coverage (in rupees)?

Sources: Questions of the Table 10.2 are taken from the questionnaires of various rounds of the following surveys: Indian Human Development Surveys (IHDS)[5]; Study of Global Ageing and Adult Health (SAGE)[6]; National Sample Survey Office (NSSO)[7]; and Gateway to Global Aging Data (LASI)[8]

a This question is also asked for high BP, heart disease, diabetes, leprosy, cancer, asthma, polio, paralysis, epilepsy, mental illness, STD or AIDS, accident, other long-term morbidity.
b Same question is repeated for "diabetes or high blood sugar," "Cancer or a malignant tumor," "Chronic lung disease such as asthma, chronic obstructive pulmonary disease/Chronic bronchitis or other chronic lung problems,," Chronic heart diseases such as Coronary heart disease (heart attack or Myocardial Infarction), "congestive heart failure, or other chronic heart problems," "Stroke," "Arthritis or rheumatism," "Osteoporosis or other bone/joint diseases," "Any neurological, or psychiatric problems such as depression," "Alzheimer's/Dementia, unipolar/bipolar disorders, convulsions, Parkinson's etc.," "High cholesterol."
c Same question is asked for "going to toilet without help," "dressing without help," "hearing normal conversation," "speaking normally," "seeing distant things [with glasses, if any]," and "seeing near object such as reading/sewing [with glasses, if any]."
d This question is repeated for "Difficulty in speaking or swallowing," "Difficulty with your vision," and "Difficulty in thinking or finding the right words to say."
e All these questions are repeated for expenses incurred during the last 15 days for out-patient treatment of ailment.
f This questions are asked for long-term morbidity as well.
g Same question is repeated for "Sitting for 2 hours or more"; "Getting up from a chair after sitting for long period"; "Climbing one flight of stairs without resting"; "Stooping, kneeling or crouching"; "Reaching or extending arms above shoulder level (either arm)"; "Pulling or pushing large objects"; "Lifting or carrying weights over 5 kilos, like a heavy bag of groceries"; and "Picking up a coin from a table."
h Same question is asked for out-patient care.

two problems: (a) response bias due to the high attrition rate of the sample and (b) non-representativeness of the elderly population as the inclusion of 60 years and above individuals are very small in each state. NSS overcomes the shortcomings mentioned earlier as it includes a substantially large sample and social, demographic, economic, and health characteristics of the elderly population. However, the successive rounds of NSS are directly not comparable, particularly to investigate the change in the health status of the senior citizens—because NSS surveys do not contain panel structure in sample design.

The findings of the chapter suggest that all the micro-level datasets have certain strength and weakness of micro-level data. Accurate estimation of health problems of the senior citizens, based on a single dataset, at the national level in India is difficult. Most of the surveys, except LASI, have included older adults as a sample subgroup and lack either representing the actual population or including all necessary geriatric health variables. This chapter suggests conducting nationally representative surveys with a significant focus on elderly people based on the findings. In addition, for estimation of health problem of the senior citizens, it is suggested to include age-specific health variables, direct and indirect determinants of health like lifestyle, demand for healthcare services etc.

Notes

1. http://niti.gov.in/content/life-expectancy.
2. Panchayat wards are used instead of villages.
3. For detail see: http://www.censusindia.gov.in/vital_statistics/SRS_Report_2015/5.Chap%201-Introduction-2015.pdf.
4. https://www.ncaer.org/uploads/photo-gallery/files/1459408358About%20IHDS.pdf.
5. https://ihds.umd.edu/
6. World Health Organization (2006). WHO SAGE Survey Manual: The WHO Study on Global AGEing and Adult Health (SAGE). Geneva, World Health Organization.
7. http://mospi.nic.in/NSSOa
8. This analysis uses data or information from the LASI Pilot micro data and documentation. The development and release of the LASI Pilot Study was funded by the National Institute on Ageing/National Institute of Health (R21AG032572, R03AG043052, and R01 AG030153).

References

Arokiasamy, P., Bloom, D., Lee, J., Feeney, K., & Ozolins, M. (2012). Longitudinal aging study in India: vision, design, implementation, and some early results. In *Aging in Asia. Findings from new and emerging data initiatives* (pp. 36–74). National Academics Press, Washington, DC.

Agrawal, S. (2012). Effect of living arrangement on the health status of elderly in India: Findings from a national cross sectional survey. *Asian Population Studies*, 8(1), 87–101.

Alam, M. (2007, July 25–27). Ageing in South Asia: An overview and emerging issues for policy planning and research. Bangkok: Seminar on the Social, Health and Economic Consequences of Population Ageing in the Context of Changing Families. Available at http://citeseerx.ist.psu.edu/viewdoc/download?doi=10.1.1.561.9635&rep=rep1&type=pdf

Barik, D., Desai, S., & Vanneman, R. (2018). Economic status and adult mortality in India: Is the relationship sensitive to choice of indicators? *World Development, 103*, 176–187.

Bharati, K., & Singh, C. (2013). Ageing in India: Need for a comprehensive policy. *IIM Bangalore Research Paper*, 421.

Beydoun, M. A., & Popkin, B. M. (2005). The impact of socio-economic factors on functional status decline among community-dwelling older adults in China. *Social Science & Medicine, 60*(9), 2045–2057.

Brinda, E. M., Rajkumar, A. P., Enemark, U., Prince, M., & Jacob, K. S. (2012). Nature and determinants of out-of-pocket health expenditure among older people in a rural Indian community. *International Psychogeriatrics, 24*(10), 1664–1673.

Chambers, R. (1995). Poverty and livelihoods: Whose reality counts? *Environment and urbanization, 7*(1), 173–204.

Desai, S., Dubey, A., Joshi, B. L., Sen, M., Shariff, A., & Vanneman, R. (2009). India human development survey: Design and data quality. *IHDS Technical Paper, 1*, 1–27.

Goel, P. K., Garg, S. K., Singh, J. V., Bhatnagar, M., Chopra, H., & Bajpai, S. K. (2003). Unmet needs of the elderly in a rural population of Meerut. *Indian Journal of Community Medicine, 28*(4), 165–166.

Goldman, N., Korenman, S., & Weinstein, R. (1995). Marital status and health among the elderly. *Social Science & Medicine, 40*(12), 1717–1730.

Haines, M. R. (1995). Disease and Health through the ages. In J. Somon, *The state of humanity* (pp. 51–60). Basil Blackwell, Oxford.

He, W., Goodkind, D., & Kowal, P. (2016). *US Census Bureau, international population reports*. P95/16-1, An Aging World: 2015.

Ingle, G. K., & Nath, A. (2008). Geriatric health in India: Concerns and solutions. *Indian Journal of Community Medicine: Official Publication of Indian Association of Preventive & Social Medicine, 33*(4), 214–218.

Kabir, M. (1992). Effects of social-change on the health of the elderly: Evidence from a micro study. *Journal of Family Welfare, 38*(1), 44–55.

Kabir, Z. N., Tishelman, C., Agüero-Torres, H., Chowdhury, A. M. R., Winblad, B., & Höjer, B. (2003). Gender and rural–urban differences in reported health status by older people in Bangladesh. *Archives of Gerontology & Geriatrics, 37*(1), 77–91.

Li, W., Liu, E., & BeLue, R. (2018). Household water treatment and the nutritional status of primary-aged children in India: findings from the India human development survey. *Globalization and Health, 14*(1), 1–8.

Mohanty, S. K., Chauhan, R. K., Mazumdar, S., & Srivastava, A. (2014). Out-of-pocket expenditure on health care among elderly and non-elderly households in India. *Social Indicators Research, 115*(3), 1137–1157.

Pal, R. (2012). Measuring incidence of catastrophic out-of-pocket health expenditure: with application to India. *International Journal of Health Care Finance and Economics, 12*(1), 63–85.

Patil, A. V., Somasundaram, K. V., & Goyal, R. C. (2002). Current health scenario in rural India. *Australian Journal of Rural Health, 10*(2), 129–135.

Prakash, I. J. (1999). *Ageing in India*. Geneva: World Health Organization.

Rajan, S. I., Mishra, U. S., & Sarma, P. S. (1999). Indian Elderly: Some Views of Populance. *Indian Journal of Social Work, 60*, 487–507.

Reddy, P. H. (1996). The health of the aged in India. *Health Transition Review, 6*, 233–244.

Sen, K. (1994). *Ageing: Debates on demographic transition and social policy*. Zed Books. London.

Sengupta, M., & Agree, E. M. (2002). Gender and disability among older adults in North and South India: differences associated with coresidence and marriage. *Journal of Cross-Cultural Gerontology*, *17*(4), 313–336.

Soneja, S., Nagarkar, K. M., Dey, A. B., Khetrapal, K., & Kumar, V. (1996). Socio-economic status and its relationship to parameters of social morbidity among elderly patients seeking outpatient medical care. In: Kumar V, editor. *Aging: Indian perspective and global scenario*. All India Institute of Medical Sciences, New Delhi. 137–139.

Srinivasan, K., Vaz, M., & Thomas, T. (2010). Prevalence of health-related disability among community dwelling urban elderly from middle socioeconomic strata in Bangaluru, India. *Indian Journal of Medical Research*, *131*, 515–521.

Strawbridge, W. J., Camacho, T. C., Cohen, R. D., & Kaplan, G. A. (1993). Gender differences in factors associated with change in physical functioning in old age: A 6-year longitudinal study. *The Gerontologist*, *33*(5), 603–609.

UNDP. (2000). *United Nations Expert Group Meeting on Policy Responses to Population Ageing and Population Decline*. New York: United Nations: United Nations Population Division. ESA/P/WP.163.

Verbrugge, L. M., & Patrick, D. L. (1995). Seven chronic conditions: Their impact on US adults' activity levels and use of medical services. *American Journal of Public Health*, *85*(2), 173–182.

Vedantam, A., Subramanian, V., Rao, N. V., & John, K. R. (2010). Malnutrition in free-living elderly in rural south India: Prevalence and risk factors. *Public Health Nutrition*, 13(9), 1328–1332.

World Health Organization. (2001). *International Classification of Functioning, Disability and Health*: ICF. World Health Organization.

World Health Organization. (2015). *World Report on Ageing and Health*. World Health Organization.

11 Conclusion

Future Research Directions for Eldercare Issues in China and India

Jagriti Gangopadhyay

The main aim of this edited volume was to contribute to the discourse of gerontology through a comparative lens. Gerontology as a discipline has always been very interdisciplinary and scholars of demography, economics, sociology, and anthropology have played a key role in shaping the discipline. Similarly, the contributions in this edited book are also multidisciplinary and through each of the chapters, we have tried to show that aging is a complex and diverse process. We particularly, chose the comparative lens, as there is a dearth of scholarship on comparative studies in the discipline of gerontology. Though China recognized its elderly population early on and devised policies for its aging population long back and India continues to be identified as a youth dominated country, nonetheless, individual studies on both these countries have highlighted that the problems being faced by the older population of both these countries are quite the same. Despite similar cultural practices and demographic patterns, a comparison of eldercare issues between the two countries: China and India, is missing. It is also important to point out that this edited book, never intended to applaud the policies of one country over the other. Instead, through this volume, the goal is to present the major eldercare issues plaguing both China and India. The other important contribution of this book is that it highlights eldercare issues that are prominent in the urban areas of both countries. Since aging as a concern has been over-researched in the rural parts of China and India, this book intends to contribute to policymaking and expand the scope of research in gerontology with special emphasis on the urban and affluent elderly.

In closing, I would like to summarize some of the most important issues raised in all of the chapters and shed some light on policy perspectives and the future of gerontological research in China and India.

Filial Piety: A Cultural Process

In the first section of the book, both the chapters discuss the cultural belief of filial piety in great depth. Analyzing Government texts, Zhang, in his chapter, demonstrates how the notion of filial piety goes beyond the concept of family and is also embedded in the Chinese Government's policies and projects. Relatedly, Gangopadhyay, in her chapter, relies on qualitative interviews and illustrates how

DOI: 10.4324/9781003254256-16

the cultural tradition of filial piety is fulfilled in a neoliberal India. In particular, this chapter highlights how the older generation continues to feel an emotional void, in spite of cohabiting with their adult child and their families. Both these contributions establish the significance of filial piety as a cultural practice in India and China. However, as Zhang points out, the culture of filial piety is practiced not only by Chinese citizens, but by their Government as well to uplift the morale of the public. Furthermore, in the other chapter, Gangopadhyay indicates that filial piety is mostly a cultural practice that is followed by the elderly and the Government of India through legal norms obligates the adult children of these elderly, to provide caregiving arrangements for their older parents. Despite the legal structures, cases of elder abuse and abandonment continue to rise in India and there is a huge policy lacuna with regard to elder abuse in India. Based on the findings of both these chapters, it may be suggested that acknowledgment of filial piety as an important cultural belief by the State and policymakers could aid in improving the emotional wellbeing of older parents.

Institutionalized Care

China is already grappling with an aging population and India's elderly population is constantly increasing. As discussed, in both countries, legally eldercare depends upon the adult children and their families. However, with the change in family structures and increasing migration patterns, institutional care in various forms has become a reality in both countries. Institutional care in the form of old age homes, eldercare residences, community dwellings for the elderly and assisted living centers are gradually rising in China as well as in India. In this section, the two chapters contributed by Peng, Mang, and Kulaixi (China section) and Ghatak (India section), outline the various issues faced by the elderly opting for institutional care. For instance, in their chapter, Peng et al. reveal how the rise of elderly care institutions is facing the opposition of their neighboring residents and has led to the development of an attitude, which is popularly known as "Not in my backyard." Elaborating on the stigma faced by the elderly in China, this chapter highlights how the absence of understanding of death, misery, and aging among the general population has resulted in the lack of respect and dignity for the elderly in China. Measuring the "quality of life" in the old age homes in the metropolitan city of Kolkata, Ghatak uses a mixed-methods approach to explain how the quality of life differs among older men and women residents of different old age homes. Specifically, Ghatak finds that the older women are more adjusting and appreciative of their care facilities as opposed to their male counterparts. In particular, Ghatak points out that as older women are used to being caregivers, they are less skeptical and are more grateful as care receivers in an institutional setting.

As indicated in both the chapters, with the growth of the biomedical perspective of anti-aging across the globe (Kampf & Botelho, 2009), dialogues around later-life care, age-related disabilities, and death are missing in the media and popular culture narrative. Older adults not only face stigma as discussed by Peng et al. in their chapter, but they also face isolation and loneliness in their later lives. Likewise, as Ghatak argues in her chapter that lack of dignity and respect continue to remain the main complaints of older adults in India as well.

In contrast to the cultural value of filial piety, institutional care is considered to be against the traditional norms of caregiving in China and India. In particular, studies have noted that older adults moving to institutional care often express their loss of ties with their adult children (Lamb, 2020; Liu et al., 2019). However, the rise of institutional care is significant and as pointed out by Ghatak, nuances such as the intersections between gender and aging need to be taken into account while framing policies for institutional caregiving in India. Additional measures also need to be taken to deal with the stigma associated with community dwellings, old age homes, and other forms of institutional care available in China and India.

Family-Based Care

Tied to the idea of filial piety, family-based care is the dominant model of care in both China and India. Though this section has contributions only from Chinese scholars, I will also draw from Gangopadhyay's chapter on family care to throw light on the role of the family in providing care to their elderly in urban India. Elaborating on how filial piety has changed in modern China, Yu and Fang suggest that with escalating employment demands, competition, and increasing geographical distances, filial piety as an ideology is changing in China. Similar to Yu and Fang's research, Gangopadhyay also argues in her paper that perceptions of filial piety are different among the older and the younger generation. Influenced by the requirements of neo-liberalization, the younger generation of India also have very little time for their older parents, owing to their hectic work schedules. Apart from this very competitive work environment, as pointed out by both Yu and Fang as well as Gangopadhyay, caregiving dynamics have also changed with a large number of women entering the workforce. As a result, family-based care is no longer a duty fulfilled only by the women of the family. Consequently, family care is divided and shared by both male and female family members. Additionally, Gangopadhyay, also highlights in her chapter that these changing caregiving roles have also marked a cultural shift in urban India, wherein a lot of older parents are choosing to live with their adult daughters and debunking the son-preference myth of India.

Extending the idea of caregiving experiences, He and Wu, in their chapter, focus on the important issue of end-of-life care. Using qualitative meta-synthesis on articles examining caregiving experiences of caregivers providing care to cancer patients in India and China, He and Wu found that family caregivers in both countries require medical knowledge and training to provide adequate care to patients suffering from a terminal illness. However, a direct comparison between the two countries highlighted that China fares much better with regard to health infrastructure and facilities, in comparison to India. Despite the rise of institutional care, the importance of family care cannot be ignored in both China and

India. Though modernization and neo-liberal policies have had their impact on the cultural practice of filial piety, nonetheless, as suggested by all the contributors, filial piety as an expectation continues to persist among the older generation and is also promoted by the Government of China as explained by Zhang in his chapter. Hence, it is imperative for policymakers in both countries to take note of family-based care and suggest measures to improve this form of care.

Marginalized Eldercare Groups

Given the extensive emphasis on family support for later-life care, there is very little scholarship around older adults living alone or on older adults without any adult chapter. In this section, contributions from Chowkhani and Wua and Qiua reflect on the elderly living alone in urban India and the elderly who have lost their only child and are the only caregivers of their grandchildren in China. As eldercare groups, these are very pertinent as the law and policy rarely take them into consideration. Wua and Qiua, in their study, highlight how the older adults who have lost their only child, have to cope with their loss as well as fulfill their grandparenting responsibilities. In particular, this study found that in the process of looking after their grandchildren, the older adults become functional again and this caregiving responsibility enables them to accept their loss. Exploring similar questions, Chowkhani, in her chapter, examines the various self-care strategies adopted by older adults living alone in India. In particular, Chowkhani demonstrates how these older adults have developed their own social support systems to navigate illness and failing health. Against the backdrop of the pandemic, COVID-19, Chowkhani highlights how these older adults were at an advantage as they were used to living alone and doing things on their own.

One of the biggest challenges of filial piety as a cultural process prominently present in both countries is that family care emerges to be the most prevailing form of care, both legally as well as socially. Consequently, older adults who are childless, unmarried, or have lost their only child are deprived of traditional forms of support. Hence, as discussed by Chowkhani and Wua and Qiua in their respective chapters, they either create their own social network ties or rely on grandparenting duties to fulfill their emotional needs.

As the aging population of both these countries continues to rise, these groups of older adults without any kin support are also increasing. As a result of China's one-child policy, the majority of older adults have only one child. Thus, the loss of that child because of a disaster or accident or suicide results in the elderly parents experiencing helplessness and being deprived of familial care (Song, 2014). Moreover, older adults opting to live alone is gradually rising in India. Though Chowkhani primarily focuses on older adults who are single, nonetheless, the number of elderly living alone is also rising in urban India. Several older adults in urban India, irrespective of having children are choosing to live alone to be able to remain independent in their final days (Gangopadhyay, 2020). These two chapters of this edited book counter the cultural ideology of filial piety and present some of the core issues of such eldercare groups. Hence, these eldercare groups need to be taken into consideration and be included in academic scholarship, media coverage, and policy issues in both countries.

Data and Elderly Care

The final contribution from Dona Ghosh investigates the existing data sets that are studied to make policies for the aging population of India. In this chapter, Ghosh examines the major databases in India and highlights their inadequacies and significance in identifying the major eldercare issues in India. Ghosh's chapter is useful and warrants careful reading as she lists out in detail the major data sources representing the Indian elderly. In particular, Ghosh suggests that each of the micro-level datasets has some strengths and some weaknesses. Drawing from Ghosh's chapter, it may be suggested that most of the datasets are useful to understand the main issues of the elderly, however, they rarely answer "why" these problems need to be taken seriously for future course of action. Hence, Ghosh's chapter makes an important argument and to improve the wellbeing of older adults in India, the deficiencies in the datasets should be addressed and more measures should be taken to enhance the later-life experiences of the elderly in India. It is important to note that in this edited book, the intersection between data and the elderly have been presented only from the perspective of India. Since China has been dealing with its elderly population for a longer period as opposed to India, their datasets are much more established and validated. Additionally, owing to the one-child policy, China's elderly concerns are much more pronounced and embedded in policymaking. Thus, to meet the physical and emotional requirements of the elderly in India, the State, the market, and the policymakers, first need to acknowledge the growing aging population of India.

Though this edited book has covered the major forms of caregiving arrangements that are available for later-life care, in the next section, I shed light on some of the future areas of research that would expand the scope of gerontology as a discipline.

Future Research Agendas

Broadly in this edited volume, we have covered the relevance of filial piety in modern China and India, followed by the contemporary forms of caregiving arrangements dominant in both countries. Hence, in this section, we discuss some of the major areas which need to be developed as potential research questions to contribute to policymaking and academic scholarship.

One of the most important issues that needs immediate attention from the research community is the rise of paid caregiving services in both countries. Zhang and Goza (2006), in their study, discuss how the one-child policy of China makes it difficult for one single child to provide care for two parents and four sets of grandparents. In particular, in their study, Zhang and Goza suggest a number of alternatives for both urban and rural elderly that will reduce the caregiving burden for the single child. Emphasizing the significance of the neighborhood committee system, Zhang and Goza recommend that volunteers of these committee systems are quite inexpensive and very effective in their provision of eldercare. Given the example of Shanghai, Zhang and Goza stress the need to develop more such programs to shift eldercare from the family to other forms of social support groups. Apart from this very important paper by Zhang and Goza, most research on eldercare in China has either focused on family care or institutional care. Other forms of emerging care, such as paid caregiving, assisted living, market-based care, care provided by support groups, and external network ties, are important and need to be examined by the gerontological research community. Though filial piety continues to dominate as a cultural value, nonetheless, it is vital to examine these other forms of care as well to understand the changing caregiving arrangements in modern China.

Similar to China, India too is witnessing major demographic transitions and the family as a unit of care is diminishing in a neoliberal Indian society. Like China, other types of caregiving arrangements are coming up in India as well. For instance, market-based care, paid caregiving, and external groups providing care are gradually being adopted by several financially stable older adults in India. Though a few scholars have focused on these newer versions of caregiving in urban India (Gangopadhyay, 2020, 2021; Roy & Ayalon, 2021), much more research remains to be done in this area. Though legally, the caregiving responsibility rests on the family, a lot of the elderly are now shifting to paid caregiving for their later life needs. Hence, this kind of caregiving deserves a careful research analysis. Relatedly, owing to migration patterns, virtual care is the other form of caregiving that is gaining currency in India. Several adult children, residing in other cities and countries, rely on information and communication technologies (ICTs) to provide care to their older parents (Ahlin, 2018; Ahlin & Sen, 2020; Gangopadhyay, 2021). This too is a major area of research that can be explored by scholars of gerontology.

The other line of research that has received widespread attention in gerontology is the study of aging practices and intergenerational relationships among the Chinese and Indian diaspora. Several scholars have examined how caregiving relationships, cultural values, network groups, and kin ties are shaped among Chinese and Indian elderly immigrants in different transnational contexts (Brijnath 2009; Chappell & Kusch, 2007; Gangopadhyay 2021; Lai, 2009; Lamb, 2009; Tang 2011; Zhou, 2012). These studies are extremely significant and have raised relevant issues being faced by the elderly Chinese and Indian diaspora outside their own homeland. However, equally important are studies that adopt a comparative lens and examine cross-cultural issues of growing old in different countries. There is a scarcity of such studies in gerontological scholarship and comparative studies are required to understand the major issues being faced by the elderly across the world. Though some scholars such as Broom (2016), Kunkel et al. (2014), Lamb (2009), and Gangopadhyay (2021) have presented a global narrative of aging, however, more comparative research is needed to comprehend the growing concerns of the elderly population around the world. Scholars of gerontology should take note of this research gap and take steps to address this gap as well.

China and India: A Policy Perspective

Following the discussion on future areas of research, the final section of this edited book highlights some of the major policies adopted by both countries for their aging population. By representing some of the core policies of both countries, this book also aims to take forward the discussion on the formulation of policies for eldercare. In the process, this book will also demonstrate how a representation of cross-cultural policies is useful to gain an understanding of aging issues across different countries.

Elderly Policies in China

Demographic changes and socio-economic transitions have effected the cultural norm of filial piety in China. Consequently, the Government of China has implemented certain policies that will enable the elderly to move beyond their family members and rely on external support systems. Through the Urban Employee Basic Medical Insurance Scheme (since 1998), the New Rural Cooperative Medical Scheme (since 2003), and the Urban Resident Basic Medical Insurance Scheme (since 2007), China provides basic health insurance to its elderly population (Feng et al., 2013). In addition to providing health insurance, China also started the New Rural Pension Insurance pilot program in 2009 in 10% of the Chinese countries (Feng et al., 2013) and by 2020, this program was further extended to the entire nation covering all rural elderly (Chen et al., 2020). Through this program, which provides pension income to the elderly parents, the State intends to raise the income of the older parents and reduce the financial burden of the adult children in rural China (Zhao et al., 2021). Additionally, China also has institutional care provisions for the elderly with no children, no income, and no relatives. These elderly reside in residential care homes and these homes are run by the State, municipalities, local governments, or collectives (Feng et al., 2013).

Apart from the State-funded residential care homes, institutional care is also rising among financially independent urban elderly. These care homes are mostly run by the private sector. In their study, Qian et al. (2018) illustrate that shifting to pay and stay institutional care is more common among empty-nest singles and empty-nest singles residing in urban areas of China. In contrast, the rural elderly prefer to continue co-habiting with their adult children and their families. Also, the lack of availability of institutional care in rural China and the low-income status of the rural elderly acted as barriers for the rural elderly to access institutional care (Qian et al., 2018).

Finally, the other very important care service that is gaining ground in China are the community-based elderly care services that meet the health, emotional and physical needs of the elderly in China. In a recent study, Xia (2020), based on the 2018 wave of the Chinese Longitudinal Healthy Longevity Survey, found that these community-based elderly care services provide daily care, medical aid, and emotional support for the elderly. Though limited in supply, there is a huge demand for these services, particularly among the elderly with serious disabilities (Xia, 2020).

Despite the implementation of various policies and programs, studies have noted that elder abuse (Dong, 2015), coping with loneliness (Luo and Waite, 2014), and shortage of caregivers for the elderly (Mather, 2020) are some of the major concerns of the elderly population in China. Hence, the Government of China needs to look into these growing concerns of its aging population with urgency.

Elderly Policies in India

Following an analysis of elderly policies in China, it is important to reflect on the policies of India as well. In 1999, the Government of India had implemented the National Policy on Older Persons was formulated to provide financial and food security, healthcare, shelter, and other needs of older persons. The major goals of the policy are as follows:

- Protection of older women from biases against age, gender, and widowhood.
- Remove dependency and provide opportunities for productivity, choice, and creativity among senior citizens of India.
- Develop age integration to nurture the bond between the young and the old.
- Stress on the role of social and community services for older persons, with a particular focus on older women.

Despite this policy, older adults across India continue to face financial, physical, medical, and emotional hurdles. Since, legally, the responsibility of the elderly rests on their adult children and their families, this policy has done little to improve the wellbeing of India's aging population (Paul & Asirvatham, 2016; Verma & Khanna, 2013). In particular, there is no universal pension scheme or national pension scheme which will ensure eldercare in India. As a result, cases of elderly abuse and abandonment are on the rise in rural and urban India (Shankardass, 2018). Relatedly, another scheme, known as the National Programme for the Health Care of the Elderly (NPHCE), which was launched in 2010 to provide a geriatric unit and beds to be made available for patients at government primary health centers and sub-district facilities, has also failed to meet its goals (Ugargol, 2021). However, most of the States have been slow in responding to this initiative by the Central Government. Hence, this policy too has not been adequately implemented and the elderly residing in rural India continue to suffer owing to poor public health infrastructure (Govindarajan, 2017).

Similar to China, India too is witnessing the rise of institutional care. However, most of the institutional care facilities, popularly known as old age homes in India are run and managed by private individuals or trusts. Hence, they are quite expensive and only the wealthy elderly can access their services (Matra, 2017). Though the government-funded old age homes provide shelter, medical aid, recreational facilities, and food to the abandoned elderly, nonetheless, they hardly meet the expectations of their elderly residents. Lack of funds results in inadequate healthcare, power failures, and variety in food (Sharma, 2018). Hence, an urgent need to reform these old age homes is needed to improve the living conditions of these elderly.

Finally, India does not take into account its elderly population who are childless, unmarried, and without any kin. Most policies and the law, as discussed extensively in this edited volume, require the family to provide eldercare. As India's aging population continues to grow, it is important to take note of their demographic trends, later-life needs, and well-being to improve the aging experiences of India's elderly.

In this section, the goal was to present the different types of policies that have been implemented in both countries. Through this presentation of policies, the aim was not to applaud the initiatives of a particular country but to highlight the eldercare requirements of China and India.

Final Remarks

This edited book was conceived and shaped amidst the global pandemic of COVID-19. During the first wave of the pandemic, the elderly across the globe were affected. In particular, the pandemic highlighted some of the many struggles being faced by the world's elderly population. This edited book, through a comparative lens, has presented some of the major forms of eldercare and some of the key challenges being faced by the elderly population of India and China. Additionally, in closing, this book has also reflected on future areas of research and the core elderly policies being followed in both countries. In the coming years, most research will be around the pandemic and given the vulnerability of the elderly population, they will play a key role in the research focusing on the intersections between the pandemic and aging issues. Against this backdrop, this book was developed to begin a dialogue around eldercare in the pre-pandemic times. Additionally, we also hope to have contributed to policymaking which would be beneficial for both China as well as India. Finally, we end with the expectation that this book adds to the gerontological scholarship and more such comparative studies are undertaken to provide a holistic understanding of aging issues around the globe.

References

Ahlin, T. (2018). Frequent callers: "good care" with ICTs in Indian transnational families. *Medical Anthropology*, 39(1): 69–82. https://doi.org/10.1080/01459740.2018.1532424.

Ahlin, T., & Sen, K. (2020). Shifting duties: Enacting "good daughters" through elder care practices in transnational families from Kerala, South India. *Gender, Place and Culture*, 27(10): 1395–1414. https://doi.org/10.1080/0966369X.2019.1681368.

Brijnath, B. (2009). Familial bonds and boarding passes: Understanding caregiving in a transnational context. *Identities*, 16: 83–101. https://doi.org/10.1080/10702890802605836.

Broom, A. (2016). *Dying: A Social Perspective on the End of Life*. United Kingdom: Routledge.

Chappell, N. L., & Kusch, K. (2007). The gendered nature of filial piety: A study among Chinese Canadians. *Journal of Cross-Cultural Gerontology*, 22: 29–45. https://doi.org/10.1007/s10823-006-9011-5.

Chen, S., Chen, Y., Feng, Z. et al. (2020). Barriers of effective health insurance coverage for rural-to-urban migrant workers in China: A systematic review and policy gap analysis. *BMC Public Health*, 20: 408. https://doi.org/10.1186/s12889-020-8448-8.

Dong, X. Q. (2015). Elder abuse: Systematic review and implications for practice. *Journal of the American Geriatrics Society*, 63: 1214–1238.

Feng, Z., Liu, C., Guan, X., & Mor, V. (2013). China's rapidly aging population creates policy challenges in shaping a viable long-term care system. *Health affairs (Project Hope)*, 31(12): 2764–2773. https://doi.org/10.1377/hlthaff.2012.0535.

Gangopadhyay, J. (2020). Examining the lived experiences of ageing among older adults living alone in India. In M. K. Shankardass (Ed.), *Ageing Issues and Responses in India* (pp. 207–219). Singapore: Springer. https://doi.org/10.1007/978-981-15-5187-1_13.

Gangopadhyay, J. (2021). *Culture, Context and Aging: Narratives from India and Beyond*. Singapore: Springer.

Govindarajan, V. (2017). Seven years ago, India promised health care units for the elderly. Where are they? *Scroll*. Accessed at https://scroll.in/pulse/849561/seven-years-ago-india-promised-health-care-units-for-the-elderly-where-are-they.

Kampf, A., & Botelho, L. A. (2009). Anti-aging and biomedicine: Critical studies on the pursuit of maintaining, revitalizing and enhancing aging bodies. *Medicine Studies*, 1: 187–195. https://doi.org/10.1007/s12376-009-0021-9.

Kunkel, S. R., Brown, J. S., & Whittington, F. J. (2014). *Global Aging: Comparative Perspectives on Aging and the Life Course*. New York: Springer.

Lai, D. W. L. (2009). Filial piety, caregiving appraisal, and caregiving burden. *Research on Aging*, 32(2): 200–223. https://doi.org/10.1177/0164027509351475.

Lamb, S. (2020). Old-age homes, love, and other new cultures of aging in middle-class India. In Jay Sokolovsky (Ed.), *The Cultural Context of Aging: World-wide Perspectives*, 4th ed. (pp: 466–491). Westport, CT: Praeger.

Liu, Z-W., Yu, Y., Fang, L., Hu, M., Zhou, L., & Xiao, S-Y. (2019). Willingness to receive institutional and community-based eldercare among the rural elderly in China. *PloS ONE*, 14(11): e0225314. https://doi.org/10.1371/journal.pone.0225314.

Luo, Y., & Waite, L.J. (2014). Loneliness and mortality among older adults in China, *The Journals of Gerontology: Series B*, 69(4): 633–645. https://doi.org/10.1093/geronb/gbu007.

Mather, M. (2020). Aging and health in China: What can we learn from the world's largest population of older people? *Today's Research on Aging*, Issue 39. Accessed at https://www.prb.org/resources/china-aging-worlds-largest-population-older-people/.

Matra, A. (2017). The very high cost of living in old-age homes. *India Today*. Accessed at https://www.indiatoday.in/lifestyle/culture/story/cost-old-age-home-delhi-ncr-the-golden-estate-lifest-1032213-2017-08-27.

Paul, N. S., & Asirvatham, M. (2016). Geriatric health policy in India: The need for scaling-up implementation. *Journal of Family Medicine and Primary Care*, 5(2): 242–247. https://doi.org/10.4103/2249-4863.192333.

Qian Y, Qin W, Zhou C, et al. (2018). Utilisation willingness for institutional care by the elderly: A comparative study of empty nesters and nonempty nesters in Shandong, China. *BMJ Open*, 8: e022324.

Roy, S., & Ayalon, L. (2021). "Goodness and kindness": Long-distance caregiving through volunteers during the COVID-19 lockdown in India. *The Journals of Gerontology: Series B*, 76(7): e281–e289. https://doi.org/10.1093/geronb/gbaa187.

Shankardass, M. K. (2018) Perspectives on abuse and neglect of the elderly in India. In: Shankardass, M., & Irudaya Rajan, S. (Eds), *Abuse and Neglect of the Elderly in India*. Singapore: Springer. https://doi.org/10.1007/978-981-10-6116-5_2.

Sharma, N. C. (2018). Old age homes lack ambulances, medical facilities: Study. *Livemint*. Accessed at https://www.livemint.com/Politics/O9Ku9C2g8OExw0ELAMUm2I/Old-age-homes-lack-ambulances-medical-facilities-study.html.

Song, Y. (2014). Losing an only child: The one-child policy and elderly care in China. *Reproductive Health Matters*, 22(43): 113–124. https://doi.org/10.1016/S0968-8080(14)43755-8.

Tang, M. (2011). Can cultural values help explain the positive aspects of caregiving among Chinese American caregivers? *Journal of Gerontological Social Work*, 54(6): 551–569. https://doi.org/10.1080/01634372.2011.567323.

Ugargol, P. V. (2021). Government needs to focus on care for those in their sunset years. *Deccan Herald*. Accessed at https://www.deccanherald.com/opinion/in-perspective/government-needs-to-focus-on-care-for-those-in-their-sunset-years-1029656.html.

Verma, R., & Khanna, P. (2013). National program of health-care for the elderly in India: A hope for healthy ageing. *International Journal of Preventive Medicine*, 4(10), 1103–1107.

Xia, C. (2020). Community-based elderly care services in China: An analysis based on the 2018 wave of the CLHLS Survey. *China Population and Development Studies*, 3: 352–367. https://doi.org/10.1007/s42379-020-00050-w.

Zhang, G., & Goza, Z. (2006). Who will care for the elderly in China?: A review of the problems caused by China's one-child policy and their potential solutions. *Journal of Aging Studies*, 20(2): 151–164. https://doi.org/10.1016/j.jaging.2005.07.002.

Zhao, M., Zhu, Z., Kong, C. et al. (2021). Caregiver burden and parenting stress among left-behind elderly individuals in rural China: A cross-sectional study. *BMC Public Health*, 21: 846. https://doi.org/10.1186/s12889-021-10892-9.

Zhou, Y. R. (2012). Space, time, and self: Rethinking aging in the contexts of immigration and transnationalism. *Journal of Aging Studies*, 26(3): 232–242. https://doi.org/10.1016/j.jaging.2012.02.002.

Index

Note: *Italicized* folios indicate figures, **bold** indicate tables and with "n" indicate endnotes.

action strategies: for coping with loss 160; for personal growth of grandchildren 166–167
activities of daily living (ADL) 126, 139n1, 178
adult daughters: and debunking son-preference myth of India 221; filial piety (India) 43; not expected to look after their aging parents 34; older adults preference to co-reside with 44
adult health 175
adult sons: adult daughters *versus* 43; filial piety (India) 43; joint family structure 34; older adults co-residing with 34; responsibility of later-life caregiving resting on 44–45
ageism: impede in development of institutionalized eldercare 6; stigmatization and 113–114
aging: development in China 108; feminization 130; global 175; identities 34; longitudinal study 178–179; modern fears of 117; negative attitudes toward 114; pandemic and 227; parents 34, 89, 91–92, 94; physical 113; in place 108–109; population 1, 4, 6–7, 89, 107, 111, 139, 174, 179, 220, 222–223, 225; problem 107, 119; processes 33; psychological 113; QOL of the elderly 138; self-acceptance of 114; society 13, 17, 20; stigmatized perceptions of older adults 6; *see also* successfully aging alone
anthropometrics 175, **194–195**
anticipatory care **134**, 136–137
attitudes: of aging 114; of children 89; institutional and cultural 109; negative toward aging 114; nimbyist/NIMBY 6, 114–115; public 20
Australia 37, 96

Bai, C. 5
balance of interests 118
Basic Old-Age Insurance for Urban and Rural Residents 1
Beautiful Home & Nursing Home 112
behavior: in adolescence 166; civil 13; civilized 20, 26; elderly-oriented social 22; and filial culture 118–119; of filial piety 93; health-seeking 174; moral 16–17, 25; NIMBY 110–111, 118–119; older adults 114; public 22, 26; to public service facilities 110–111; social 24; stigma against older people 114
Bian, Y. 26
bias 58, 68; cognitive 114; response 216
biomarkers 175, **194–195**
blood relationship support 160–161
Bowling, A. 125, 133
Buddhism 80

Canada 37, 97, 111
care *see* formal care
care burden 68, 72, 74, 76, 80, 90, 92, 94
care gains **73**, 74, **78**, 79
caregiver: adult-children 90, 92; adult children as 33; of cancer patients 74; family 55–59, 68, 80–82, 95; filial piety and 95; identity 7, *159*, 164–165; informal 57; new ways of living as 167–168; older adults and 98; primary 91; professional 56
caregiving: "best caregiving option" 92; institutional 45; later-life 32, 34; paid 40, 45, 224; patient-centered skills and care needs 68; responsibilities 93; transnational 33
caste system, India 45–46n3
census, India 177

Index 231

Census Enumeration Blocks (CEBs) 178
Central Civilization Office (China) 16
Checklist for Qualitative Research 58, 68
Checklist for Systematic Reviews 58, 68
Chen, W. W. 95–96
Cheng, Z. 156
China: aging society 17; elderly policies in 225–226; family caregivers of elderly cancer patients 68; immigrants 96; one-child policy 7, 14–15; pension systems 1; socialist modernization 18; social security 3–4; spiritual civilization 18; Three Loves 18; universal health insurance coverage 2
China National Health and Fitness Commission 1
China Women's News 21
Chinese State Council 89
civilizational project 13–14, 16–19, 22, 26
CNKI 56
Cochrane Library 56
cognitive adaptation theory 131–132
cognitive bias 114
cohabitation: joint 32; multigenerational 93
collectivism 91, 93–94
Communist Party of China 16
community-based eldercare institutions 107; *see also* "Not In My Backyard" (NIMBY)
co-morbidity 173
Confucianism 15, 19, 80, 89
Confucius 89
(re)constructive care 135–136, 138
Convoy Model of Social Relations 132
COVID-19 227; in India 145–153; lockdown 6
CPC Central Committee (China) 16
Critical Discourse Analysis 16
cultural backdrop 31–32
cultural dimension of identity of losing 165–166
cultural gerontology 35–36
cultural shift 43, 221
Cumming, E. 35
Cummins, R. A. 125

data: collection 35, 112, 156–158; and elderly care 223; filial piety (India) 39–40; loss-of-only-child families 158–159; sources 156–158; Wanfang Data 56

death: of an only child 161–168; of child 7, 159–160; registration 177; taboos on 113, 117
demographic profile: of India 124; of sample 129–130
demographic shifts 1, 5
DePaulo, B. 146–147, 151–152
desires 33, 91
discourse(s): analysis 14; biomedical 149–150; on Chinese traditional identity 23; filial 81; Foucauldian analysis 59; "re-Orientation" 18–19; strategies centered on raising grandchildren 163–164; strategy for caregiver construction 166–167; theory 16; xiao 16
Disengagement Theory, filial piety (India) 35–36, 42–43
diversification in fulfilling filial piety 94
Diwan, S. 33
Dong, X. 97

economic development 108–109, 111
Education and Health Questionnaire 178
eldercare/elderly care 173–216; data and 223; in filial piety (India) 32–33; inclusion of variables on health of elderly **181–215**; micro-level dataset on health 175–179, **179**; policies in China 225–226; policies in India 226–227
Embase 56
emotional amplification 114–115
emotional identity as older adults having only child 162–163
engagement, filial piety (India) 42–43
entrusting future to grandchildren 161

family-based care 89, 221–222
family caregivers of elderly cancer patients 55–82; care burden 68, 74; care gains 74; characteristics of articles 59, **60–67**, 68; Chinese caregiving 68; exclusion criteria 58; extraction process 58; inclusion criteria 57; Indian caregiving 74; patient-centered caregiving skills and needs 68, 74; quality appraisal results **69–70**; quality assessment 58, 68–74; research limitations 82; research methodology 56–58; research results 58; search strategy 56–57, **57**; selected articles 58, *59*, **71–73**, **75–78**; selection process 58

232 Index

family-state isomorphism 15, 20, 25–26
Fang, S. 156
fertility rate 1, 173
filial expectations 40–42
filial nationalism 15
filial piety 219–220; culture 106–110; *see also* xiao (filial piety), China
filial piety (India) 31–46; adult daughters 43; adult sons 43; Cosmopolitan Manipal 36–37; cultural backdrop 31–32; cultural gerontology 35–36; cultural shift 43; defined 31; Disengagement Theory 35–36, 42–43; eldercare in 32–33; engagement 42–43; filial obligations in 33–35; law in 32–33; neoliberal India 36–37; policy implications 45; research findings 40–42; research limitations 40; research methodology 37–40; results 40–42; son preference in 33–35; *see also* xiao (filial piety), China
filial-piety-based family care in China 89–98; academic research 98; challenges of 91–93; in Contemporary China 93–95; family care in overseas Chinese societies 95–97; filial-piety-based care 90; health effect of filial piety 90; policy 98; research 98; traditional filial piety 89–90
financing healthcare expenditure **214**
First Stage Units (FSU) 176
Five Concerns, Four Beauties program 18
Fong, V. 15
formal care 3, 6, 126–127
Foucault, M.: discourse theory 16
Fourth Survey on the Living Conditions of the Elderly in Urban and Rural China (2015) 4
Furexin Senior Residence 112
Future Workplace 37

Gabriel, Z. 125, 133
Gangopadhyay, J. 146, 150–151
Ganguly, B. B. 1
gender division 94–95
geriatric health 174, 216
global aging 175; *see also* aging
Goffman, E. 113
grandchildren: entrusting future to 161; raiser identity 161–162; raising after loss 161–164; separating future from 164
grandparenting: duties 34, 222; responsibilities 40–42
Greenhalgh, S. 17
Grew Literature in the Health Sciences 56
grief: medicalization of 159–160; somatization of 159–160
Growing Old (Henry and Cumming) 36

He, L. T. 3, 81
healthcare: expenditure **211–213**; expenditure financing **214**; geriatric 174; utilization **200–209**
health state 175, **181–193**
Henry, W. E. 36
high modernist 22; civilizational projects 14, 26; social behavior 24
Hong Kong 96
Household Consumer Expenditure Survey (HCES) 2
Hsueh, K. H. 31
Hu Jintao 18–19

identity: of caregiver of the elderly 164–168; Chinese traditional 23; Consent forms 147; emotional 162–163; grandchild raiser 161–162
Ikels, C. 15
imagined community 26
immigrants: Asian Indian 33; Chinese 96–97; India 33–34, 224
India 139; caste system 45–46n3; COVID-19 in 145–153; demographic shifts 5; elderly policies in 226–227; family caregivers of elderly cancer patients 74; Longitudinal Aging Study in India (LASI) 179–180; National Family Health Survey (NFHS) 178; National Sample Survey 176–177; population aging 1; *seva* 3; social security 2–4; *see also* successfully aging alone
Indian Human Development Survey (IHDS) 177–178
informal care 127
institutionalized care 126, 220–221
instrumental care 133–134, 137
International Agency for Research on Cancer (IARC) 55
intimacy indifference 160–161

intimate relationships: care alliance 167; caregiving alliance 159; reconstruction of 163–164
intra-generational–interpersonal relationship 128, 131–133, **132**
Iversen, T. N. 113

Jamuna, D. 126
Japan 96
Jen, C. H. 95
Jiang, Z. 113
Jiangnan Eldercare Home 112
Joanna Briggs Institute's (JBI) critical appraisal tools 58, 68
joint cohabitation 32
joint participation 118, 156

Kadam, N. N. 1
Kahn, C. 152
Kemp, C.L. 34
Kislev, E. 147
Korea 96
Kronos Incorporated 37

Lahad, K. 147
Laidlaw, K. 114
Lamb, S. 33, 44
law: in filial piety (India) 32–33; single people's existence in old age 145
Lefebvre, H. 115
Lei, X. Y. 5
Lei Feng 22
Li, M. 97
life expectancy: in China 1; and decreases in fertility 92, 173; in India 173; between males and females 130; prolonged 5
Lin, Y. 55
Link, B. G. 113
Longitudinal Aging Study in India (LASI) 179–180
Longitudinal Study Programme 175
Lorde, A. 146
loss-of-only-child families 155–169; action strategies for coping with the loss 160; blood relationship support 160–161; constructing grandchild raiser identity 161–162; cultural dimension of identity of losing 165–166; data analysis 158–159; data collection 156–158; data sources 156–158; discourse strategies centered on raising grandchildren 163–164; discourse strategy for caregiver construction 166–167; emotional identity as older adults having only child 162–163; entrusting future to grandchildren 161; group for the first time 161–162; identity of caregiver of the elderly 164–168; intimacy indifference 160–161; literature review 155–156; medicalization of grief 159–160; new ways of living as caregiver 167–168; raising grandchildren after 161–164; research process 156–159; self-healing stage 159–161; separating future from grandchildren 164; social adaptation 159–168; somatization of grief 159–160

Maintenance and Welfare of Senior Citizens Act, 2007 (India) 32–33, 145
Manipal: filial piety (India) 36–37; health facilities 40
marginalized eldercare groups 222–223
May Fourth Movement (China) 15, 109
Medical Facility Questionnaire 178
medicalization of grief 159–160
MEDLINE 56
Meinhof, M. 15
Ministry of Health and Family Welfare (MOHFW) 178
Ministry of Human Resources and Social Security (China) 1
Mishra, A. 146
missing children 164–165
modern fears of aging 117; *see also* aging
modernization 31–32, 124; China 18, 32; neo-liberal policies 222; socialist 18
moral stigma 113; *see also* stigma
motivations 91; older parents 40, 161
Mu, G. 7
multigenerational cohabitation 93

National Family Health Survey (NFHS) 178, 180
National Pension System (NPS), China 1–2
National Sample Survey Office (NSSO) 176–177
neoliberal India 36–37; *see also* India
New Cooperative Medical System (NCMS) 79
New Culture Movement (China) 15
Nolan, M. 137

"Not In My Backyard" (NIMBY) 107–119; ageism 113–114; aging in place 108–109; balance of interests 118; behavior and filial culture 118–119; data collection 112; effect of 110; emotional amplification 114–115; filial piety culture 106–110; influence of culture on 112–113; joint participation 118; modern fears of aging 117; preference behavior to public service facilities 110–111; from psychological distance to 115–116; research findings 112–116; research methodology 111–112; research sites 111–112; special features and convertibility as 116–117; stigmatization 113–114; subjective distortion 114–115; traditional taboos on death 117

Ocean Express Tsubaki Xuanmao Senior Living Apartment 112
Office of Registrar General of India 177
O'Hare, M. 110
old-age home, Kolkata 124–139; care 127; demographic profile of sample 129–130; dimensions of receiving care in **133–134**, 133–136; interpretation 129; intra-generational–interpersonal relationship 128, 131–133, **132**; quality of life of elderly 125–128, 136–137, **136**; rationale of study 126–127; research method 127–128; research results **129**; research variables 127–128; social adjustment 128, 130–131
Old Age Homes (OAH) 124–125
one-child policy, China 7, 14–15

pandemic in 2020 146–147; see also COVID-19
Pang, E. C. 97
"*paraya dhan*" 44
parent–child relationships 35, 40–42, 95, 109
paternalism 109
patient-centered caregiving skills and needs 68, 74
patriarchy 109
perceptions 91; cultural 80–81; filial piety 79, 97; negative 114; negative societal 4; psychological 115; subjective 116
performance tests **194–195**
Perry, E. J. 18
Phelan, J. C. 113

physical stigma 113; see also stigma
population aging 1, 4, 6–7, 89, 107, 111, 139, 174, 179, 220, 222–223, 225; see also aging
practice ability and division 92–93
preference behavior to public service facilities 110–111
preservative care 134–135, 138
preventive care 137
preventive health and risk factors **195–200**
Primary sampling Units (PSUs) 178
PRISMA flow diagram of article selection process 59
Probability Proportional to Size with Replacement (PPSWR) 176
public service facilities 110–111
PubMed 56

quality assessment 58, 68–74
quality of life (QOL) 55, 127–128, **209–210**; of elderly 125–126, 136–137, **136**; see also old-age home, Kolkata

receiving care 133–136, **133–134**
reciprocal care 135, 138; see also care
reciprocalization of the content 93–94
Reddy, L. K. 126
relationships: intergenerational 6, 95, 168; intra-generational–interpersonal 137–138; parent–child 35, 40–42, 95, 109; social 125–126
"respectable professions" 147
risk factors and preventive health behaviors **195–200**

Sample Registration System (SRS) 177
Scott, J. C. 22
Second Stage Strata (SSS) 176
self-care 146–147; connected to lifestyle improvement 146; during the COVID-19 lockdown 6; moral precedence 150; singlehood 149, 152–153
self-healing stage 159–161
self-isolation 146, 155
separating future from grandchildren see grandchildren
seva 3
Sharma, K. 34
Shih, Y.-K. 15
Simple Random Sampling (SRS) 176

singlehood: successfully aging alone 146–147, 152–153
social adaptation 159–168
Social Adjustment Scale (SAI) 130, **130**
social constructionist theories 138
social insurance 5
social involution 167–168
socialist modernization 18; *see also* modernization
social security 1; China 3–4; ethical deficiency 119; health insurance 79; India 2–4
social stigma 113; *see also* stigma
social transformation 114
socioemotional selectivity theory 132
somatization of grief 159–160
Songhe Nursing Home 112
son preference, filial piety (India) 33–35
spatio-temporal analysis 156
spindle code scoping **158**
spiritual civilization 18, 26
stigma/stigmatization 111, 113–114; *see also* "Not In My Backyard" (NIMBY)
structuralist-functionalist 124
subjective distortion 114–115
subjective well-being 175, **209–210**
successful aging model 151
successfully aging alone 145–153; pandemic in 2020 146–147; research methodology 147–148; self-care 146–150, 152–153; singlehood 146–147, 152–153; social support among older long-term single people 150–152; *see also* aging
supervisory care 137; *see also* care

Taiwan 95–96
Three Loves program 18
Tianlu Lake Senior Care Center 112
Tornstam, L. 109
total dependency ratio 5
tradition: in Bengali families 124; China 18–20; national cultural 26; patriarchal 91; public moral 25; revitalization of 19; taboos on death 117

Ultimate Stage Units (USU) 176
United Kingdom 96
Urban Employee Basic Medical Insurance (UEBMI) 79
Urban Frame Survey (UFS) 176
Urban Resident Basic Medical Insurance (URBMI) 79

van Heugten, K. 81
Vienna International Plan of Action on Aging 124
VIP database 56
volunteering: in China 14; *xiao* and 22–25; Yishui volunteering program 24

Wanfang Data 56
Wang, D. 117
Wang, W. 117
Wang, Z. 15
Web of Science 56
WeChat 14, 16, 25
westernization 91; *see also* modernization
work culture 37
World Health Organization (WHO) 55, 127, 146, 175

xiao (filial piety), China 13–26; defined 14, 20; extension of 19–22; in literature 14–15; as part of civilizational project 16–19; research methodology 16; sample 16; volunteering and 22–25; *see also* filial piety
Xi Jinping 16, 19, 22

Yan, J. 95–96
Yeh, K. H. 96
Yishui (Shandong) 23

Zhang, L. 5, 17
Zhang, S. 107
Zhao, Y. 107
Zhou, Z. 113